A Cardiologist Examines Jesus

Dr. Franco Serafini

A Cardiologist Examines Jesus
The Stunning Science Behind Eucharistic Miracles

Translated by
Dr. Umberto Villa, B.S., M.B.B.S.
and
Fr. Brendan Purcell, M.A., S.T.L., Ph.D.

SOPHIA INSTITUTE PRESS
Manchester, New Hampshire

Sophia Institute Press

Box 5284, Manchester, NH 03108

1-800-888-9344

www.SophiaInstitute.com

Sophia Institute Press® is a registered trademark of Sophia Institute.

paperback ISBN 978-1-64413-477-1

ebook ISBN 978-1-64413-478-8

Library of Congress Control Number: 2021946447

Fourth printing

He gave medical knowledge
to human beings,
so that we would praise him
for the miracles he performs.

—Sirach 38:6, GNT

To Bl. Carlo Acutis
(1991–2006),
a young man
in love with the Eucharist
who mysteriously labored and interceded in Heaven
for this book to be written

Contents

A Cardiologist Examines Jesus

Introduction

I am a physician—more precisely, a cardiologist. As we shall see, this will come in handy.

I should also immediately declare my "conflicts of interest," as is usual nowadays in medical conferences and scientific publications: I am Roman Catholic. I initially thought I could manage writing something "aseptic" and impartial. I thought that the implied sublime and embarrassing truth would come across to the reader by simply reporting scientific facts, without needless comments by the narrator. I couldn't manage this: like a football supporter in the wrong stadium corner, every time my favorite team scored, I could not help shouting and raising my hands despite being stared at by everyone else around me. So I won't hide my own Catholic point of view, although—my word of honor—this was not a reason for me to censor, attenuate, exaggerate, or otherwise even slightly modify the reported data that are fully verifiable in the annotated bibliographies at the end of each chapter.

In the next few pages, I shall browse through a few eucharistic miracles: just five, plus one that I later disregarded. What these events have in common is that they all have undergone rigorous scientific analyses in recent or very recent times. I am not a theologian and therefore wish for my small investigation to be exclusively medical.

I critically sifted through a sieve the clinical, laboratory, histologic,[1] and genetic tests performed on these mysterious and anomalous tissues derived from consecrated hosts.

This meant looking for articles and original publications as well as eliminating a large amount of false and misleading devotional material often embellishing the narratives around these miracles. Whenever possible, I dispelled doubts and clarified inaccuracies by personally contacting the South American and Polish researchers who took up the investigations firsthand. I even traveled to some of these places to interview witnesses and verify details in person.

Well, the result of my work was surprising at the very least.

We shall see an emerging pattern repeating itself with reassuring or baffling punctuality (depending on your point of view): a consistent pattern, from one event to the next, regardless of the historical time or the geographic location. The next step will then be to try to advance some reflections in the field of this very unique discipline: one whose foundations are yet to be laid, a subject we could call "bio-theology," "experimental and applied theology," or whatever other name we like. We will venture into an unexplored land where bewildering and inexplicable phenomena take place, even if documented with the best technology at our disposal. This journey will truly challenge our open-mindedness, our willingness to accept an incredible, thorny, and embarrassing Christian mystery breaking into our

---

[1] Histology is the study of microanatomy: the study and characterization of cell types and the body tissue types done by observation under the microscope.

everyday world. We shall wander in an underground landscape, every now and then accompanied by dodgy companions: blundering scientists, crazed mystics, bamboozling ufologists. At times, we shall be surprised to appreciate that the dogmas and truths of the Faith are indeed like beacons in the night. They will paradoxically shine the light we will need to make sense of phenomena that we could never otherwise fully explain through reason alone.

We should acknowledge that hundreds of Church-recognized eucharistic miracles have happened throughout the centuries. These are most likely only the tip of a massive concealed and forgotten iceberg consisting of thousands of events. Caesarius of Heisterbach, a German monk in 1200, listed up to sixty-seven miraculous events related to the Eucharist in his *Dialogus miraculorum* (*Dialogue on Miracles*). Most impressively, all of them took place just around Cologne, over his lifespan, all of them stuck in his memory. French monk St. Paschasius Radbertus had already written *De corpore et sanguine Domini* (*On the Body and Blood of the Lord*) in the ninth century. This was perhaps the first essay on the Eucharist in the history of the Church, and it listed a substantial number of known miraculous events. St. Thomas Aquinas, too, in his *Summa theologica*, dedicated a specific article (III, q. 76, a. 8) to the phenomena of eucharistic miracles, which were obviously not so rare even then.

Very well, let's clear away this misapprehension at once: this book is not about legends from the depths of the Middle Ages.

Eucharistic miracles keep happening even today, in our time, with generous abundance—so much so that I had to hurry up in writing an extra chapter on an event that just took place in Legnica, Poland, about which the local bishop issued an official statement on April 10, 2016. May the editor not hold it against me, but this book is born condemned to being out of date: it will always require updated editions.

One Last Hesitation

Please allow me, before starting this incredible journey, to share one last moment of hesitation, one last backward glance.

Why should we carry out scientific tests on eucharistic miracles? Is it really necessary?

It is not a trivial question. This must certainly seem like the only sensible way to go for people like ourselves, living surrounded by technology. After all, we trust—or better, we think we can trust—science and medicine to be the foundations of our lives. Therefore, this scientific approach must seem obvious, or at least very "reasonable." Inexplicable events took place in Buenos Aires and Sokółka, but we have scientists and laboratories, so let's get the miracles analyzed! Are we sure that our ancestors would have reasoned just the same way had they had access to our means? What are we looking for?

In fact, all these miracles are already talking to us in language and symbolism that is fully understandable: as Catholics, we cannot see anything other than the Blood—the most precious Blood redeeming and saving us from death and Hell—when looking at the faithful adoring a host exuding a red liquid. Is it really that important that red blood cells be counted under the microscope, or that protein electrophoresis be carried out in the laboratory? The miraculously appeared, jellylike dark mass obviously wants to remind us of the Real Presence of that one Body. What does the knowledge that such substance is actually heart muscle tissue—rather than pancreatic tissue or skin—add to our adoration?

Also, what tests should we run? Who would have the power to order them? How far should we venture into this, and where would morbid curiosity begin?

Why not quantify cholesterol and glucose levels? What were those pious women feeding Jesus with? What about liver transaminases? Did they make him drink too much? Dear reader, could you understand how far we might go?

Still, Church authorities have always requested laboratory tests for all such miraculous signs in the last twenty to twenty-five years. Clearly, this is now considered common practice: scientific review is an established component—and perhaps the main one—in the protocol followed by the Church to recognize a miracle. Bishops would only acknowledge the supernatural origin of these events after thorough scientific investigations.

This whole topic prompts a reflection on the ambivalent role of science for modern mankind. It is a tool to understand nature, a very powerful extension of our eyes and hands, emancipation from the burden of work and disease. No one would question that! At the same time, however, science and technology hem us in with their power and unquestionable authorities: they deprive us of an element of spontaneity and, ultimately, of freedom.

Scientific analysis also notoriously yields contradictory results. At times it even gives rise to a counterproductive boomerang effect. Even in good faith, researchers can make mistakes or, otherwise, lie in bad faith. Investigations can be inconclusive. I quite empathize, then, with the Lanciano friars on the morning of November 18, 1970, at the end of Prof. Linoli's assessment and sampling of their local miracle. Those Franciscans must have been wondering: "What have we done? Was it really us who destroyed the miracle our forefathers managed to hand down for thirteen hundred years?"

I should point out another little-desired but otherwise non-negligible element of their dilemma: scientific analysis always requires that a fragment of the miraculous material be taken to be either heavily processed or often destroyed. Who would dare excise a fragment of what will be demonstrated to be the heart of our Redeemer by holding a scalpel in a steady hand? Who would have the nerve to do so, knowing the sampled material will be destroyed? Who would want to sacrifice even only one drop of His Blood? Would you, reader, have this courage? Even if the sample taken were no greater than a few millimeters, the excision could not possibly be painless and will leave a mark, a permanent loss. Also, where should the incision be made? How much should be taken?

Enough hesitations! If a miracle happened, if a sign was allowed to be seen, it had to be because Heaven deemed it useful and appropriate at that time and in that place. Eucharistic miracles are truly for all of us, and they happen to sustain our faltering faith.

The concept of a selfless gift is inherent in the language of the Eucharist, in the same way that the host is broken and offered to us without reservation. Similarly, eucharistic miracles, too, become food for our contemporary souls and rational minds. These miracles "know us"; they know we live in a time when science and technology dominate, and they have already anticipated well before happening that we would look at them under the microscope, analyze them with genetic probes, and pick at them with chemical and immunological reagents. They lend themselves to our curiosity, and in the end, test results also become integral parts of the actual miracles.

Clearly, authorization to perform scientific testing must first come from the legitimate local Church authority: the bishop of the diocese where the event took place. Such authorization is usually only granted after carefully assessing the likelihood of the supernatural origin of an event, the credibility of the witnesses, and the lack of contradiction in their accounts. The Church does not abandon the faithful to themselves on such delicate matters and indeed does hold the ultimate power to make official statements about the miraculous nature of these events.

The Relationship between Science and Faith

The whole topic of eucharistic miracles research should be recognized as a new and original chapter in the sometimes-tormented relationship between science and faith. Especially in the last few centuries, this relationship has been mostly confrontational, and we could turn this into an endless discussion. Mankind has always been foolishly trying to be the master of himself. However, the advent of science—despite its many unquestionable benefits—exacerbated this grandiose human delusion. Hence, the ancient tormented discomfort felt by all Christians—that of being in the world without belonging to it—has also been exacerbated. To tell the truth, the same discomfort can indeed be felt in many societal contexts besides that of science, such as the social, political, and economic ones.

The world is a field where the good wheat and the weeds live together: we already see that within our inner selves. Thus, there is no need to discuss the chief world systems. Through faith, we know that we will eventually make sense of everything only within the framework of an *eschatological* perspective, a divine plan.

Science and faith will only find a simple equilibrium and an obvious division of roles in a much better society than the one we currently live in. This is what Ortega y Gasset was hoping

A Cardiologist Examines Jesus

for in his brilliant essay "The State's Origin in Sport," which he began with his provoking but uncriticizable statement: "Scientific truth is characterized by exact and rigorous forecasts, although experimental science achieves these praiseworthy standards by keeping its focus on problems of secondary importance, leaving the ultimate and most decisive issues unanswered." Indeed, just a few lines down, the Spanish philosopher rebuked science for acting very much like the character of the fox in Aesop's tale "The Fox and the Grapes." This is because there is a tendency among scientists to brand as "mythology" all the fundamental questions they don't know how to tackle, thus taking refuge in agnosticism. In this regard, I am pleased to remember the solemn and poetic opening to the encyclical *Fides et ratio* by Pope St. John Paul II, dedicated to this theme: "Faith and reason are like two wings on which the human spirit rises to the contemplation of truth."

Let's get this straight: the problem isn't science itself. I am a physician keeping very much up to date with recent medical progress, especially in my own specialization of cardiovascular diseases. Throughout the relatively few years in my own medical career, I nevertheless witnessed the establishment of increasingly finer diagnostic modalities, new, more effective, and safer drugs, as well as new and less invasive techniques. I see patients either living better lives or making complete recoveries, and I am proud of that. Still, I do not ask medicine to give me the answers to the meaning of life, the reason why we need to suffer and inevitably die despite our remarkable medical progress. I do not expect these answers to be published in the next edition of the *New England Journal of Medicine*, the most prestigious medical magazine in the world.

However, I do believe that modern science did not just develop by chance in the West, the cradle of Christianity. A rational

Introduction

God created an ordered and comprehensible world so that a rational man could understand the nature surrounding him to become its master (Gen. 1:28). It is no coincidence that many of the best scientists came from the ranks of Catholic clergy, such as Copernicus, Spallanzani, Mendel, or Lemaître (who "discovered" the Big Bang), just to mention a few.

Therefore, the real problem is *scientism* rather than science itself: This claims that science is the only acceptable means to discover the truth. Scientism lures people into its trap by fascinating them with undeniable technological achievements, though once trapped, they relinquish their truth-seeking minds and delegate even their most fundamental life choices to "scientific experts." Everything begins at school: nearly all Italian pupils have—at some point—been afflicted with some theatrical or film version of that biased ideological masterpiece that is *The Life of Galileo* by Bertolt Brecht. It is drummed into us that science arises from man's freedom of thought, as if it were the only way for him to break free from the oppressing obscurantism and dogmatic backwardness imposed by religious clergy: there are plenty of documentaries, books, and magazines—each targeting specific audiences—to ensure there is no escape from the one and only dictatorship of scientism.

I shall stop here to avoid boring the reader any further and to return to our subject. Eucharistic miracles are an embarrassing stumbling block for the scientist ideology: Flesh and Blood breaking into the sterile and sacred ground of the goddess Reason. After four centuries, we are witnessing Galileo's telescope scene "flipped upside down." In the 1600s, the old Aristotelians at the court of Cosimo de' Medici in Florence despised the telescope and refused to look through it, lest they had to acknowledge Galileo's discoveries: Jupiter's satellites and the moon's craters.

A Cardiologist Examines Jesus

When eucharistic miracles are investigated instead, those roles are inverted: the rigorous and closed-minded scientists—champions of freedom of research—are the ones who refuse to look through their own microscope, lest they see a mysterious fragment of "suffering" heart muscle tissue. This attitude of fear and loathing—mostly from the academic scientific world—was clearly exemplified by the miracle of Sokółka: the local professors of anatomical pathology conducting the investigations were persecuted by their own university and publicly attacked by their own superficial—if not incompetent—colleagues. The latter expressed judgments on the miraculous samples without ever actually having seen them.

What was reported by Ron Tesoriero in his book *Unseen* was very interesting and revealing, and we shall discuss it further in the Buenos Aires chapter: on December 15, 2005, he met with Prof. Susanne Hummel at the University of Göttingen, in Germany, together with his colleague Mike Willesee. Prof. Hummel is possibly the greatest world expert in ancient DNA analysis. Not by chance will I also mention one of her innovative and impeccable works in my blood groups chapter. The meeting was extremely tense: The two researchers brought a sample taken from a Buenos Aires host in which a California-based laboratory had identified traces of human DNA, without managing to determine its profile. They asked for Prof. Hummel's cooperation, and her invaluable supplemental investigations, but they preferred not to reveal the origin of the sample to ensure the impartiality of her tests. However, Prof. Hummel insisted that if she wasn't told the origin of the specimen, she would not undertake her study. Let's put ourselves in her shoes: What were those two trying to hide if—without regard to expenses—they had come on purpose, all the way from Australia, to request genetic tests?

Introduction

What sort of controversy were they trying to involve her in? The two eventually gave in. They revealed the suspected miraculous origin, and the German scientist's courteous smile turned into an icy grimace. She would not perform any tests, as she was already confident they would yield negative results: at most, only fungal or bacterial contaminants could possibly be found. Perish the thought! With an impetus of disarming sincerity, the professor concluded that had it been demonstrated that a host had turned into human blood or flesh, this would have caused too much embarrassment to the University of Göttingen: maybe even its partial closure, as some of its programs and activities were openly founded on atheism.

In order to hear a sensible and completely opposite statement, we must then turn to Prof. Sulkowski, a scientist we shall talk about in the chapter dedicated to the Sokółka miracle: "If a new important social issue arises, one that requires a scientist's involvement, if there is a need for his knowledge, he not only has the right, but also the duty to be involved.... We have the duty to investigate every scientific problem."

Four centuries after Galileo, we are finally closing the circle: ideological prejudice changed sides and is now the dominant scientific school of thought in the most prestigious universities. However, the study of eucharistic miracles brilliantly unmasks the haughtiness, intellectual sloth, and conformism of a certain type of science.

One last note, before concluding: Eucharistic miracles should also be defended from the friendly fire of various scientists and popularizers who dish up studies and publish inaccurate articles. Even if they do this in good faith, their "works" are biased, unable to withstand serious and rational criticism, and ultimately end up being absolutely counterproductive. The most obvious example, which I personally unmasked, is the elusive World Health Organization-United Nations report published by Prof. Giuseppe Biondini in 1976 in support of the otherwise crystal clear and scientifically incontrovertible investigations by Prof. Linoli on the miracle of Lanciano. Viewing the report only requires obtaining permission from the Conventual friars of Lanciano, always friendly and available. It is a slapdash document clumsily mixing rigorous and well-written scientific data—mostly obtained from Egyptian mummies and not from the tissue specimens of Lanciano—with ramblings supporting the miracle written in a hazy and bombastic Italian. The damage is enormous: this "UN report" pretends in its excerpt to be an original study of the sacred relics, claiming the undertaking of a whopping five hundred analyses on the relics themselves. That way, it presents itself to the naïve faithful as an even more superior investigation than the one performed by Linoli. However, its far-fetched conclusions are easily unmasked by the experts. Unfortunately, this foreign material has crept into the "official" scientific documentation on the miracle of Lanciano: even today—forty years later—both devotional and more "formal" publications continue to reference this cheap ideological fake, presenting it as if it were of comparable quality to Linoli's work.

Well, understood then, let's keep our eyes open, pay attention to what we hear, and remain vigilant. Enjoy the read!

1

Lanciano (Eighth Century)

An Ancient Miracle

The name of this charming town of thirty-five thousand inhabitants, in the Chieti province of the "strong and gentle" region
of Abruzzo, is closely associated with one of the most important
eucharistic miracles. Lanciano indeed hosts one of the most
ancient eucharistic miracles whose relics are still preserved. It
is so ancient that a precise historical documentation regarding
the original event has been lost over the centuries. However, the
inhabitants of Lanciano managed not to lose sight of the origins
of this miracle until modern age through oral tradition and very
strong uninterrupted devotion.

What happened exactly? In all likelihood, a Basilian monk
was celebrating Mass in Lanciano at the church of Sts. Legonziano
and Domiziano between AD 700 and 750. In Greece and the
Byzantine East, Basilian monks were following St. Basil's Rule, according to the spirituality of the Desert Fathers and St. Anthony
the Abbot in particular. Between AD 600 and 700, many Basilians were fleeing from persecutions — mostly by Persians or the
Byzantine emperor himself if he was an iconoclast — and found
refuge in Italy. In Lanciano, one of these monks, whose name has

not been passed on, was celebrating Mass. I shall then turn to a 1631 manuscript—written in good-quality Italian nine hundred years after the miracle—which clearly explains the events:

> In this city, in the convent of St. Legonziano, where the Monks of St. Basil lived in about seven-hundred AD, was … a monk who, not very steadfast in his faith, well educated in the sciences of the world, but ignorant in God's ones, lived day by day doubting if the true Body of Christ was in the consecrated host and likewise if the true Blood was in the wine.
>
> Still, never abandoned by divine grace in constant prayer, he kept praying to God that he would heal this wound in his heart.…
>
> Thus, one morning, in the midst of his Sacrifice, after uttering the most sacred words of consecration, while more than ever before caught up in his old mistake, he saw (Oh marvelous and unique favor!) the Bread turned into Flesh and the Wine turned into Blood.…
>
> Behold the Flesh and the Blood of our most beloved Christ.
>
> At these words the anxious people hastily ran with devotion to the Altar and terrified, not without overflowing tears, began shouting for mercy.

After many centuries, without undergoing any process of decay—which is evidently in itself a mysterious fact—a double relic has been handed over to us made of

- a fleshy rounded tissue, dark brown and yellowish in color, about 6 centimeters in diameter, thicker on the edges and thinning out centrally into a large cavity in the middle

• five solid fragments of unequal volume, yellow-brown
color, of clotted blood weighing altogether 16 grams
At present, the relics are contained and sealed in an elegant silver
double monstrance crafted in 1713, which allows full view of the
precious contents through a window and a crystal chalice. They
are kept in a marble case on top of the main altar in the church
of St. Francis, under custody of the Conventual Friars Minor.

A *Blackout* of Eight Centuries

There are currently no reliable historical documents about the
origin of these relics. The first written text explicitly mentioning
a eucharistic miracle preserved in Lanciano dates back only to
1574, during the first ecclesiastical review of the relics themselves, requested by Archbishop Antonio Gaspar Rodriguez.
Giacomo Fella, a historian from Lanciano, in 1620 wrote of
the sworn declaration he received from two Conventual friars
of Lanciano, Fr. Antonio Scarpa and Fr. Angelo Siro. The two
remembered the existence, up to sixty years earlier, of a Gothic
manuscript book written in Greek and Latin and covered by two
small boards, which was certainly decisive in determining the
origin and dating of the miracle.

Well, the manuscript book was kindly shown to two passing
Basilian monks who were hosted in Lanciano. Since the times
of the Trojan Horse, it has not been advisable to trust Greeks! I
am joking, but the following day, early in the morning, the two
Basilians disappeared for good without saying goodbye, and with
them disappeared the precious book, which mentioned a former
fellow brother of theirs whose lack of belief had stained the good
name of their order.

Thus, the Gothic manuscript book no longer exists and neither does a notarized declaration confirming the theft of the

book itself, which the historian Fella had recommended should be written as evidence of the theft.

Oral tradition about the remote event was put down in writing in the elegant 1631 document that I already cited, or in stone on a monument of the same year, but the first eight centuries since the miracle of Lanciano remain a "black hole" for historians. A black hole, yes, but one nevertheless lit up by archived documentation demonstrating the strongly convergent interest of the Franciscans, the diocesan clergy, the brotherhoods of both the ancient church of St. Legonziano, where the miracle happened, and the more recent 1258 church of St. Francis built on top of St. Legonziano, where the relics were moved later on—a common interest that brought about tensions and disputes, even to the extent of papal edicts being issued to confirm the custody of the St. Legonziano-St. Francis compound (and hence of its precious, yet never mentioned, content).

Around the eleventh century, a theological dispute grew up in the Church about the presence of Christ in the Eucharist; it led to a flourishing of treatises that set the foundations for the later definitive definition of the concept of *transubstantiation*. That refers to the transformation of the substance of bread and wine into the substance of the Body and Blood of our Lord during Mass at the moment of consecration despite remaining under the visible species of bread and wine.

An important theological contribution was provided in 1073 by Guitmund of Aversa, a Norman monk who wrote *De corporis et sanguinis Christi veritate in Eucharistia* (*On the Truth of the Body and Blood of Christ in the Eucharist*). In a passage there, he recalled a miracle he was told about by his teacher and friend Lanfranc of Pavia. During his infancy, Lanfranc had heard that in Italy "a miracle had taken place in the hands of a priest who, while celebrating Mass, saw the true Flesh on the altar and the true Blood in the chalice. He was afraid to consume them and thus called on the bishop for advice. The bishop, along with other fellow bishops who came together for the event, took the chalice containing the Flesh and the Blood, carefully sealed it, and set it in the center of the altar for it to be perpetually preserved amongst the most important relics." Fr. Nicola Petrone, a Conventual Franciscan that recently studied the miracle's history, believes the miracle mentioned by Lanfranc is referring to the one in Lanciano, which is unlike any others known to us from the early Middle Ages in Italy because it is fully complete and has survived through so many centuries.

The 1574 Inspection

Since 1574, the miraculous tissues have undergone inspections nearly every century, ordered either by the Church or the Franciscan authorities. The first one, in 1574, should certainly be remembered: the monstrances were opened in front of the people, and the relics were inspected and weighed. On this occasion, a mysterious event took place that was destined to be memorable: the five blood clots, clearly different sizes to the naked eye, turned out to be of identical weight on the scale. Not only that, but when all the clots were weighed together simultaneously, they still weighed the same as each clot weighed alone.

Writing this in 2016, I believe in the intelligence of my ancestors and must guard against ridiculing them, since they were so much better than me at facing much more difficult lives with courage and moral strength. Merely by chance, my father and grandfather were born in Atessa, a township bordering Lanciano. My family name also originates from there, and I cannot even rule out that one of my forefathers could have been present on that day in Lanciano. If this miracle of the same weight doesn't occur today, it would have been even less likely back then in 1574, when such instruments were even more commonly used. How would one make a mistake when using a weighing scale, particularly in such an important moment and in front of all the fellow citizens? As a Roman Catholic, I believe in much more "incredible" things, and I cannot see why I should not give credit to perhaps one of my forefathers telling me about a mysterious fact that he witnessed in person. Besides, the theological meaning of the event is crystal clear: each of the smallest drops of consecrated wine already contains in its wholeness the complete and indivisible substance of the Blood of our Lord; the smallest drop, just as a chalice full of wine contains the One whom the whole universe cannot contain. In 1563, the Council of Trent had just ended, having defined the dogma of transubstantiation: Heaven was once again conveying an unequivocal sign from Lanciano.

In the following inspections, such a miracle no longer took place. For instance, in 1886 the weights of the five fragments amounted to 8.00, 2.45, 2.85, 2.05, and 1.15 grams, besides 5 milligrams of pulverized fragments.

In 1809, the liberty, equality, and fraternity of Napoleon's laws also arrived in Lanciano: the convent of St. Francis was shut down and turned into barracks, the nine friars went missing, and the dining hall became a town hall. For some time, part of the former convent even hosted a Masonic lodge. The church of St. Francis became the parish church. With order being re-established in the Restoration period, only in the following century were conditions once again suitable for the Conventual Franciscans to return to Lanciano in 1952.

The 1970 Inspection

Later on, in the 1960s, the crisp air of the Second Vatican Council was perhaps being felt. Uncertainty about the distant origins of their treasure—somewhat lost in the foggy early Middle Ages—began to weigh on the Franciscans. They began to think of planning a new and modern inspection of a robust scientific character. Archbishop Msgr. Pacifico Perantoni, also a Franciscan, hesitated at first but then convinced himself. A researcher was needed to carry out the analytical work: an expert in the scientific field as well as one of the highest moral character. That man was Prof. Odoardo Linoli, forty-eight years old, an anatomical pathologist and the head of the "Spedali Riuniti" hospital in Arezzo.

On the morning of November 18, 1970, at 10:15 in the sacristy of the church of St. Francis, the archbishop broke the 1886 seals and, in front of many witnesses, opened the monstrance on a table covered in "white linen." In a moving ceremony, Prof. Linoli asked the archbishop "to be allowed to touch" the Flesh, and the bishop consented. The texture was hard, almost wooden. The case containing the Flesh was clearly not airtight: the tissue of the Flesh was covered in white, dry stains, detaching easily. Those stains were molds, not starch, as immediately ascertained under the microscope. There were also residues of small insects and maggots. It was a discouraging moment described by the secretary, Fr. Castiglione, in his report: "After examining the tissue of the Flesh, Prof. Linoli expressed his concern to be unable to identify valid elements to draw scientific conclusions through laboratory tests. He advanced the hypothesis that the Flesh tissue was already lacking all characterizing features." The prominent forehead of the professor began perspiring beads of sweat. He then asked the archbishop "to be allowed to collect a few small fragments," and the bishop consented. By applying great force with his scissors, he snipped away two minuscule samples from the edge, a total of 20 milligrams of tissue.

It was then time for the Blood: five clots, free of contaminants, of hard and uniform texture. A suggestion was made to weigh the clots separately and altogether, exactly as in 1574. A weighing scale was not among the available instruments, so a person borrowed one from the local pharmacy. The total weight was 15.85 grams, and naturally, each clot was of a different weight. Linoli then asked the archbishop "to sample a small fragment," and again, the bishop consented. The detached fragment weighed 318 milligrams. The inspection was over. At that time, it was the friars who were feeling discouraged: "We friars, astonished, were staring at each other. Everyone's facial expression revealed unmistakable disappointment and disillusionment." An eyewitness wrote: "Perhaps due to our merit or fault, the end of the eucharistic miracle of Lanciano had come about. We were feigning calmness though deep inside we were extremely apprehensive and already expecting the worst."

After returning to Arezzo, Prof. Linoli carried out a batch of baseline tests over the following hundred days: those were quite possibly the most exciting of his life. As directly transcribed from the article he published the following year in Quaderni Sclavo, his tests were aimed at

- ascertaining the histological structure of the wood-hard tissue handed down as Flesh
- ascertaining if the hardened, stony, claylike substance handed down as "Blood" could indeed be characterized as blood
- establishing which biological species the Flesh and Blood belonged to
- identifying the blood group of both tissues

• investigating the protein and mineral components of
the Blood

The work was not easy. The histological structure needed interpretation: cellular nuclei did not stain with conventional dyes,
nor were there any enhancing transverse striations (although
this was to be expected in a longtime preserved tissue). Thus,
Linoli asked for extra help from Prof. Ruggero Bertelli in Siena
to confirm that the muscle tissue originated from the heart.

There were no red or white blood cells in the blood specimen
either, and some of the test results were inconclusive. Others
needed adaptations in the analytical protocol to account for
the unique nature of the ancient and highly dehydrated sample.

Still, one step at a time, with patience and persistence, a
full and amazing result began to take shape, perhaps beyond
everyone's expectations. On two occasions, Prof. Linoli felt the
need to anticipate and share his satisfaction about his preliminary results with the Lanciano friars. He wrote two telegraph
messages. On December 11, 1970, he wrote: "In principio erat
Verbum, et Verbum caro factum est," citing from the prologue
to the Gospel of John: "In the beginning was the Word, and the
Word became flesh." If style is what defines a person, then his
style was telegraphic by necessity, but it must have greatly warmed
the trembling hearts of those Franciscans on that very Christmas.
Again, on February 11, 1971, he wrote: "Further research allows
confirmation of the presence of cardiac striated muscle. Alleluia."

On March 4, 1971 — one of the coldest days of the century in
Italy — Prof. Linoli finalized a scientific report in snow-covered
Lanciano. It summarized the following points:

1. The Blood of the eucharistic miracle is true blood and
the Flesh is true flesh.
2. The Flesh is made of heart muscle tissue.

3. The Blood and the Flesh belong to the human species.
4. The blood group is AB and is identical in the Blood and the Flesh: hence, in all likelihood, both belong to the same Person.
5. Blood proteins could be fractionated in the ratios of normal fresh blood.
6. Chloride minerals, phosphorus, magnesium, potassium, and sodium were detected in reduced quantities in the blood, whereas calcium was present in excess.[2]

The more technical details (which we will carefully examine in several following chapters: Heart, Blood, and AB Blood Group) became the subject matter of a thorough scientific publication accompanied by extensive photographic evidence: an impeccable one, even by modern standards.

In addition to the above-mentioned conclusions, Prof. Linoli also mentioned the following:

- The structure of the Flesh does not lend itself to the hypothesis of a "fake" specimen maliciously crafted in previous centuries: only a very expert hand in anatomical dissection could have tangentially cut through the surface of a hollow organ so neatly to obtain such a thin cross section or "slice" from a cadaveric heart (as deduced by the mostly longitudinal course of the bundles of muscle fibers seen in the histological samples).
- The specimens — the Blood in particular — would have rapidly undergone putrefaction if originating from a corpse.
- However, salts of preservative substances were never detected in the tissue samples.

---

[2] Likely due to environmental contamination.

Thirty years later—while interviewed in his Arezzo home in March 2001 by Mike Willesee and Ron Tesoriero (whom we shall formally meet in the Buenos Aires chapter)—Linoli candidly confessed that after the time when these results came through, "for a few months [he] felt as if [he] was walking thirty centimeters above the ground."

The Supplemental 1981 Inspection

In the decade following the 1970 inspection, the Franciscan brothers asked Prof. Linoli to further examine the miraculous Flesh, both macroscopically and microscopically. Thus, new histologic sections[3] were obtained from a small fragment not used in 1970 that was still preserved in Lanciano.

In the new microscope slides, the myocardial structure[4] of the muscle fibers was even more clearly delineated. Moreover, new and original structural details could be seen: the endocardium, the internal lining of the heart, was clearly visible as well as areas of adipose tissue;[5] arterial and venous blood vessels and even bundles of vagus nerve fibers[6] could be appreciated. It was a series of microscopic findings that—taken as a whole—outlined the picture of a complete human heart.

The macroscopic study was also surprising. Linoli's focus was on the fourteen small circular holes punched along the entire

---

[3]   Histologic sections are prepared from sampled tissue by different methods. The end result, however, is a microscopically thin tissue slice that is fixed onto a glass slide to be examined under a microscope.

[4]   *Myocardial* means belonging to myocardium: the medical term for heart.

[5]   *Adipose tissue* is the medical term for fat.

[6]   The vagus nerve provides inhibitory innervation to the heart, which slows down heart rate.

external edge of the relic, as if, in a remote past, it had been necessary to fix the Flesh with fourteen nails onto a wooden support to counteract the retraction and shrinkage of rigor mortis.[7] Thus, the Flesh would have retracted toward the outer nails, giving rise to the hollow space currently present in the middle. However, according to the professor, this cavity was also partly pre-existent. Therefore, still to this day, the relic macroscopically resembles a complete heart cross section, or possibly a cross section just through the left ventricle.[8]

Prof. Linoli added one last penetrating observation: if the Flesh we venerate today had undergone rigor mortis, evidently at the time of the original miracle it would have been alive. In fact, rigor mortis begins one to three hours after death and ends thirty-six to forty-eight hours later.

He actually continued to reflect on this in the following years and, on the twentieth anniversary of the inspection, felt the urge to reveal a macroscopic aspect of the Flesh that he had previously missed: A full heart transverse section can actually be recognized in the overall makeup of the miraculous Flesh. A remnant of the left ventricle can be glimpsed in the thicker lower portion while the thinner upper portion is the right ventricle. Time caused the loss of anatomical parts such as the interventricular septum, which physiologically divides the two ventricles, hence resulting in the remaining single cavity. Dehydration and spontaneous mummification caused a reduction in size, as the current size is smaller than one of a living heart.

[7] Rigor mortis is a normal post-death phenomenon leading to transient generalized stiffening of all body muscles.

[8] The human heart is divided into four chambers: two atria and two ventricles. The left ventricle is the largest and most powerful contractile chamber of the adult heart.

Therefore, the Flesh of Lanciano begins to resemble the image a cardiologist visualizes on an ultrasound screen: it is a parasternal short-axis view,[9] obtained as if ideally "cutting" the heart along the frontal axis. The left and right ventricles would then be seen next to each other beating together and maintaining an ovular shape.

Scientific Standard

As already stated, Prof. Linoli's investigations are scientifically impeccable. The report is incredibly detailed and describes materials and methods: the most up-to-date and validated ones at the time. He did not hide the difficulties he encountered (such as the negative results of the hematin and hemochromogen tests[10]) and faithfully adhered to the objectives he laid out at the beginning of his study.

Whenever methodologically possible, he introduced control samples (such as human or animal blood, or sheets of untreated blotting paper) to bring out the soundness of his method and enhance the validity of his results. His photographic evidence is complete.

Any weaknesses? The whole investigation was carried out by Prof. Linoli alone. There was no supervisory committee: he took the samples, and these were analyzed by him and him alone.

Nowadays we would certainly organize a chain of custody for the specimens, possibly even video-record its most crucial

---

[9] A parasternal short-axis view of the heart reveals the cross-sectional image of a heart that has been horizontally cut across by an imaginary plane.

[10] Broadly speaking, these tests screen for the presence of the iron-containing heme pigment molecule present in hemoglobin, the oxygen-carrying protein present in red blood cells.

moments, and the study would be done by multiple experts. Reciprocal surveillance would eliminate the risk of fraud. Even better, blinding methodologies would be applied to the experiments, such as not revealing the origin of the samples to the researchers. We shall see that this was the procedure followed by Dr. Castañón in Buenos Aires in 1999 and in Tixtla in 2009. The trust put in Prof. Linoli's integrity was itself part of the heart-wrenching decision by the Franciscans to test the sacred relic. Let's put ourselves in the friars' shoes: for the first time in Church history, modern medical science was allowed to analyze an extraordinary specimen—supposed to be nothing less than the Body and Blood of our Lord—and the friars even accepted its partial destruction in the sampling process. They must have had great courage: the risk that the analyses would have demonstrated a fraudulent origin or more simply yielded inconclusive results was very high (considering how ancient and degraded the tissue was). So much boldness on their part had to be understandably balanced with their trust in a nonhostile scientist at least. Personally, given the historical context, I find their prudent attitude quite understandable.

The Elusive WHO-UN Report

Between 1973 and 1976, a certain Prof. Giuseppe Biondini involved a World Health Organization committee in further research to try and win greater "scientific support" for Linoli's work. The quality of this new study report—which I personally consulted at the Shrine of Lanciano—is more than disappointing and does not deserve any further publicity.

In Conclusion

It can't be denied that Prof. Linoli's scientific studies restored both public attention on the miracle and its visibility. However, even before those studies, it was never really forgotten at any time in history, and today interest in it is alive more than ever: every year, tens of thousands of pilgrims come to Lanciano from all over the world to venerate the relic or adore a Presence (both attitudes are equally allowed by the Church). Indeed, the miracle of Lanciano is one of the best examples of a happy and fruitful encounter between medical science and the Catholic Faith.

Bibliography

Linoli, Odoardo. 1971. "Ricerche istologiche, immunologiche e biochimiche sulla carne e sul sangue del miracolo eucaristico di Lanciano (VIII secolo)." *Quaderni Sclavo di Diagnostica* 7 (3). Original report by Professor Linoli no longer available. A PDF copy is possessed by the author and can be made available upon request.

Linoli, Odoardo. 1992. *Ricerche istologiche immunologiche e biochimiche sulla carne e sul sangue del miracolo eucaristico di Lanciano (VIII secolo).* Italy: Edizioni S.M.E.L. Research findings from 1971 integrated with data from the 1981 research and reflections on the macroscopic structure of the Flesh by Prof. Linoli. Available for sale at the Shrine of the Eucharistic Miracle in Lanciano.

Wikimedia. 2018. "File:Eucharistic Miracle of Lanciano – public documentation – L'Osservatore Romano.JPG." *L'osservatore Romano.* Accessed July 11, 2021. Newspaper article in which Prof. Linoli presents the scientific findings obtained from his second round of research.

Petrone, Nicola. 1990. *Il miracolo eucaristico di Lanciano.* 2nd ed. Lanciano: Litografia Botolini presso Libreria S.M.E.L. Supported by Church imprimatur, updated with the studies from 1981.

Sammaciccia, Bruno. 1973. *Il miracolo eucaristico di Lanciano: La scienza ha fornito le prove.* 4th ed. Lanciano: Litografia Botolini.

The first book narrating full story of the eucharistic miracle of Lanciano in the light of Prof. Linoli's findings. Supported by Church imprimatur.

La Lampada. 2010. "Bollettino: Santurario del miracolo eucaristico," *La Lampada* III (20).

In this issue of the periodical newspaper published by the shrine of Lanciano, Fr. Petrone hypothesized that the miracle described by Guitmund of Aversa was very likely to be the miracle of Lanciano. No longer available online. A PDF copy is possessed by the author and can be made available upon request.

2

Buenos Aires (1992, 1994, 1996)

A Dutiful Premise to Understand the
Buenos Aires, Sokółka, and Legnica Events

What should a priest do when a consecrated host has been dirt-
ied—either accidentally or by desecration—and can hardly be
consumed anymore? Ancient Church policies actually provide
answers to even the most incredible circumstances that could
arise during the celebration of the Holy Sacrifice of the Mass,
including the celebrant's death. In 1962, Pope St. John XXIII
approved the latest revision of the *Missale Romanum* (*The Roman Missal*) where, in the "*De defectibus*" ("About the Defects")
chapter, par. X, no. 7 reads as follows: "If something poisoned
touched the consecrated host,... it may be put in a chalice full
of water, as stated above in regards to the Blood at no. 6." No.
6 stated: "So that the species may dissolve and such water be
poured into the sacrarium."

Thus, the complete dissolution of the visible unleavened
bread host is awaited. Once the species are missing due to being dissolved in water, the substance of the Body of our Lord is
then also said to be missing. Only at that stage can the water be
discarded, although not into the common sewer but rather into

the sacrarium: an outlet draining into the ground within the boundaries of the consecrated church premises.

Interestingly enough, this is a new 1962 addition to the previous Missal version suggesting instead that "the same be preserved in a separate place inside the Tabernacle until the species have degraded and only then be poured into the sacrarium."

A Fivefold Miracle

Five miraculous eucharistic events took place between 1992 and 1996, all of them in the same Buenos Aires parish. No human argument can explain this abundance of gifts: Couldn't these miracles have been more "equitably" distributed around this world of ours, one that is so hungry for visible signs of God's presence? It was as if the words of the glorified Christ of the Apocalypse were re-echoing: "Behold, I stand at the door and knock." Christ's knocking at that same door in Buenos Aires has indeed been persistent.

Still, most people hardly know about these events, even in Argentina. In Italy, they have only been recently discussed after Pope Francis's election and just since the media—Catholic bloggers in particular—shifted their focus to that diocese "at the end of the world" where Francis came from. One of the best Italian Catholic journalists, Maurizio Blondet, spent two weeks in Buenos Aires in 2014 for an exclusive inquiry that then led to his book *Un cuore per la vita eterna* (*A Heart for Eternal Life*), which I strongly suggest as a reference to learn more about the facts.

Speaking from my own Buenos Aires travel experience (exactly at that time for family reasons), if you asked a local taxi driver to take you to St. Mary's Church on Avenida La Plata 286, he would most likely interrupt you with a gesture of understanding, saying: "Yes, the church." No, you are not thinking of the same answer. Even in Argentina, few people know the facts we are about to discuss. "The church with the clock!" would be his enthusiastic reply: he would always check the time when driving in front of it.

Imagine being in the center of Buenos Aires, in a very ordinary and unimpressive neighborhood: not a rundown one, but certainly far from the quainter and more elegant quarters visited by most tourists. The red brick neo-Romanesque church of St. Mary's is most likely barely a hundred years old. It has a common but dignified look, like that of the surrounding neighborhood. In 2006, a reserved eucharistic adoration chapel was added to the left-side nave. Every third Friday of the month at 8:00 p.m. and every fourth Saturday of the month at 11:00 a.m., there are scheduled sessions to explain the facts of the events that took place there to the visiting faithful.

After a long wait, since my family and I did not visit on one of the monthly sessions, the parish priest sent us over to a layman: a delightful gentleman who thoroughly and discreetly explained the 1990s events to us in slow and understandable Spanish. At the end, he opened a tabernacle on the wall behind the elegant monstrance holding the Blessed Sacrament in the adoration chapel. The decorated monstrance in front of the tabernacle is a modern one, made of glass paste and metal. Its design resembles the *nahui ollin* flower, a simple four-petal flower symbolizing the presence of God's power for the ancient Aztecs. The same flower is also found on the dress of the Virgin of Guadalupe, more precisely over her womb, as a reminder of Mary's pregnancy. After a few moments of moving religious silence, he then took from the tabernacle another simple monstrance holding the tiny 1992 blood crust between two glass plates and showed it to us by illuminating it with a small flashlight.

A Cardiologist Examines Jesus

The Facts

1992

On the evening of Friday, May 1, 1992, Carlos Dominguez, a lay minister of the Eucharist, noticed two crescent-shaped host fragments lying on the corporal[11] in front of the tabernacle. Quite possibly they could have fallen out of the ciborium[12] earlier on. He mentioned it to the parish priest, Fr. Juan Salvador Carlomagno, who told him to begin the dissolving procedure explained before, thinking they were no longer fresh and edible. The two host fragments were thus immersed in water in a small ceramic container that was then locked inside the tabernacle.

On the morning of May 8, Fr. Juan checked the container for the first time and was astonished. He spoke about what he saw with the other priests living in the same parish: Fr. Eduardo Pérez Dal Lago, Fr. Eduardo Graham, and Deacon Marcelo Pablo Tomaino. Three blood clots had formed in the water, initially covered in a white "fuzz" that later disappeared. There were blood streaks on the walls of the container, as if they had been produced by some sort of "explosion" of the hosts themselves. They advised the diocesan curia: Cardinal Antonio Quarracino (Bergoglio's immediate predecessor) was absent, and so they discussed the matter on the phone with Msgr. Eduardo Miras, the auxiliary bishop of Buenos Aires, who recommended a medical evaluation. As we shall see, the latter confirmed the apparent nature of the substance as blood. Marcelo Antonini, a professional photographer, was also summoned, and he documented the ongoing specimen changes that happened over the following days.

---

[11] The square cloth on which the sacred vessels are meant to rest.
[12] The sacred vessel that contains the consecrated hosts and is kept inside the tabernacle.

On Sunday, May 10, during both the 7:00 p.m. Mass, celebrated by the parish priest, and the 8:15 p.m. Mass, celebrated by Fr. Graham, a new miraculous event took place twice. The paten[13] holding the consecrated host was stained with blood—not just one but rather two distinct patens: a bronze one and a tin fish-shaped one.

St. Mary's parish priests were living through moments of joy and fear. What was happening? Why was this specifically happening to them, at their very hands? I must recommend reading the touching spiritual diary written by Fr. Eduardo Pérez on those very days and found in Blondet's book. The young thirty-year-old priest had a deep personal involvement in the mystery of the Real Presence at the time. While waiting for an official statement by Church authorities, St. Mary's priests decided not to talk about the events outside their very small circle, even if it was quite difficult to maintain discretion.

Meanwhile, in Fr. Pérez's words, "the 'blood-thing' remained shiny, like liver flesh, although bright red and not purplish, without the slightest smell of going off." After some time, the water in the container evaporated and a little crust was left over at the bottom before detaching a few years later. That was the small red crust—at most a couple of centimeters in size—that I also had a chance to see.

1994

At the children's morning Mass on Sunday, July 24, 1994, the lay minister distributing the Eucharist noticed a running drop of blood on the inner rim of the ciborium. The episode was not

---

[13] The metal plate holding the bread during the Liturgy of the Eucharist.

destined to have much resonance, as it was squeezed in between the "major" 1992 and 1996 events. While in Buenos Aires, I saw a photograph of that ciborium with a blood streak on its internal wall, and I retained an indelible memory of it. The one who lived and witnessed the episode in person certainly did not consider it a "minor" event!

1996

At the end of the distribution of Holy Communion at the 7:00 p.m. Mass on Sunday, August 18, 1996, one of the faithful turned to the priest celebrant, Fr. Alejandro Pezet, with great embarrassment. She had noticed a host hidden in the base of a candlestick in front of the crucifix, which is still to this day in the right-side nave. Fr. Alejandro took a look and picked up the host that had certainly been abandoned by someone with desecrating intents. He thought of consuming it himself, but it was too dirty and dusty. Therefore, he asked Emma Fernandez—a seventy-seven-year-old lay minister of the Eucharist—to immerse it in water and lock it in the tabernacle according to the usual procedure. The insightful reader must now be feeling a déjà vu. Mrs. Fernandez, the only lay person who had access to the tabernacle, indeed saw something strange in the round glass container she had left in it and discussed what she saw with Fr. Pezet on August 26. After immediately involving Fr. Eduardo Graham, Fr. Pezet also noticed that the host was transforming into something else, something red in color that was destined to grow in the following weeks. Of course, he knew about the facts of 1992 and 1994, although he hadn't been at St. Mary's at the time. Because of this, he immediately suspected a supernatural cause for what was happening. He informed the curia, and Jorge Mario Bergoglio, one of the four auxiliary bishops of Buenos Aires at the time, recommended taking professional photographs to begin with. As in 1992, the photographs taken on August 26 and September 6 by Marcelo Antonini are readily available both in the texts referenced in my bibliography and online. The dissolving host was less and less distinguishable, although the water was made more and more turbid by a red "cloud-like" substance and darker "jelly-like" clumps whose texture resembled that of clotted blood. Darker "mold-like" blooms were seen on the surface of these presumed blood clots.

After about a month, the leftover "foreign material" was transferred to a closed bottle of distilled water: not exactly the best storage medium to preserve a living tissue! Unfortunately, it remained in distilled water for at least three years until Dr. Castañón's investigations began.

The Scientific Assessments

1992–1995

In May 1992, the parish priest Fr. Carlomagno told Msgr. Miras what was happening. The bishop himself recommended that medical evaluations be carried out. Two doctors were involved very early on, an oncologist[14] and a hematologist.[15]

DR. BOTTO

Following Fr. Pérez's account of the events, an initial investigation was assigned to Dr. Isabel Botto, an oncologist living close to the parish. She attempted drawing up with a syringe some of what

---

[14] An oncologist is a physician specializing in the treatment of cancer.
[15] A hematologist is a physician specializing in the treatment of blood diseases.

looked like blood from the central mass in the ceramic vase from May 1, but couldn't do so because of its hardened consistency. She then collected the material making up one of the reddish streaks staining the walls of the container. Along with a laboratory technician, Alicia Martines, she analyzed her sample at the Sanatorio Evangelico El Buen Samaritano. The positive reaction to a hemoglobin detection test confirmed that the substance was blood; however, she did not specify whether the analytical kit she used could also confirm its human origin. Dr. Botto admitted that more in-depth analyses by a medical examiner were warranted at that stage. She even claimed she had seen muscle cells and "living fibrous tissue" under her microscope. Fr. Pezet himself asked if those cells could be heart muscle cells, and she answered that it was possible, although further testing was needed.

Dr. Sasot

Two medical reports were presented, or I should say photographed, in Dr. Castañón's book. They were typewritten and signed by Dr. Adhelma Myrian Segovia de Sasot. Behind such an impressive name was a hematologist working at Dr. J. M. Ramos Mejia Hospital in Buenos Aires. Three distinct investigations can be deduced from her writings:

1. In a "June 1992" report, with no mention about the exact date, she described the macroscopic evolution of a material "taking the shape of a clot" in a ceramic container. Its texture also felt like that of a clot to touch. The substance remained fairly stable until holy water was added to it just a few days later. In June, after just one month, Dr. Sasot mentioned that the dried-up clot was about to detach itself from the container (as actually happened in the following years).

She initially described its microscopic appearance at low 16x magnification as made up of multiple layers: lower dark red ones, and lighter-colored superficial ones. The latter appeared to be made of transparent threads resembling the textbook appearance of mitochondria. Her description of the layered structure was indeed quite imprecise and relying on analogies. Of course, she did not actually claim that the superficial layers were made of mitochondria: these energy-producing organelles contained in many cell types could not possibly be seen at low 16x magnification. Someone — most likely herself — made a little drawing on the margin of one of the pages of her report: a squiggly sketch resembling a cross section of the inner membranes of a mitochondrion. I think she drew it as a visual representation of the structure she was seeing through her microscope.

She then continued on, describing the superficial layers of her specimen by mentioning at least three formations reminding her of "water droplets." I am not quite sure about what sort of scientific conclusions could be drawn from these descriptions of hers: I must admit I translated and transcribed her notes hoping that some histopathology[16] expert may read them one day and perhaps shed some light on her arcane writings.

Suddenly, however, her report ceases to be vague and imprecise. She literally makes the reader jump off the chair by writing: "One of the times I observed it, I noticed an area that *seemed to be rhythmically beating*" (in Spanish: *parecia latir rit-micamente*). Unfortunately, she didn't have access to a camera or video camera at the time of her observation. So we are just

---

[16] Histopathology is the specialty of diagnosing diseases based on the observation of diseased tissue specimens.

left openmouthed by reading about something so fantastic and unbelievable.

Finally, Dr. Sasot concluded her report by noting that she regretted having to discontinue her observational work due to health problems.

2. Still in June 1992, Dr. Sasot described the laboratory tests done on an alleged blood sample taken from a paten. The substance had been analyzed three days after making its appearance. Hence, she must have been referring to one of the two miracles on the evening of May 10. A simple though unequivocal test was performed to examine what was thought to be a drop of blood: a blood film[17] prepared with the standard May-Grunwald and Giemsa stains.[18] This common blood test yielded a full differential white cell count,[19] expressing the relative percentage proportions of the five major types of white blood cells. The differential count demonstrated an excess of lymphocytes[20] (47 percent) compared to neutrophils[21] (49 percent), as expected in

---

[17] A blood film (also called blood smear) is a thin layer of blood smeared on a glass slide, which is then stained to visualize the various blood cell types in it under the microscope.

[18] These are commonly used standardized mixtures of fixating and coloring agents. They stain various populations of white blood cells in different ways so as to make them clearly distinguishable to the eyes of a scientist.

[19] This is indeed an extremely common blood test, prescribed by doctors as part of routine screening blood work at many medical consultations and checkups.

[20] Broadly speaking and not exclusively, lymphocytes are white blood cells specialized in fighting viral infections.

[21] Broadly speaking and not exclusively, neutrophils are white blood cells specialized in fighting bacterial infections.

a typical physiological response to a viral infection, but also in the context of intense psychophysical stress.

Furthermore, the blood film revealed nonspecific debris, vacuolated cells,[22] and abundant bacterial contamination by cocci.[23] Using a nonmedical term, all these abnormal blood film findings were suggestive of a "state of suffering" of the analyzed blood sample. At least that was what could be seen in June 1992, after an unknown period of time—in the order of days—since the blood's appearance.

Finally, without clear explanations, Dr. Sasot concluded her June 1992 report by certifying that the analyzed sample was of human origin.

3. Lastly, there is also a "hematology report" by Dr. Sasot dated October 29, 1995. It is a summary of all the positive conclusions she could draw and directly demonstrate—as a competent specialized hematologist—from her work on a material whose origin she had actually not been told about, at least initially. The sample she analyzed—still available to her in 1995—was a small tissue portion preserved in a test tube filled with holy water that had been given to her at some point in time. In all likelihood, it must have been taken from the ceramic container of the first 1992 miracle, although this wasn't specified. She outlined the following list of conclusions, which would unequivocally demonstrate that the analyzed substance was blood, at least according to her, when taken altogether:

---

[22] Vacuoles are small inner cellular blebs that tend to appear when cells are physiologically stressed or dying.

[23] A coccus is any bacterium with a spherical, ovoid, or generally round shape. Most people will have heard of the *Staphylococcus* and *Streptococcus* species commonly responsible for skin and respiratory infections.

- A differential white cell count with a mild lymphocyto-sis[24] was obtained after May-Grunwald Giemsa staining: this was very similar to the previous May 10, 1992, result.
- Bacterial and fungal contamination was observed.
- Sodium and potassium were present.
- The presence of LDH enzyme[25] could be appreciated.
- The sample had a "physiological" protein electropho-resis profile,[26] except for a decreased amount of gamma globulins,[27] a finding observed in patients with compro-mised immune systems.

Finally, at the end of this report, there was mention of inter-est in performing further blood group identification analysis as well as other tests looking for the presence of DNA. Notably, Dr. Sasot believed that all these extra tests could have been easily performed by continuing to use that same small amount of sample.

My overall opinion on the 1992 investigations? Lots of good-will, but few available means and poor research coordination. Why waste the very precious sample material with multiple and pointlessly repeated tests? Why did no one seek to obtain the most important identification opinion when faced with an unknown

---

[24] A lymphocytosis is an excess of lymphocyte white blood cells.

[25] LDH stands for *lactate dehydrogenase*, a protein enzyme molecule located inside nearly all living cells that is involved in mediating energy producing chemical reactions.

[26] Protein electrophoresis is an analytical method used to separate all proteins in a given sample based on their molecular size. Proteins migrate different distances on a gel matrix based on their size when an electric field is applied. Once separated, their relative amounts can also be quantified to yield an electropho-retic profile.

[27] Gamma globulins are the antibodies used by the immune system to fight infection.

biological tissue: that of a histopathologist? Unfortunately, because of this, we will never know if those muscle tissue–like fibers—perhaps even spontaneously contracting—were truly what they were thought to be. Why is there no photographic documentation nor any proper laboratory notes to be consulted? Why should we have to make do with rough descriptions and doodles on the edge of a page? I can appreciate why no DNA investigations were carried out: PCR technology[28] was not so easily available in the 1990s. Such DNA tests would have been very expensive and perhaps would have entailed sacrificing too much material. But still, why did nobody try to identify the blood group? It would have been a trivial, although crucial and cheap, test to perform on fresh blood. Was the human origin of the analyzed tissues truly and incontrovertibly demonstrated? No specific procedure was ever mentioned in this regard. What about the sample storage conditions? Certainly, when dealing with a sacred relic, one would want to count on its supernatural incorruptibility. However, even the poorest laboratory in the world would at least have access to a freezer and would certainly not rely on the antiseptic and preservative properties of holy water. To tell the truth, and as partial justification for the haphazard nature of these investigations, it should be noted that Archbishop Miras did nominate an expert for the 1992 events: Msgr. José Luis Mollaghan. He was the one who, at a certain point, understandably forbade further sampling to preserve the integrity of the miracle. He requested that the investigators and the faithful be content with the conclusions that had been drawn at the time.

---

[28] PCR technology, short for *polymerase chain reaction* technology, is a technique to make many copies of even trace amounts of DNA found in a given sample.

A Cardiologist Examines Jesus

1995–2005

Jorge Mario Bergoglio had been the new archbishop of Buenos Aires since 1998. When asked in writing by Fr. Luis Maria Rodrigues Melgarejo, who succeeded Fr. Carlomagno as parish priest at St. Mary's, Bergoglio decided to allow further scientific testing on the eucharistic relics in July 1999. Dr. Castañón, a supernatural events researcher, took an interest in the eucharistic events at St. Mary's in the following months. Finally, on September 28, Bergoglio approved the new evaluation protocol proposed by Castañón with caveats of discretion and confidentiality to be maintained at all times during the course of the investigations.

Who is Dr. Ricardo Castañón Gómez? He is a clinical psychologist and expert in psychosomatics, biochemistry, and neuropsychophysiology. He is also a great communicator, and his YouTube conferences are very enjoyable to listen to. He captivates audiences for hours in parish halls of city suburbs just as well as at major North American conventions. Originally from Bolivia, he also studied in the United States and Europe. In 1992, he began to take an interest in mystical phenomena from a medical point of view, starting off with skeptical opinions and then ending up as a Catholic convert. At the time he was involved, there was certainly no shortage of research "material" for him, especially in South America: apparitions, miracles, stigmata, weeping or bleeding statues. In a Fox interview in 1999, he stated he had followed fifty cases but could only exclude a supernatural origin in six of them. Unfortunately, browsing the list of the most famous visionaries he studied (Nancy Fowler, Patricia Talbot, Julia Kim, Catalina Rivas), I personally would reverse his proportion of genuine to sham cases. This subject of fake mystical phenomena, or truly inexplicable phenomena — whose origins can and are likely to be diabolical—is certainly an interesting one, although it would deserve a detailed discussion I will not pursue here.

For many years, Dr. Castañón availed himself of the cooperation of two wealthy Australian professionals: lawyer Ron Tesoriero and television presenter Mike Willesee, a well-known public figure in Australia. Together, they created a common task force, an implacable war machine studying mysterious phenomena. They professionally filmed verbal accounts given by witnesses in the presence of a notary public, video-recorded the sampling of biological materials from original relics, and took care of forwarding those samples to a wide network of laboratories staffed by the best experts and scientists all over the world. Their policy was to maintain a "clear, unbroken and documented chain of custody," an uninterrupted and documented handover of material to be studied under "blinded" conditions—that is, by keeping the origin of the samples unknown to the researchers analyzing them. All of these expensive investigations were entirely self-financed by the Grupo Internacional para la Paz, founded by Castañón himself.

This was the special "agency" that Archbishop Bergoglio entrusted with investigating the events at St. Mary's Parish. On October 5, 1999, in front of witnesses and TV cameras, Dr. Castañón took two samples.

1. A first and very small sample was taken from the tiny dried crust still visible nowadays in Buenos Aires: the remnant of the first 1992 event. The label accompanying the sterile sealed test tube stated: "8 de mayo de 1992 Muestra 5 de Octobre de 1999."

2. A second sample was obtained from the remnant of the 1996 events: brown, semisolid material in distilled

water. Similarly, the label stated: "26 de Agosto de 1996 Muestra humeda 5 de Octobre de 1999."

According to the usual custodial process, the two vials were personally handed over on October 21, 1999, by Tesoriero himself to Forensic Analytical in Hayward, California. The following can be read in the May 1, 2000, report, signed by Vanora M. Kean, Ph.D., about test no. 19990441 performed on the two samples:

- Item no. 1-1, the dry 1992 sample, was examined under a stereo-microscope: an unidentified dark and brown-reddish material was seen with a hair, or a hair fragment, seemingly adhering to its edge. A preliminary orthotoli-dine blood identification test[29] yielded a negative result. A 2x3 millimeter portion was excised from the original 3x5 millimeter fragment, to exclude the suspicious hair-like formation, and was sent off for DNA analysis: a small amount of human DNA was indeed detected, although the following DNA profiling analysis failed to identify any of the standard STR[30] sequences.

- Item no. 1-2, the 1996 sample, was also examined un-der the stereo-microscope. While still wet, the presence of whitish fibrous material along with a brown-reddish substance adhering to it was noted, although no known morphological features could be recognized. After drying, darker particles became apparent, and an orthotolidine

---

[29] The orthotolidine test is a presumptive test looking for the presence of blood that involves the reaction of the o-tolidine molecule with blood hemoglobin in the presence of hydrogen peroxide.

[30] STR analysis, short for *short tandem repeat* analysis, is a DNA profiling technique commonly used in forensic medicine to iden-tify the DNA of the individual the analyzed sample belongs to.

test was performed on these, with negative result. One-third of the entire sample was used for DNA profiling. Once again, a small concentration of good-quality high-molecular-weight human DNA was isolated in the sample. However, PCR technique failed to identify and replicate any of the ten standard genetic profiling markers (nine STRs plus the X and Y amelogenin[31] genes) for *muestra humeda* no. 1-2 too. Notably, even if the DNA was reported to be of human origin, the final report could not but hypothesize a nonhuman origin for it as, once more, no human DNA profile could be determined by means of standard STR analysis. We shall return to this subject later on in a dedicated chapter on DNA.

No investigations were carried out to determine the blood group. These could have been performed even in the absence of blood, as the ABO antigens[32] can also be present in other tissues (in fact, for Lanciano, the Flesh was AB as well as the Blood). Dr. Castañón told me in person that the fragments were too small and priority was given to demonstrating the presence of DNA, a more "powerful" and specific finding than the ABO group. As requested, the leftover material from the two samples was sent via FedEx on March 2, 2000, to Dr. Robert Lawrence of

---

[31] Amelogenin genes are DNA sequences residing on sex chromosomes. They are important for the synthesis of tooth enamel and for determining a suspect's sex in forensic medicine. Because of this, they are always included in DNA profiling tests along with standard STR analysis.

[32] An antigen is any substance that can be detected by the immune system and triggers an immune response. Blood groups are defined by the presence or absence of specific antigens such as A, B, and O on the surface of blood cells.

Delta Pathology Associates in Stockton, again in California. Dr. Lawrence, a medical examiner from San Francisco, could thus prepare some microscope slides of these mysterious tissues and began to study them. The tissue that grabbed the researcher's attention was the 1996 one: it was not easily identifiable and appeared to be infiltrated by a large number of white blood cells, as would happen with inflammation. In particular, in a December 7, 2000, video-recorded interview, he specified that the white blood cells were active and living at the time the sample was taken. In addition, he stated that how those white blood cells had survived in water without dissolving after more than just a few minutes, one hour at the most, once separated from the living organism they came from, or after its death, was simply inexplicable. I should remind the reader that these samples came from a tissue preserved in water, without nutrients. Distilled water alone is actually incompatible with life due to osmotic reasons,[33] but still, living white cells were present at the time of sampling, even if the material had been kept under these conditions for more than three years. Surprises, however, weren't over yet.

The tissue was infiltrated by inflammatory cells and thus not easy to identify. Dr. Lawrence dared suggesting it could have been in keeping with clusters or fragments of keratinized cells[34] — hence

---

[33] Osmosis is the spontaneous movement of water across cell membranes from regions of low solute concentration to regions of high solute concentration. By definition, distilled water has no solutes dissolved in it. Thus, distilled water would inevitably seep into solute-containing living cells. For this reason, living cells would swell and eventually rupture if exposed to distilled water.

[34] Keratin is the key structural protein material in skin, hair, and nails.

epidermis, the most superficial skin layer or, more accurately, inflamed skin, infiltrated by white blood cells.

The same slides were shown to other professionals in the following months and years. In Australia, Dr. Peter Ellis at the University of Sydney and Dr. Thomas Loy at the University of Queensland confirmed Dr. Lawrence's interpretation about the epidermal origin. In Sydney, however, Dr. John Walker believed it could have been muscle tissue. Even the no-longer-young Prof. Linoli in Arezzo, who researched the miracle of Lanciano, was involved: according to him, it was possible it could have been myocardial tissue.

There was a need for a more authoritative and definitive opinion. Thus, the research team decided to turn to Prof. Frederick Zugibe, chief medical examiner and cardiologist in Rockland County in New York. His academic profile, made up of scientific discoveries and numerous publications, together with his thirty-year experience of ten thousand autopsies, is impressive at the very least. On April 20, 2004, the investigators Ron Tesoriero and Mike Willesee were in Prof. Zugibe's New York office, and the microscope slides were still the ones prepared by Dr. Lawrence. The meeting was filmed, Tesoriero holding the video camera and Willesee interviewing. Prof. Zugibe wished to know the origin of the material to be examined, but the two Australians initially kept quiet. Zugibe insisted, but Willesee explained it was better that way for him and the inquest. Zugibe scrutinized the samples under the microscope and his words were recorded. He began by saying: "I am a heart specialist. The heart is *my business*. This is heart muscle tissue, coming from the left ventricle, near a valvular area." He took a better look and specified: "This cardiac muscle is inflamed; it has lost its striations and is infiltrated by leukocytes."[35]

---

[35] *Leukocyte* is the medical term for white blood cell.

Leukocytes are not normally in the heart but leave the circulating blood and head toward a site of trauma or a wound. This person's heart has been wounded and has suffered a trauma. The blood flow has been compromised and part of the myocardium has undergone necrosis.[36] It resembles what I see in road accidents, when the heart is subject to prolonged resuscitation maneuvers, or it resembles what I find when someone has received severe blows to the chest.

Tesoriero and Willesee felt a shiver when Zugibe talked about the presence of leukocytes: the immune system–mediated inflammatory reaction normally takes place as an ordered sequence, and leukocytes can only be found if nourished by an organism that is still living. He affirmed: "This was a live sample at the time it was taken!"

After a moment of silence to compose himself, Willesee dared to ask: "How long would these leukocytes survive for, if the tissue were set in water?" The answer reechoed the one by Dr. Lawrence four years prior: "They would dissolve within a few minutes and no longer exist."

At that point it was the two Australians who surpised the professor by revealing to him that the slide came from tissue kept for a month in tap water and for three years in distilled water: "Absolutely incredible! Inexplicable by science!" Later he would specify that after such a long period in water, not only would white blood cells disappear, but also any other human cell would lose any recognizable morphology. Only in hindsight, and to his amazement, they revealed to him that the tissue originated from a consecrated host.

---

[36] *Necrosis* is the medical term for disorganized and unregulated cell death. This is opposed to apoptosis, which is organized and well-controlled cellular suicide.

In the final report, written in March 2005, Prof. Zugibe specified that the microscope slides contained myocardial tissue with loss of fiber[37] striations, nuclear pyknosis,[38] and mixed aggregates of various inflammatory cells, related to both chronic inflammation,[39] such as the predominant macrophages,[40] and acute inflammation, such as polymorphonuclear cells.[41] The direction of the myocardial fibers suggested that the original site was in a ventricular region, relatively close to a valvular area.

These degenerative alterations were compatible with a recent myocardial infarction,[42] either secondary to obstruction of

---

[37] *Fibers, muscle fibers,* and *muscle cell* are all terms with identical meanings and can be used interchangeably.

[38] Pyknosis is the shrinkage and densification of the nucleus of the cell that occurs in both necrosis and apoptosis.

[39] Chronic inflammation — that is, long-standing, well-established, and ongoing inflammation — is pathologically different from acute inflammation. Acute and chronic inflammation differ from one another because different populations of white blood cells with different functions and purposes are involved in each type of inflammation.

[40] Macrophages are specialized white blood cells capable of engulfing and digesting cellular debris, foreign substances, and microbes. They are much more involved in chronic inflammation.

[41] Polymorphonuclear cells are a family of white blood cells including neutrophils, but also basophils and eosinophils. Neutrophils specialize in killing bacteria, basophils are involved in allergic reactions, and eosinophils are specialized in attacking parasites. Polymorphonuclear cells tend to play a greater role in acute inflammation.

[42] *Myocardial infarction* is the medical term for what is commonly known as a "heart attack." It is the death and subsequent degeneration of a region of heart muscle, most commonly due to an impairment of adequate blood supply to the affected tissue.

a coronary artery[43] after thrombosis[44] or secondary to severe chest trauma in the region overlying the heart. Moreover, it was possible to estimate that the duration of "cardiac strain" must have been in the order of a few days with respect to the time when the tissue was taken. This was based on the presence of chronic inflammatory cells and the type of cardiac cellular alterations we just described.

But how could it be possible that the same slide would look like epidermis to one expert of forensic medicine and myocardium to another?

The answer is in the profound alterations the 1999 *muestra humeda* tissue was subject to. These resulted in muscle fibers losing their typical striations. They separated from one another, bent, broke, were infiltrated by a very large number of leukocytes, and thus no longer resembled the classic images in the atlases of anatomical pathology.

Prof. Zugibe's reputation was so strong that five years later, on February 28, 2008, at a meeting in San Francisco, Dr. Lawrence admitted to having made a mistake and acknowledged that the tissue was definitely inflamed myocardium.

The Inadequate Visibility of the Event

On March 17, 2006, Dr. Castañón was able to officially present a conclusive report on the investigations begun in 1999 to Jorge Mario Bergoglio, who had become the cardinal archbishop of Buenos Aires in the meantime. At that stage, an official statement

---

[43] The blood vessels supplying the heart itself are called coronary arteries. Obstruction of these arteries is the most common cause of myocardial infarction.

[44] Thrombosis is the formation of a blood clot.

by the cardinal would have been expected, considering that an-other report on the 1992 events had already been submitted to the Buenos Aires Curia and the Vatican. The presence of blood was clearly confirmed in the 1992 tissues, whereas the presence of live and "suffering" myocardial tissue was confirmed in the 1996 ones. In his book, Blondet voiced Fr. Eduardo Pérez Dal Lago's disappointment:

> I had hoped that by having these answers at hand, Bergo-glio would have announced: "Corpus Christi." Instead no, he only authorized adoration of the relics in the chapel of St. Mary's church and, only since 2002 — ten years since the event — the periodic exposition of what we must call a "eucharistic sign" rather than a eucharistic miracle.

Indeed, the curia has kept an ambivalent attitude over the years. On the one hand, it supported and encouraged St. Mary's Parish in deepening its devotion to the Blessed Sacrament and welcoming those who visit by their own initiative and actively seek information about the events that took place. In 2006, a new chapel was inaugurated in the left-side nave, dedicated to eucharistic adoration, perpetual for the first few years and today only during daytime. As I already mentioned, the parish wel-comes any visiting pilgrims for two hours on the third Friday of the month at 8:00 p.m. and on the fourth Saturday of the month at 11:00 a.m. The stories of the 1992 and 1996 events are told, and I believe the small blood crust — which is all that remains from the first 1992 miracle — is exposed.

I was told that Cardinal Bergoglio himself used to visit St. Mary's for an hour of eucharistic adoration about once a year. The parish also published a card showing Cardinal Bergoglio seen from behind and turned in prayer toward the tabernacle behind the unmistakable four-petal monstrance. The comment that the current pope made after seeing himself on the card is written on the back: "This is the best picture of a bishop I have ever seen: it represents him the way he must be."

Still, it must be acknowledged that very little has been done to make these miraculous events known at least beyond the parish boundaries, since they are certainly not very well known even in Argentina, let alone the rest of the world. A pilgrim driving on the A14 motorway on the way to Lanciano can see road signs directing to the Shrine of the Eucharistic Miracle tens of kilometers ahead of the exit. Instead, at St. Mary's in Buenos Aires, discretion is absolute: You could walk through the church entrance without noticing a single sign or indication. You have to know of the miracle already and need to directly ask someone for more information. Only then, with great courtesy and a lovable smile, would the unknown parishioner answer that yes, a miraculous event took place in the church. He would bring out some brochures and check if the parish priest is available for a meeting. To tell the truth, a few years ago, two engraved stone slabs were finally placed at the entrance of the adoration chapel reading the following:

> St. Mary's community dedicated this chapel to permanent Adoration. The Eucharistic Sign is kept here along with all the sacred vessels from the 1992, 1994 and 1996 events.
>
> We hope this Sign will be for others what it has been for us: a path to the discovery of Eucharistic Adoration.... Meetings on the events of the Eucharistic Sign take place every third Friday.... No booking is required. At these meetings, members of the community will speak about what happened, we will talk about the events, and pray

together. This is the way in which the parish community, together with its bishop, decided to share these facts with our brothers and sisters in Faith, considering this to be a more adequate and preferable way of talking about these events compared to any other means of communication.

Notably, the word *sign* is consistently repeated. It certainly isn't any less powerful or embarrassing compared to *miracle*, although it certainly is a lot more vague.

The firm unwillingness to use today's powerful and pervasive media, preferring rather a direct and interpersonal approach, is an interesting choice. Even the text in the brochure I was offered comes across to the reader in a rather politically correct style with no hint of assertiveness. It read: "In a discerning climate we keep asking which paths we are to follow.... We believe that in handing down these facts, we must respect freedom of faith. No one can oblige someone to consider them in a way or another. Everyone in the Faith has the obligation to welcome what God inspires him with in prayer, together with a fraternal attitude of sharing in freedom."

I don't wish to venture into a territory outside my expertise, but I cannot help asking myself: Are we sure we are interpreting the heavenly will correctly? Something amazing happened in Buenos Aires five times in a row, so the message should be strong and clear. There was blood, and a fragment of a live suffering heart. In a faith perspective, if these signs did happen, we evidently must have needed them. Why fearfully whisper what ought to be shouted at the top of one's lungs? Why "hide the lamp under a bushel," just to make an authoritative citation?

The result of keeping such a low profile is inevitable: outside St. Mary's Parish, few know about this miracle, and charter flights for religious tourists in Latin America (and the United States) head elsewhere—to Bethany, in Venezuela, where a visionary I do not fear calling hysterical certainly did not cultivate the virtue of humility or practice concealment to the same degree, even if her beatification process is underway.

Last but not least, the latest contribution to the censorship of the Buenos Aires events was cyberterrorism. Starting in autumn of 2015, the St. Mary's Parish website was blocked by professional Islamic hackers. What could have been a reference point for any visitor looking for safe and reliable information no longer existed. No way to find out about details such as reception times, a brief summary of the facts, and a confirmation that St. Mary's Parish is actually a concrete reality of everyday life. Instead, the fixed image of a mosque and its reflection onto a body of water at sunset with the throaty and unsettling voice of a muezzin was replacing the parish website. The perpetrators were a Turkish group of professional hackers known as "Ayyidldiz Team." They could actually boast impressive undertakings demonstrating their skills: For example, they hacked into the Israeli Iron Dome defense system in 2014. They also blocked the UN and Coca-Cola websites and those of various European institutions. In January 2016, they even mocked the website of the Russian ministry of defense by replacing its Russian flag with a Turkish one.

One last thought: Why were such capable cyberterrorists even interested in blocking the website of a poor Catholic parish? Why were they trying to harm an unknown institution insignificant in the world scene? Would you bet that the enemy, the one who never sleeps, had much clearer ideas than the children of light on what was truly worth striking?

Finally, after about a year, the official parish website reappeared on the web with new formatting in autumn of 2016.

Bibliography

Maranatha.it. *Missale Romanum de defectibus*. Sestri Levante, Italy. Accessed July 11, 2021. https://www.maranatha.it/MobileEdition/T15-MissaleRomanum1962/testi/ddefpage.htm. Full text, translated in Italian but also available in other languages.

Del Guercio, Gelsomino. 2015. "L'Ostia danneggiata o rovinata va utilizzata oppure no?" Aleteia. Accessed July 11, 2021. https://it.aleteia.org/2015/12/02/come-comportarsi-ostia-caduta-terra-bicchiere-acqua-sacrario/.
A liturgist explains the canonical norms to be applied in the event of a host falling on the ground or getting dirty.

Blondet, Maurizio. 2014. *Un cuore per la vita eterna*. Effedieffe.
First and only report written in Italian about the miracles in Buenos Aires. Particular care is given to the 1992 events, including the original testimony given by Fr. Eduardo Pérez Dal Lago. In the second part of the book, he questions himself on the reasons behind such little awareness about these facts.

The Eucharist: In Communion with me. 2002. Video. Trans Media Productions.
The video has been created by Dr. Castañón's Australian collaborators and is available online for sale. The interview with Prof. Linoli at min. 10:41 is particularly interesting. At min. 13:21, Dr. Lawrence talks about the presence of leucocytes infiltrating the Buenos Aires tissue. At min. 13:56 there is an original recording of the samples collection in Buenos Aires on October 5, 1999.

Castañón Gómez, Ricardo. 2011. *Más allá de la razón*, 3rd ed. Mexico: Centro Internacional de Estudios Humanos.
A not-to-be-missed book written by the person who directed the investigations on the Buenos Aires events in 1999. There

are photographs of important documents such as the clinical reports and laboratory tests in its appendix.

Tesoriero, Ron. 2007. *Reason to Believe*. Australia: Ron Tesoriero. Autobiographical report and reflections on some miraculous events, some of which have been personally investigated by the author. Chapter 12 covers the Buenos Aires events.

Tesoriero, Ron, and Lee Han. 2013. *Unseen New Evidence: The Origin of Life Under the Microscope*. Australia: Ron Tesoriero. A book collecting the relatively recent personal reflections by the Australian lawyer. Chapter 8 is a collection of facts regarding the Buenos Aires events. The appendix lists the precious copies of laboratory tests and reports.

Parroquia Santa Maria. 2020. Parroquia Santa Maria. Website. Accessed July 11, 2021. https://parroquiasantamariacaballito. com.ar/.
Official St. Mary's Parish website. The site was hacked by a fundamentalist Turkish group, but it was reactivated in 2016.

3

Tixtla (2006)

The Facts

Tixtla is a town of twenty-three thousand inhabitants in the state of Guerrero, in southwestern Mexico. Unfortunately, in the last decades it has been plagued by crime, drug trafficking, political instability, and even recurrent flooding. It is about 100 kilometers inland from the more famous Acapulco, the beach resort town that used to be all the rage for Hollywood's jet set.

In Tixtla, Fr. Leopoldo Roque, of St. Martin of Tours parish, organized a spiritual weekend retreat for his parishioners in October 2006. For that, he invited a famous preacher he knew: Fr. Raymundo Reyna Esteban, informally known as "Fr. Rayito." Gifted with eloquent speech, fifty-year-old Fr. Rayito looked like a gentle giant, well over six feet tall. At the time, he was living in Tijuana, on the opposite side of the country, near the American border in a neighborhood that was also troubled by crime, drug trafficking, and illegal migration. There, he had founded "The Missionaries of Jesus and Mary," based on a charismatic-type spirituality. He was quite competent with the latest social media (indeed, he was managing both a radio and a TV channel and was quite active on the web) besides being an exorcist.

A Cardiologist Examines Jesus

On Sunday, October 22, 2006, he concelebrated the Mass concluding the spiritual retreat. There were about six hundred people who could not fit inside the church. Hence, the Mass was celebrated at the nearby town hall. Two nuns were helping with the distribution of the Eucharist for Holy Communion. While holding a ciborium[45] full of consecrated hosts, Sr. Arely Marroquín, one of the two, suddenly paused and turned pale in front of the faithful who were queueing up to receive.

A few years later, the local paper *Diario 21* published an account of the events that took place on that day by giving the names of the eyewitnesses and reporting their interviews. One of them was the woman in front of whom Sr. Arely had paused her distribution of Holy Communion. According to this woman's recollection, the nun had returned to the altar with teary eyes and had shown the ciborium to Fr. Rayito after kneeling, without uttering a word: one of the hosts was stained with blood. It had a moist, friable texture, so much so that a small fragment had come off it by gently touching it. Fr. Rayito and Fr. Leopoldo quickly talked to one another until Fr. Rayito loudly spoke out—"This is a miracle!"—and publicly showed the host that was stained by a few drops of fresh blood. With his booming voice, he began singing "*Que viva mi Cristo, que viva mi Rey*," a hymn well known to all Mexicans. There were people who applauded and people who wept.

In hindsight, Fr. Rayito remembered that moment as "shocking, but also simple, sublime and eternal at the same time."

In the following weeks, Msgr. Alejo Zavala Castro, the bishop of the local diocese of Chilpancingo, set up a committee of inquiry

---

[45] *Ciborium* is the name of the sacred vessel holding the consecrated hosts.

made up of four priests. At the time, their investigations were limited to establishing facts through interviews. Seventeen statements were given by different people who all agreed with the sworn testimonies of those who were directly involved.

In a later interview, Fr. Rayito revealed he had actually already experienced a similar episode firsthand. As a young priest serving in the Dominican Republic, he had previously found himself holding a bleeding host in his hands. For some time, he had "rejoiced" in that mysterious event with his brethren. Later on, however, to obey his bishop's orders, he had placed the miraculous host in water until its complete dissolution and disappearance. I shall not go into the details of the very questionable and, I would say, atrocious decision by that bishop. Instead, I will focus on the mystery of the phenomenon happening again. We have already talked about five miraculous eucharistic events occurring in the same Buenos Aires parish in only four years. Furthermore, Dr. Castañón has been following up on a fourth potential miracle that took place in the hands of the same priest, with investigations still underway. This is another spiritual mystery of predilection and insistence by the Spirit on certain souls or elected places, one that is highly embarrassing for our modern egalitarian sensitivity. This stubborn insistence truly reechoes biblical narratives and the lives of the saints.

The Investigations

In Tixtla, too, Dr. Castañón Gómez's intervention, supported by his Grupo Internacional para la Paz, turned out to be very important, similar to his decisive contribution in Buenos Aires, under the authority of Bishop Bergoglio. In 2009, Castañón was in Chilpancingo for a conference and made contact with the local bishop, Msgr. Zavala Castro. Dr. Castañón had actually already been told about what had happened in nearby Tixtla three years before. His meeting resulted in a fruitful relationship: Dr. Castañón described the bishop as very well-balanced: neither naïve nor without prudent skepticism. He was well aware of the potential significance of the Tixtla events and was open to the possibility of an unforeseen supernatural event. He was not in a hurry to recognize a miracle in his diocese either. Above all, his desire was to establish the true facts. Msgr. Zavala Castro entrusted Dr. Castañón with overseeing the investigations on the Tixtla host and authorized him to take small samples of the material. The bishop also made a particular request of the researchers: that they try their best to determine if the blood-like substance had been added to the host from the outside, or if it actually originated from the inside. The bishop's concern was understandable: apart from characterizing the "mysterious" substance, it was also just as crucial to rule out a fraud. As we shall see later on, Msgr. Zavala's request was fully satisfied.

The Grupo Internacional para la Paz's war machine was set in motion again, ten years after Buenos Aires. It was Dr. Castañón himself who sampled three millimeter-sized fragments of the apparently bloodstained host. Then a series of investigations began that were only finally concluded on February 25, 2013. Dr. Castañón's association relied on several forensic medical laboratories in Mexico, Guatemala, Bolivia, and the United States that specialized in immunohistochemistry[46] and genetics. During the course of the analyses, the same findings were often verified multiple times, by multiple alternative and complementary analytical

---

[46] Immunohistochemistry is an analytical technique employing antibody molecules as probing agents and using molecular markers to characterize tissue samples.

methods performed by different scientists. The scientists themselves were also unaware of each other's undertakings and worked under "blinding" conditions—that is, without knowing the origin of the material. As always, all costs were generously shouldered by the Grupo Internacional para la Paz.

The results that were obtained were many and converging. I shall try to group together results from different laboratories "horizontally" across the board, sorting them out by subject matter and partially following the order of the discussion in Dr. Castañón's report:

1. *Human blood was found.*

    a. The "Gene-Ex" laboratory in La Paz (Bolivia) documented the presence of hemoglobin. Hemoglobin, I shall remind nonexperts, is the iron ion–containing protein required to transport oxygen and carbon dioxide in the organism, and it is exclusively contained inside red blood cells and no other cell type. The reader can find a bibliography link to watch a videoconference presentation showing Dr. Susana Pinell performing a capillary immunochromatography test[47] specific for human hemoglobin 21:02 minutes into the recording. We can see the instant in which a fragment of the material comes in contact with the test kit and the resulting positive chemical reaction taking place after a few seconds. I should stress once

---

[47] Capillary immunochromatography involves running a liquid sample along the surface of a pad with reactive molecules that show a visual positive or negative result when coming into contact with the sample. Very well-known examples of this technology are the widely available urine pregnancy tests.

more that although hemoglobin is present in the red blood cells of all vertebrates, the test she performed was specific for hemoglobin of human origin.

b. Red blood cells could be recognized on microscope tissue slides as appropriately tinged by the conventional hematoxylin and eosin stain performed by both Dr. Juan Ruben Chavez Hernandez at the Corporativo Médico Legal laboratory in Mexico and Dr. Orlando Rodas Pernillo at the PatMed laboratories in Guatemala. More precisely, there were areas of clustered acidophile material[48] that resembled red blood cells undergoing autolysis—that is, spontaneous self-degradation. In some areas, the material was shapeless and less distinguishable. Such clusters were compatible with thrombotic phenomena, meaning that those red blood cells could have been part of a clot. Among them, some leukocytes belonging to different cellular subpopulations[49] could also be recognized: neutrophils, macrophages,[50] and basophils.[51] On one of the

---

[48] Acidic material stained by acidic dye that was evidence of acid-mediated cellular self-digestion.

[49] White blood cells, also known as leukocytes, are the organism's immune system cells circulating in the blood. They are made up of multiple different types of specialized white cells that play different roles in tissue trauma, inflammation, and infection.

[50] Macrophages are also white blood cells specialized in engulfing various pathogens and debris. They are usually recruited to sites of tissue trauma, inflammation, or infection to "mop up the battlefield" after other types of white blood cells have performed their "fighting duties."

[51] Basophils are another white blood cell subclass. They are usually involved in allergic reactions.

slides, a macrophage full of fatty material could even be recognized.

c. Dr. Eduardo Sánchez Lazo at the Corporativo Médico Legal laboratory performed immunohistochemistry tests probing the tissues with selected antibodies aimed at identifying the presence of specific molecular substrates more accurately. He managed to confirm the presence of myeloperoxidase and of glycophorin A. Myeloperoxidase is an enzyme[52] that is only present in certain leukocytes, specifically in granulocytes of the myeloid cell line.[53] Glycophorin A is instead a glycoprotein[54] that is only present on the cell membrane of red blood cells and determines their "minor" MN blood group.[55] Overall, these were very specific findings providing further confirmation about the presence of blood cells in the examined tissues.

[52] An enzyme is a protein whose role is to greatly expedite the rate at which a cellular chemical reaction can take place.

[53] All blood cells derive from multipotent bone marrow stem cells. As they develop, they differentiate into different types of cells with specific functions. The granulocyte family includes neutrophils, basophils, and eosinophils. Granulocytes are named after the granules characterizing their microscopic appearance. Instead, the myeloid family is a broader category of white blood cells, including both granulocytes and monocytes, the latter being the cell precursors to macrophages.

[54] A glycoprotein is a protein molecule chemically linked with a more or less complex sugar chain molecule.

[55] As opposed to the "major" A, B, AB, and O blood groups most readers will know about, there are also many other, lesser-known "minor" blood groups, such as the MN one.

2. *The blood group was AB*. Two independent laboratories, Corporativo Médico Legal in Mexico and Gene-Ex in Bolivia, demonstrated the presence of A and B antigens[56] with immunofluorescence techniques[57] on the tissues examined. In the Bolivian report, the result was documented with color photographs. There was more to it, though: for the first time in the world, the Gene-Ex laboratory could also determine the Rh blood group[58] of those "mysterious" tissues. The Rh group was found to be negative. We shall go back to this finding in a dedicated chapter.

3. *There were cellular fibers belonging in all likelihood to heart muscle*. The microscope slides were still those prepared at the Corporativo

[56] An antigen is any substance that can be detected by the immune system to trigger an immune response. Quite often antigens are proteins or sugar molecules externally exposed on the surface of body cells or foreign microbes. Immune system cells can bind to them either to recognize them as "tagging" cells or biological components that are part of the organism (self) or to identify them as foreign material to be eliminated (nonself).

[57] Immunofluorescence involves binding specific molecular targets on a tissue sample with special man-made fluorescing antibodies acting as fluorescent biochemical probes that light up when exposed to light.

[58] Of the thirty-nine known human blood group systems, the Rh, or Rhesus, blood group system is the second most important one after the ABO system. It is determined by the presence or absence of the Rh antigen on blood cells. The importance of the "major" ABO and Rh groups is due to the high severity and often fatal immune system–mediated transfusion reactions that occur if blood of a given major blood group is given to an individual whose own major blood group type is incompatible. "Minor" blood groups, like the previously mentioned MN group, can also be incompatible with one another, but the detrimental immune reactions elicited by such incompatibilities are usually much less severe and often clinically tolerable.

Médico Legal and PatMed laboratories mentioned at point 1. Abundant bundles of elongated fibers were present and were well-stained by the hematoxylin and eosin dye. It should be anticipated that, as with all the other eucharistic miracles we encountered, it was not easy to determine the cardiac nature of the tissue: the fibers were particularly degraded by autolytic pathological phenomena.[59] Once again using a nonmedical term, we could say that these phenomena are suggestive of a "suffering" tissue. Striations and intercalated discs[60] were missing. The DNA containing cell nuclei were also not consistently centrally located in each cell.[61] Still, the overall appearance of such elongated and mostly parallel fibers, with multiple and immediately adjoining bifurcations with neighboring muscle cells, could not but resemble a myocardial morphology. Additional information from immunohistochemical tests would be decisive to overcome these histopathological diagnostic difficulties: this would mean coupling visual structural observations with findings proving the presence of heart muscle–specific substrates on those fibers. Notably, the final report by Corporativo Médico Legal, directed by Dr. Sánchez Lazo, stated that immunohistochemical tests did

---

[59] *Autolysis* means self-digestion and degradation. Autolysis occurs in inflamed, infected, or otherwise traumatized tissues to eliminate cells that have been damaged beyond repair.

[60] These microscopic features are normally present in healthy heart muscle tissue. They are the distinguishing features of intact cellular contractile apparatuses and heart-specific structural elements connecting heart muscle cells with one another to allow for the transmission of the electrical contraction signal.

[61] The central location of cell nuclei is a distinguishing feature specific to heart muscle tissue. Indeed, the cell nuclei of other types of muscle cells in the body are not normally centrally located.

confirm the cardiac nature of the tissue, although he did not provide further details. In his video-recorded conference presentation — at minute 1:12:35 into the conference — Dr. Carlos Parellada instead announced the lack of otherwise expected reactivity to desmin and myosin molecular probes[62] specific for muscle cells on his PatMed microscope slides. However, he attributed this negative finding to the advanced autolysis and degeneration of the putative muscle fibers.

4. *Other various histological findings:*

    a. There were clusters of adipose cells.

    b. Degraded protein structures seemingly belonging to mesenchymal cells were identified on the microscope slides studied by Prof. John Compagno in California. Mesenchymal cells are incompletely differentiated, hence still multipotent cells retaining some properties of embryonic stem cells. They can differentiate into many adult tissue types, such as bone, muscle, cartilage, bone marrow, and connective tissue cells. The documented positivity to the vimentin[63] marker test in the tissues examined by Prof. Parellada seemed to point in the same direction.

    c. Plant cells were also obviously present. They were recognized by their typical thick and non-collapsible cell walls. Those cells could not be stained with the common reagents for animal tissues but could still be recognized every now and then in the "background."

---

[62] Desmin and myosin are proteins specific to the contractile apparatus of a muscle cell.

[63] Vimentin is a cell skeleton protein specific to mesenchymal cells.

As expected, they were part of the wheat flour making up the host surrounding and supporting the analyzed tissues examined thus far.

5. *There was human DNA, but no genetic profile could be obtained.* Two distinct laboratories — Dr. Sánchez's Corporativo Médico Legal in Mexico and biologist Eyda de Campollo's I2QB3 (Instituto de Investigaciones Químicas, Biológicas, Biomédicas y Biofísicas) at the Mariano Gálvez University in Guatemala — performed DNA studies on two paraffin-preserved samples. They both reached the same conclusions. The Mexican report specified that genetic material was present, but no protein-coding gene sequences could be identified in it, nor could any useful genetic markers be amplified in order to establish a genetic profile such as those that could be used for a kinship study.

Similarly, the November 9, 2012, Guatemalan report stated that no complete genetic profile could be obtained by attempting to amplify[64] the usual fifteen STRs and amelogenins DNA sequences[65] required for standard DNA profiling. This was attributed

---

[64] DNA *amplification* refers to the process of DNA PCR (polymerase chain reaction) analysis. PCR is an analytical technique producing many DNA copies from trace amounts of DNA in a given sample. This can be achieved provided that the added DNA PCR molecular probes can bind a matching starter sequence on the DNA contained in the sample. Producing many copies or amplifying the sample's DNA is of course very useful for then running many other DNA tests on a larger amount of material that can be studied.

[65] STR stands for *short tandem repeat* DNA sequences. They are well-known sequences at various locations of the human DNA that repeat themselves in continuous stretches for a variable number of times in unrelated individuals. Along with the amelogenin sequences, they can be used to establish if one or more

to the poor quality of the DNA itself, deemed to be too degraded and fragmented. It was a result that did not surprise Dr. Castañón. The Tixtla DNA results were a repetition of the Buenos Aires ones as well as those of other cases whose study is still underway: the genetic material escapes genetic probes, and it does not lend itself to be recognized. Currently, the Grupo Internacional para la Paz considers the inability to identify a genetic profile in their tissues a type of "control variable," a sort of mysterious confirmation that they are working on a genuine and "supernatural" tissue. On the contrary, according to their past experiences, when a DNA profile identifying a specific person was found, this would invariably be the result of sample contamination: someone who had been in close contact with the material or perhaps the author of a fraud in a fake specimen.

This is a subject deserving some further reflection and will be the topic of one of the following chapters.

6. *Under a superficial layer of clotted blood, fresh blood was still present in contact with the host.* In February 2010, Ing. Fernando Rodríguez Pérez, an imaging expert entrusted by the Grupo Internacional para la Paz, came to Tixtla and visited the chapel where the miracle is preserved. He laid out his instruments a few meters away from the altar: these included a high-power ultrabright white and ultraviolet light-emitting digital microscope.

---

individuals are genetically related to one another. Amelogenin DNA sequences instead contain the required information to synthesize amelogenin tooth enamel proteins. There are different varieties of amelogenins that are made from slightly different DNA sequences, and these different sequences are located on both the X and the Y sex chromosomes. Because of this, determining DNA amelogenin sequences is a way to determine the sex of an individual whose DNA is being analyzed.

His microscope scanning study revealed that fresh blood was still present in the stained portion of the host, beneath the superficial layer of obviously clotted blood. It was an impressive finding, considering that more than three years had gone by since the miracle took place.

7. *The blood arose from within the host.* Two separate studies following different methodologies drew that same conclusion. In one of them, Dr. Sánchez Lazo analyzed the macroscopic, microscopic, and structural features of both the brownish stain and the host to understand their reciprocal spatial relationship. He elaborated on this 45:50 minutes into his conference talk, available on the web. His assessment ruled out the hypothesis that the blood could have wetted the surface of the host from the outside. If that were the case, it would have passed through and uniformly soaked the entire thickness of the underlying bread. Instead, what we would actually see in an ideal cross section of the Tixtla miracle would be the image of an "inverted cone" of blood, crossing the bread through and through only in one single middle point, slightly enlarging before reaching the exterior and then expanding on the surface of the host itself, no longer wetting it. Hence, the blood seemed to behave as if it were coming from an actual small wound: a blood vessel bleeding from a superficial point of injury, with the blood rising toward the exterior of the wound, and only on the "skin surface" would it spread out, forming a larger stain.

The second investigation on this matter is explained in Dr. Castañón's report. The thickness of the host was examined with an infrared-light technique, reaching the same conclusion: the blood came from within. He showed some photographs from the experiment but did not dwell on it with extensive explanations.

A Cardiologist Examines Jesus

Thus, the question that unsettled the diocesan bishop on the eve of the investigations was eventually answered: the red stain was not added by some ill-willed person, because the blood inexplicably oozed out from within the host, thus adding an extra and rather meaningful element to the miracle.

Some Further Remarks

The red blood cells, muscular fibers, adipose, and mesenchymal cells fixed on the microscope slides showed autolytic features, or evidence of degradation and loss of some elements of live tissues. Nevertheless, the notable exception of the presence of white blood cells, still intact and active at the time of sampling, should be highlighted. The same considerations by Profs. Lawrence and Zugibe on the leukocytes infiltrating the Buenos Aires tissues also apply to the Tixtla specimens: How could they still be there? White blood cells are extremely labile. Outside their own organism, or after its death, they would die or simply dissolve within hours. Here instead we are standing before something incredible and simply inexplicable: To begin with, the biological tissue that appeared on October 22, 2006, in the hands of Sr. Arely was never nourished or artificially grown by immersing it in a culture medium, nor was it ever treated with any preservative. Instead, it was kept at room temperature and preserved with devotion, but certainly not in sterile conditions. Nevertheless, three years later, in that same tissue, we could still find living white blood cells to the point that one of them, a macrophage, was even caught on a glass slide while doing its job, that of swallowing some fatty debris. It is well worth pointing out that the presence of leukocytes expresses the vitality of the organism from which they originate in a more general sense: white blood cells are not produced in situ, in the locally inflamed tissue, but physiologically come from elsewhere when attracted by the inflammatory response, using and relying on a functioning blood circulation. White blood cells prove that the organism they are coming from is *alive* and taking action to ensure that one of its injured and inflamed tissues is adequately repaired.

Dr. Marco Blanquicett Anaya, a Colombian cardiologist to whom Dr. Castañón presented his data in June 2014, recognized a pathological picture in the Tixtla miracle: one that was suggestive of heart muscle tissue undergoing a typical inflammatory reaction from having undergone either infarction[66] or an intense physiological stress. Moreover, myocardial tissue is known to physiologically house macrophages whose duties are to counteract excessive deposition of fats on the inner lining of the coronary arteries by swallowing them, thus preventing the formation of those notorious atherosclerotic plaques[67] responsible for heart attacks. Another inexplicable finding was shared by Dr. Parellada who, together with Dr. Castañón, in 2011 personally took a new millimeter-sized sample from the bloodstained host. The aim was to obtain new microscope slides for histopathological assessment, and, above all, to better analyze the immunohistochemistry of the freshly sampled tissues. Well, four years later, the host presented itself to the scalpel blade perfectly soft and with the same texture of a freshly made unleavened bread host,

---

[66] *Infarction* is the medical term for the pathological changes taking place in a tissue that has been deprived of adequate blood supply—in this case, a heart attack.

[67] When atherosclerotic plaques become unstable, they can detach and block a coronary vessel, thus stopping the blood supply to the downstream tissues. If the blood supply is compromised for too long, heart muscle tissue can be damaged beyond repair: a heart attack.

without any evidence of hardening or decay. On this note, my mind wanders off to a different type of eucharistic miracle, one that did not entail the effusion of blood or another kind of living biological tissue but rather involves the spontaneous preservation of consecrated hosts for decades and centuries. The most well-known and resounding one is at St. Francis Church in Siena (Italy), where hosts that were stolen and then found again have been preserved since 1730. Even today, those 223 hosts are still white, intact, and inexplicably fresh after nearly three centuries of exposure for eucharistic adoration by the faithful.

Conclusion

On May 25, 2013, in the Sentimientos de la Nación auditorium of Chilpancingo, a formal symposium was held for the presentation of the scientific data. Most of the event is available on YouTube, as pointed out in the bibliography. I cannot but recommend watching it to anyone who knows a little Spanish. At the end, amidst the applause of the moved audience, Dr. Castañón gave Bishop Alejo Zavala Castro two copies of the conclusions of the investigation, together with documents signed by each researcher involved in the project. One copy was for the diocese to keep, the other was sent to the Vatican, to the Congregation for the Doctrine of the Faith.

On October 12, 2013, the bishop issued a formal and solemn declaration recognizing the supernatural nature of the Tixtla event, declaring it a miracle.

Postscript: The Australian Documentary Undermining the Authenticity of the Tixtla Miracle

We already came across Australian journalist Mike Willesee as one of Dr. Castañón's partners investigating the Buenos Aires events. On the evening of Easter 2017, Willesee's dream came true: Channel Seven finally broadcasted on Australian television a documentary that he had been working on for years. Its title is *The Blood of Christ: Proving the Existence of God* (now available on YouTube with the title "Scientists Investigate Signs of Jesus Christ"). It was an investigation of four miraculous events that recently took place in Latin America, including both the 1996 Buenos Aires and 2006 Tixtla events. Willesee filmed places and interviews linked to those events, which were integrated with stock footage. Most importantly, he was filmed while sampling these presumably miraculous relics, including the Tixtla miracle. The focus of his documentary was an attempt at demonstrating the reciprocal authenticity of all the presented miraculous events through new genetic investigations. Unfortunately, his documentary ends almost abruptly with a jarring message and no clear interpretation of the data. On one hand, it explains how—in three out of three investigations—the DNA extracted from the white blood cells present in the samples consistently, inexplicably, but also reassuringly evaded all profiling tests commonly used for personal identification. On the other hand, however, the very last minute of the documentary drops a disconcerting bomb precisely on the fragment taken from the Tixtla relic: according to genetic testing, the DNA profile of a woman would have been found in it. Because of this, the documentary suggests that this finding would seriously undermine the credibility of the Tixtla miracle.

Mike Willesee was a great man and a great journalist. He passed away in 2019 from throat cancer. This documentary—into which he poured his heart and soul—was unfortunately completed when his disease was at a very advanced stage, with him being fully aware of that. Only a man who lived an interesting life could write an autobiography, which is what he did in his 2017

Memoirs. However, only a great man could write a second one to talk about his spiritual life and final conversion in *A Sceptic's Search for Meaning*, published in 2019. I think that one of the reasons for this second autobiography—which he truly wrote on his death-bed—must have been his willingness to correct the inaccuracies and oversimplifications in his documentary *The Blood of Christ.*

In his second autobiography, Willesee confessed some of his backstories, including Channel Seven's growing spite against his project, which was prematurely and hurriedly finished off and broadcast.

Above all, he admitted his physical and mental weakness, certainly due to the disease, as well as his regret at having been unable to take any action against the false message conveyed at the end of the documentary. In summary, Willesee stated the following, as lasting reminders:

1. The female human DNA that was detected did not come from a sample taken from the Tixtla host at all, but rather from a Jesus plaster bust that had been bleeding in Cochabamba (Bolivia) since 1995. This was what the Melbourne Victorian Institute of Forensic Medicine actually established in November 2015.

2. The investigators then sent Mrs. Silvia Arévalo's genetic profile to Melbourne for comparison, as she was the owner of the Cocha-bamba statue. On the same day, Dr. Dadna Hartman, from the Victorian Institute, confirmed beyond any doubt that the female DNA detected in 2015 exactly matched Mrs. Arévalo's profile. It should be noted that this finding did not necessarily point to a fraud. Instead, for instance, it could have been the result of a very plausible and expected contamination of the statue by skin cells belonging to its owner. Indeed, this was demonstrated to be true by more in-depth analyses carried out later on.

3. A need for more in-depth testing was then felt. The goal of further analyses had to be that of detecting the DNA content of single cells. That way the DNA of the precious and presumably miraculous white blood cells could have been analyzed on its own, as separated from other genetic material originating from any potential skin cell contaminants present in the samples. To achieve that, the Melbourne scientists themselves referred Willesee to a laboratory that had access to the required technology: the Italian Menarini Silicon Biosystems in Bologna. There, Dr. Francesca Fontana's team examined the samples collected in Tixtla, Cochabamba, and Campoalegre (the latter being another possible eucharistic miracle that was never recognized by the local bishop). The Italian laboratory confirmed that human blood was present in all three South American specimens. Moreover, it also extracted the DNA contents of single white blood cells present in each of the three samples. The result was what Willesee was expecting, although it disappointed Dr. Fontana: by excluding the possibility of skin contaminations of human origin, no individual DNA profile could be obtained from the genetic material extracted from any of the single white blood cells belonging to each of the three specimens.

4. The chronological order in which the investigations took place was clumsily or maliciously reversed so that the most accurate and definitive test results from Bologna were presented first, followed by the more generic Melbourne ones later on. That way, the barely credible and actually false result at the end of the documentary was inappropriately highlighted.

I cannot deny feeling moved by reading the end of *A Sceptic's Search for Meaning*, in which Willesee explains his regret for missing this important occasion in his life, one that should have been the height of his career, when the documentary *The Blood of Christ* ends with himself uttering his last few words as a journalist in front of a camera, those words expressing an ideological falsehood whose weight he then began to feel.

Bibliography

Castañón Gómez, Ricardo. 2014. *Crónica de un milagro eucarístico: Esplendor en Tixtla Chilpancingo, Mexico.* Grupo Internacional para la Paz.

Report about the facts and research from Tixtla with numerous photographs.

Jaramillo, J. A. 2014. "Será expuesta en la parroquia de San Martín de Tours: Colocan la hostia sangrante de Tixtla en cápsula antibalas." *Diario 21*, September 11, 2014.

Report from a local newspaper of the episodes from October 22, 2006, after eight years. The article was written on the occasion of the placement of the miraculous host in a sealed, transparent bulletproof capsule.

Jaramillo, J. A. 2013. "No se descarta un milagro: Iglesia—De humano, sangre hallada en hostia de Tixtla: Científicos." *Diario 21*, May 27, 2013.

Newspaper report from May 27, 2013: the day after the official presentation of the Tixtla miraculous host to the research studies to the scientific commission.

Monte Maria Mjm. 2013. "Conferencia Milagro Eucaristico Tixtla, Chilpancingo-25-Mayo-2013." Video recording. YouTube. Accessed July 12, 2021. https://www.youtube.com/watch?v =pUN0Gxx_y0g.

Integral 81-minute-long video of the official presentation of the research results to the scientific commission in Chilpancingo on May 25, 2013, in the presence of Bishop Zavala Castro. Dr. Sánchez and Dr. Parellada are also in the video.

Meloni, Sergio. 2014. *I miracoli eucaristici e le radici cristiane dell'Europa*, 3rd ed. ESD Edizioni Studio Domenicano.

The most complete anthology (available in Italian) of eucharistic miracles based on a worldwide successful traveling exhibit. From the third edition of the book, the more recent events from Tixtla are also included from page 516 to page 519.

7NEWS Spotlight. 2019. *The Blood of Christ: Proving the Existence of God — Sunday Night*. Documentary. YouTube (now with the title "Scientists Investigate Signs of Jesus Christ"). Accessed July 12, 2021. https://www.youtube.com/watch?v=m WmdXqIhjSs.

Documentary from the Sunday Night series broadcast on April 9, 2017, on the Australian Channel 7, in which Mike Willesee is seen taking a new sample from the miraculous Tixtla host to begin new investigations, apparently without any authorization by the local bishop.

Willesee, Mike. 2019. *A Sceptic's Search for Meaning: A Spiritual Journey*. Macmillan Australia.

Autobiography of the Australian journalist revealing precious backstories about his documentary *The Blood of Christ*.

4

Sokółka (2008)

The Facts

Sokółka is a small and quiet town of about twenty thousand people in northeastern Poland, a few kilometers from the border with Belarus. It is surrounded by hilly, wooded nonindustrial farmland. Not far from it is one last remnant of what used to be the lush European primeval forest, still inhabited by bison. The hardworking local people are very attached to their land, their patriotism tightly united with a very strong Catholic Faith. It is the homeland of Blessed Fr. Jerzy Popiełuszko (whose canonization is underway) and Fr. Stanisław Suchowolec, two beloved priests, both victims of communist repression in the 1980s.

Just two weeks before the events I am about to explain, the spotlight of the Catholic Church was set only forty kilometers away from Sokółka in Białystok, the regional capital and seat of the diocese. There, eighty thousand people had gathered. Pope Benedict XVI, connected by video-link for the Angelus in Rome, was greeting the faithful gathered in Poland for the beatification ceremony of Fr. Michał Sopoćko, St. Faustina Kowalska's spiritual director and confessor.

Two weeks later, October 12, 2008, was a Sunday like many others at St. Anthony of Padua Church in Sokółka. The 8:30

morning Mass was being celebrated by the young priest Fr. Filip Zdrodowski. He was being helped with the distribution of Holy Communion by Fr. Jacek Ingielewicz. Most likely it was he who dropped a consecrated host by mistake at that time. The series of events involved in the mishap was curious and moving. It was witnessed in great detail: one of the faithful was kneeling at the altar rail to receive Holy Communion, as is still seen today at Tridentine Rite Masses. Without uttering a word, that lady touched Fr. Jacek's leg and, with a glance, showed him the first step of the altar. The priest picked up the host. It was dirty, and he decided not to consume it but rather to immerse it in water in the vasculum, a silver container used for the cleansing of the hands that was already on the altar. So the canonical procedure that was carried out twice in Buenos Aires began there too. After a few days, the bread species would no longer be recognizable and would be poured on sacred ground. At the end of Mass, Fr. Jacek put the host-containing vasculum inside the tabernacle.

On the same day, parish priest Msgr. Stanisław Gniedziejko was either informed of the mishap or otherwise simply took notice of the water container that had been unusually stored inside the tabernacle. Thus, he asked Sr. Julia Dubowska, the parish sacristan looking after candles, sacred vessels, and the overall church décor, to pour the contents of the vasculum into a larger glass vase, adding water to it and locking it in the sacristy's safe, whose keys were only kept by the two of them. The nun diligently did what she was told but, curious about the unusual event, kept checking out the vase in the safe every day over the following week. At 8:00 a.m. on the following Sunday, October 19, Sr. Julia opened the safe and smelled a bread fragrance: she thought it was from the complete dissolution of the host, but that wasn't the case.

Later on, she opened up about her feelings at that moment: she felt like Moses in front of the burning bush. Part of the host had not yet dissolved and was partially covered by a solid red protruding stain, resembling a 1-by-1.5-centimeter blood clot. Yet the water in the container had remained clear. Sr. Julia immediately called the parish priest, Fr. Stanisław, and the other priests, who rushed over. All of them were surprised and astonished. At the time, they decided to maintain a strict silence about what had happened. On the same day, Sr. Julia photographed the glass container and its content. The photograph is still available on the web. At that same time, Fr. Stanisław informed the local Białystok Curia about the strange event, and a few days later, Archbishop Edward Ozorowski and his chancellor, Andrzej Kakareko, came to St. Anthony's Parish in person to verify the facts. The bishop asked to have the host kept in reverent custody.

So, on October 29, the vase was moved from the safe to the tabernacle of a small Divine Mercy chapel located inside the rectory where the parish priests were living, at a short distance from St. Anthony's Church. Then, on October 30, the parish priest separated the entire solid portion made up of what was left of the unleavened bread and the mysterious red clot from the water with a small spoon and laid it on a small corporal, as advised by the bishop. A very visible small red cross was embroidered in the center of the corporal. The "clot" was partially covering two of the four arms of the embroidered cross. The corporal was then inserted in a transparent monstrance and kept in the tabernacle.

By mid-January 2009, the "mysterious" material was described as already fully dried out, tightly clinging to the linen fabric on which it had been laid. Some years have already gone by, and the Sokółka relic has maintained the same look. Seen from far away, the red-colored stain blends in with the red arms of the embroidered cross, very much like an original, well-recognizable drawing.

The Investigations

The Białystok archbishop decided to proceed with scientific investigations to clarify the nature of the mysterious material. The curia demanded the utmost seriousness, urgency, and total secrecy on the matter. It entrusted the study to two experts from the University of Białystok: they were Prof. Stanisław Sulkowski and Prof. Maria Elżbieta Sobaniec-Łotowska. Both were anatomical pathologists at the same university, although in different departments, and both had impressive scientific résumés.

The tabernacle of Sokółka was opened on January 7, and Prof. Sobaniec-Łotowska took a small sample of the material, which looked like a blood clot, at least according to her. Part of the white host was also present in the sample she took, as inseparable from the "clot." The sample was then divided and one-half given to Prof. Sulkowski, who was not present on that day and was kept unaware of the origin of the specimen. In the following weeks, the material was processed and studied under both a light microscope and a transmission electron microscope.[68]

This is a summary of the results independently obtained by both researchers:

1. The sampled material was myocardial tissue. In their final report, both professors stated the following: "[The specimen] is myocardial tissue, or at least, out of all the tissues of a living

---

[68] A transmission electron microscope uses a beam of accelerated electron particles instead of a light-emitting lamp. This allows much higher orders of magnification than those achievable with light.

organism, myocardial tissue is the one which is most similar to it." The fibers actually demonstrated centrally located nuclei. Moreover, remnants of intercalated discs and bundles of delicate myofibrils[69] could be recognized under the electron microscope.

2. The analyzed material was made up of such myocardial tissue in its entirety throughout.

3. Pathological signs such as segmentation and fragmentation were present in the muscle fibers. Nonmedically speaking, these are signs of truly suffering heart muscle tissue. Segmentation is the detachment of myofibrils from the intercalated discs to which they are normally bound. It is a phenomenon resulting from the rapid repeated spasms of heart muscle cells in the context of imminent death. It should be pointed out that this is not a degenerative change taking place after death: segmentation can only happen in a living heart muscle cell in agony. The pathological meaning of fragmentation and the near-death conditions in which it occurs are very similar. It is the presence of myofibrils that are neatly broken apart at any point along their length, not limited to breaks at the sites where they attach to intercalated discs.

4. The appearance of some muscle fibers was in keeping with contraction band necrosis (CBN). This is typically characterized by thickened contraction bands spanning the short axis of heart muscle cells, parallel to intercalated discs. As we shall see in a later chapter, CBN is specifically caused by a condition known as *stress-induced cardiomyopathy*, as well as by the late reperfusion

[69] Myofibrils are the basic rodlike contractile units inside muscle cells. They are not muscle cells, but rather, they are a cell component of muscle cells.

stage of the common "heart attack." Reperfusion may occur if blood supply is restored to a portion of heart muscle tissue that had initially been deprived of it due to blockage of a culprit blood vessel.

5. Myocardial fibers and the substance of the bread host were making contact with one another in an inexplicable way. The high degree of intimate and microscopic interpenetration seen at their interface was extremely remarkable and unachievable by any kind of humanly conceived instrument or methodology available at present. Prof. Sobaniec-Łotowska pointed out that this was an astonishing finding ruling out the possibility of a man-made artifact.

6. Lastly, as with other eucharistic miracles, the persistence of myocardial tissue along with the unleavened host bread is inexplicable: both intact, without signs of decay or degradation in the absence of any preservative, after all the time first spent in water and then in air for months (and currently uncorrupted for many years, for those going on a pilgrimage to Sokółka).

The Conclusion

After considering the results of the histological analyses, the Białystok Diocese instituted a special Church committee on March 30, 2009, to investigate the fine details of the sequence of events that took place according to the accounts given by the witnesses. The conclusion was that the analyzed host had to be the same one that Sr. Julia had been looking after since October 12, 2008, with no window of opportunity for any other intervention or tampering by a third party.

On October 14, 2009, one year after the facts, the rector of the Białystok Archdiocese, Andrzej Kakareko, declared that the Sokółka event was not contrary to the Faith of the Church. Instead, he stated that it confirmed its doctrine and gave permission to the faithful to venerate the relic.

On October 2, 2011, in the presence of thirty-five thousand faithful, the monstrance containing the corporal bearing the host fragment and the sacred tissue was solemnly moved to the chapel of Our Lady of the Rosary in the parish church, where it is still exposed for daily adoration together with the Blessed Sacrament. Interest in this eucharistic miracle has been growing over the years both in Poland and elsewhere. Dozens, even hundreds, of faithful pilgrims attend every day, and the parish set up a reception center run by priests, nuns, and lay volunteers working full-time. For larger groups, they recommend booking according to the instructions on the parish website (so far, only written in Polish). Many spiritual and physical healings are also known to be linked to Sokółka. The book by Adam Białous, listed in my bibliography, mentions some physical healings from cancer as well as cardiac arrhythmias.

The Controversies

One unique feature of the Sokółka miracle, compared to other eucharistic events discussed in this book, is that of the objections and controversies it raised in lay civil society as well as the Polish scientific community. Perhaps this was to be expected. After all, Polish society and culture were very different from those of Latin America, where the Buenos Aires and Tixtla miracles found their fertile ground in the strong faith of the people. Indeed, those miracles did not stir any of the local South American intellectuals or civil authorities. They were too busy dealing with more pressing issues of finance and public order. Poland was instead a much different reality: a Western country with a free market economy in an off-center location that, despite its significant Catholic historical background, had already "opened up" to the secular "values" of the "free world" in the 2000s. There, a eucharistic miracle could not but fully express its upsetting, embarrassing, and scandalizing impact. Let's see how it did so.

Once again, it is worth dwelling on the extraordinary curricula vitae of the two researchers at the University of Białystok who were involved in the investigations. At the time, Stanisław Sulkowski was a brilliant professor in the Department of General Pathomorphology. He is still a leading expert on the immunohistochemistry of neoplastic tissues,[70] having authored at least 286 internationally valued publications referenced on PubMed[71] up to now. Prof. Maria Elżbieta Sobaniec-Łotowska was working in the neighboring Department of Medical Pathomorphology. Her primary research focus was in pediatric hepatology[72] and gastroenterology.[73] She had 108 PubMed publications as of February 2019. In 2008, they were both at the height of their careers. They were highly respected and professionally esteemed both in their own country and abroad. Despite all that, they were also both formally reprimanded by their own director and a spokesperson of the University of Białystok, Prof. Lech Chyczewski, who accused them of carrying out "illegal" and "disloyal" investigations.

[70] *Neoplastic* is the medical term to describe anomalous tissues that are either cancer or about to turn into cancer.

[71] PubMed is a mainstream, free online search engine to access scientific articles on life sciences and biomedical topics. The database is maintained by the United States National Library of Medicine.

[72] Pediatric hepatology is the medical subspecialty focused on liver disease in children.

[73] Gastroenterology is the medical specialty focused on diseases of the gastrointestinal tract.

An interesting reflection by Prof. Sulkowski on the duties of a scientist toward the community in which he lives was the following:

> If a new important social issue arises, one that requires a scientist's involvement, if there is a need for his knowledge, he not only has the right, but also the duty to be involved.... We have the duty to investigate every scientific problem. I see that as a kind of service to the society which finances our scientific activities. Just as a doctor cannot refuse to care for a patient, likewise, we have the duty to research every scientific problem, according to the guidelines of the Polish Academy of Sciences.

Prof. Sobaniec-Łotowska's approach was more practical. She reminded her supervisor that she had been working after receiving a precise written and formal request by the Białystok Curia. She could not refrain from recalling, with a note of sarcasm, that she could not fill in some forms because she could not find the medical card number of the person to whom that myocardial tissue belonged.

The ancient and still unresolved contrast between science and faith became very real in that situation, even if in a new and quite unique context.

The director of the university accused his own researchers, with whom he shared many published scientific works, of conflating the "emotional" aspect of their Catholic Faith with the rationality required by laboratory work. He could not admit that his very well-esteemed colleagues with thirty years of experience could "see" what science could not acknowledge or explain.

In October 2009, the "authoritative" voice of the tabloid magazine *Super Express* joined in the controversy. Sneaked in between a sports article and a gossip one, there was a scoop titled "Is the Sokółka Miracle a Scam?" Please, everyone, stop! Church authorities were deceiving us: it was a trivial bacterial contamination. Prof. Pawel Grzesiowski, from the Warsaw National Institute of Hygiene, was the one who could finally explain what really happened when interviewed. A bacterium, *Serratia marcescens*, which usually grows well on carbohydrate-rich media, contaminated the bread as it was dissolving in water under non-sterile conditions. While growing, *Serratia* produces a red-orange pigment called "prodigiosin," a name it was given precisely because it simulated the appearance of blood on bread and other starchy materials in many other occasions. Any unsettled Polish citizen can now go back to a quiet sleep: science will be watching over him, protecting him from disturbing obscurantism and medieval intrusions. Even the reader who has patiently followed me thus far can heave a sigh of relief and begin to think about what else he ought to be reading. My dear friend, please close this book, go to the newsstand, and get yourself a copy of *Super Express*, or whatever is its equivalent in your own country. So many truly interesting articles: "Five Foods That Burn Your Belly Fat" or "Eight Things Not to Say on Your First Date with a Girl."

Welcome to the new Orwellian world, where an "expert" who never set foot in Sokółka, with actually only thirty PubMed publications compared to the 286 by Prof. Sulkowski — if we were to make a comparison in terms of scientific authority — dared to insult his much more well-esteemed colleagues, accusing them of being incompetent. Clearly, given his great knowledge and expertise, Prof. Grzesiowski could give his qualified and objective scientific opinion about the Sokółka specimen without having actually even looked at the microscope slides himself and without knowing how they were prepared. Sadly, this false argument about *Serratia* and its prodigiosin pigment keeps coming up in publications based on "scientific skepticism," and in the reader's best interest, it should be clarified, once and for all, that any microscope, even the one they gave me as a present for my First Holy Communion as a child, can deliver justice after all this nonsense: a colony of rod-shaped enterobacteria indeed looks completely different from striated heart muscle tissue. Even in the first year of medical school, in any histology course, students are taught about distinguishing the different tissues of the human body: being unable to distinguish bacterial contamination from an organized tissue means a failing grade.

In this case, it was as if an airline pilot with thirty years of experience were accused of being unable to tell apart a runway from a potato field when landing his plane. Rightfully, Profs. Sulkowski and Sobaniec-Łotowska wanted to seek justice by legal means, but they did not pursue this only because they were otherwise advised by Church authorities. Furthermore, a bacterial contamination is ever-changing: it can change its look from day to day until it inevitably disappears when the substrate on which the bacteria are feeding is exhausted. Let's imagine, to make a trivial example, the mold growing on a jam jar forgotten in the pantry: it changes shape and color over time, and after a long while, it turns into dust and disappears. This does not apply to the Sokółka relic, which has been made visible to the public for several years now: the red stain on the corporal is completely stable and unchanged over time, without human intervention or preservatives (which, by the way, are actually meant to prevent bacterial growth).

Still, Poland just cannot stop surprising us: the Sokółka case also came with a morbid and grotesque story in its tail end that deserves to be told. We should start by saying that living in Poland must be very frustrating for a true rationalist atheist, who could really face a nervous breakdown: despite decades of communist rule and now liberal capitalism, the country just cannot break free from its ancient papist heritage. The Polish Rationalist Association could not help reacting in the face of the umpteenth clerical insult. Hence, on October 1, 2009, the president of the association, Dr. Małgorzata Lesniak, initiated a public lawsuit addressed to the district attorney of Sokółka, calling for him to begin investigating and shed light on a series of grave criminal offences, including murder, which allegedly took place in the district under his jurisdiction. The logic was airtight: if two university researchers had demonstrated the presence of a tissue sample identified as human heart muscle at St. Anthony's Parish, that must have meant that the fragment had come from somebody's heart, somebody who could not possibly still have been alive. Hence:

1. The myocardium had been certainly taken from a corpse, and the defilement of human remnants was itself a crime as per article 262, no. 1 of the Polish Criminal Code.

2. A murder could not therefore have been ruled out in that context of murky religious fanaticism, at least until a corpse was identified from which the tissue had to have been taken. However, murder, as the diligent rationalists reminded us, is legally punished as specified at article 148, no. 1 of the Polish Criminal Code.

3. The significant epidemiological hazard: even if the heart muscle tissue had been stolen during an autopsy or was of animal nature, it should not have

been stored in a tabernacle. This could have led to the potential contamination of the "foodstuff" that Polish citizens consume at religious services with tissues of unknown biological origin, and it could have exposed the population to risks of serious infections such as avian, swine, H5N1 and H1N1 influenzas, only citing a few. Hence, this must have warranted an appeal to article 165, no. 1, section 1 of the Polish Criminal Code.

4. A failure by the competent authorities to commence formal investigations had been revealed. Such omission of public duty had also been aggravated by not taking any action even if presented with objective tissue evidence of a serious crime. That alone would have been a crime in and of itself, according to article 231, no. 1 of the Polish Criminal Code.

It looks as if the Sokółka attorney general never took the rationalists' provocation too seriously, limiting the response to a simple statement highlighting that no one in the town had gone missing and that there had been no homicides.

I admit feeling sympathy for those sad and bitter Polish atheists—looking like a hardly imaginable group of teetotalers attending the Vinitaly wine festival in Verona—as they actually took an apparently inexplicable event seriously. They clung to the facts and wrote: "As it is highly unlikely those heart fragments belong to a Jewish prophet crucified 2000 years ago, they must belong to some Polish citizen who has recently died!" I find the crass shallowness of those advancing the argument of "emotional religiosity," hiding behind paperwork technicalities or putting forth the explanation of bacterial contamination, to be much more offensive.

Bibliography

Bejda, Henryk. 2012. *Cud eucharystyczny*, 1st ed. Dom Wydawniczy Rafael.

Book fully dedicated to the Sokółka events (only in Polish).

Białous, Adam. 2015. *Hostia: Cud eucharystyczny w Sokolce*, 1st ed. Edycja.

Book fully dedicated to the Sokółka events (only in Polish).

Cząstka Ciała Pańskiego (A Part of the Body of the Lord). Accessed July 12, 2021. https://sokolka.archibial.pl/index.php/czastka-ciala-panskiego/.

Presentation of the miracle on the St. Anthony of Padua Parish website.

Komunikat Kurii Metropolitalnej Białostockiej w sprawie zjawisk eucharystycznych w Sokółce (Announcement from the Bialystok Metropolitan Curia on the eucharistic phenomena in Sokółka). October 14, 2009. Accessed July 12, 2021. https://archibial.pl/komunikaty/965-komunikat-kurii-metropolitalnej-bialostockiej-w-sprawie-zjawisk-eucharystycznych-w-sokolce/.

Official public statement of recognition of the miracle by the Diocese of Białystok (October 2009).

11Gall. 2011. "*Pokazali światu hostię z Sokółki—Polska—02.10.2011*." Video recording. YouTube. Accessed July 12, 2021. https://www.youtube.com/watch?v=MwL5YtysbU4.

Press report on Polish television channel TVN24 from October 2, 2011, on the occasion of the solemn procession for the entrance of the relics in the parish church.

Love One Another! no. 23 (2012), 3–10. English version of *Miłujcie się!* Accessed July 12, 2021. https://pdf.milujciesie.pl/pl/love-one-another/266-love-one-another-2012-3.html.

Extensive summary of the Sokółka episode from a very well-known Polish bimonthly religious newspaper.

Racjonalista.pl. 2009. "Doniesienie do prokuratury w związku z tzw. cudem w Sokółce." Letter. Krakow. Accessed July 12, 2021. http://www.racjonalista.pl/kk.php/s,6832.
Statement by the Rationalist Polish Association on October 1, 2009, to the Sokółka Attorney General.

Stasiak, Bożena, and Tomasz Matuszkiewicz. 2009. "Cud w Sokółce to oszustwo?" *Super Express*. Accessed July 12, 2021. https://www.se.pl/wiadomosci/polska/cud-w-sokoce-to-oszustwo-aa-G2o6-EMv7-X3ds.html.
Online article on *Super Express* (October 29, 2009), titled "Is the Sokółka Miracle a Scam?"

Meloni, Sergio. 2014. *I miracoli eucaristici e le radici cristiane dell'Europa*. 3rd ed. ESD Edizioni Studio Domenicano.
The most complete collection of eucharistic miracle accounts based on a successful exhibit traveling around the world (written in Italian). The more recent Sokółka events have been included since its third edition from page 520 to page 525.

Tesoriero, Ron, and Lee Han. 2013. *Unseen New Evidence: The Origin of Life Under the Microscope*. Australia: Ron Tesoriero.
The Sokółka episode is in chapter 9. Ron Tesoriero and Mike Willesee went to Poland to meet Profs. Sulkowski and Sobaniec-Lotowska.

1713 silver and crystal glass shrine
containing the Lanciano relics.

The Flesh of the eucharistic miracle of Lanciano: it retains the circular shape of a host and is also the cross-sectional image of a heart. In the later years of his research, Prof. Linoli stated that the thicker part at the bottom had to be a remnant of the left ventricle, whereas the thinner, upper part belonged to the right ventricle.

The Blood of the Lanciano miracle, made up of five clotted clumps.

Following are four microscopic images (continued on the next page) of the Flesh and Blood of Lanciano, taken from Prof. Linoli's publication.

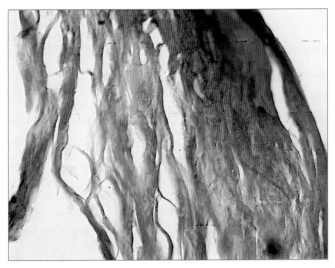

Eosin stain, x 200 magnification. Bundles of mostly longitudinal fibers, suggestive of a superficial area of the cardiac muscle.

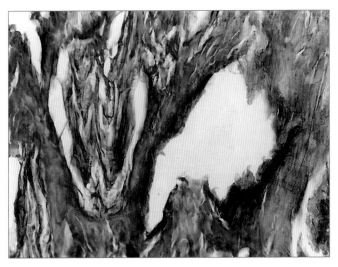

Mallory stain, x 250 magnification. Amid myocardial fibers, an arterial blood vessel can be seen on the right, and a nerve structure on the left.

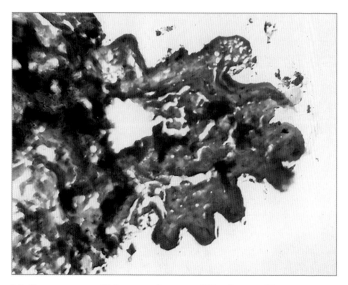

Mallory stain, x 400 magnification. The "rugged" appearance of the endocardium can be seen on the inner surface of this cross-sectional heart sample.

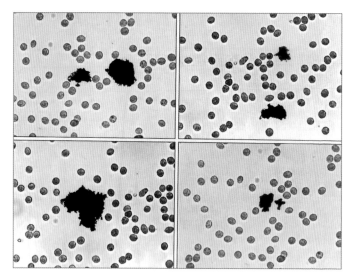

The absorption-elution test, x 80 magnification. There is evidence of agglutination with anti-A serum on the left and anti-B serum on the right. Samples of the Blood are at the top, and those of the Flesh at the bottom. Both have been demonstrated to be of the AB group.

The current appearance — like that of a small crust of blood — of the remnant of the May 1992 eucharistic miracle of Buenos Aires.

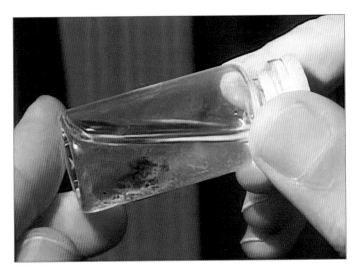

The tissue of the 1996 Buenos Aires miracle, stored in distilled water, at the time it was sampled by Dr. Castañón, three years after the event.

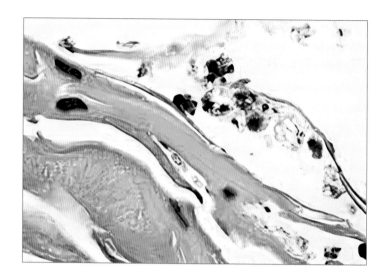

Samples of the 1996 Buenos Aires miracle. The myocardial fibers display degenerative changes: fragmentation, loss of striations, pyknotic nuclei, and considerable infiltration by inflammatory cells (macrophage and neutrophil leukocytes).

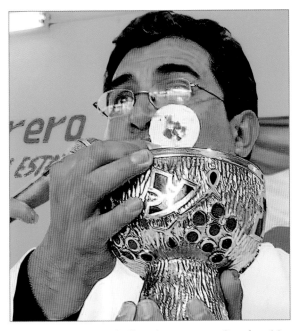

At the Tixtla town hall auditorium on October 22, 2006, Fr. Rayito shows those who attended Mass the consecrated host that had just bled.

The Tixtla ciborium, a few minutes after the event, on October 22, 2006.

Histological images of the samples taken from the eucharistic miracle of Tixtla:

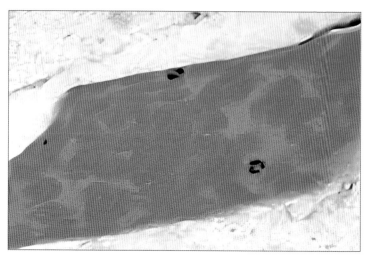

An acidophile cluster made of blood undergoing autolysis: single erythrocytes are no longer distinguishable, although a neutrophil leukocyte (lower right) and an eosinophile leukocyte (top left) can still be recognized.

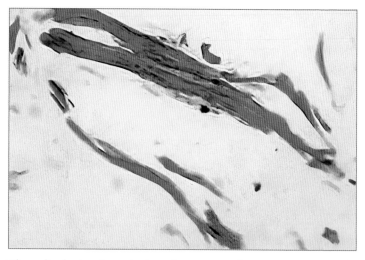

Fibers displaying degradation phenomena: fragmentation, poorly visible nuclei, lack of striations. However, the tendency of the fibers to bifurcate and anastomose with one another—typical of myocardial cells—is still evident.

A cluster of adipose cells, recognizable due to the large, white, fat-filled inner cavities taking up all of the cytoplasm in each cell.

A large and nearly square macrophage whose cytoplasm is filled with lipid material that has just been phagocytosed. Amorphous material and adipose cells can be seen at the top right. A branched, unstained structure, in keeping with a bread trabecular element, can be seen in the middle.

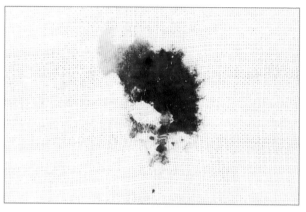

The red tissue remnant of the 2008 Sokółka miracle still joined to a host fragment (on the top left). It is currently adhering to a linen corporal, on which is embroidered a red cross that is partially covered by the miraculous tissue.

The monstrance displaying the eucharistic miracle at St.
Anthony of Padua Church in Sokółka.

Photographic sequence evidencing the formation of the miraculous tissue of Legnica in December 2013:

The appearance of red coloring extending from one edge of the host as the latter was dissolving in water.

The spontaneous detachment of the red portion, a few days later.

After two weeks, the nearly complete dissolution of the host and the persistent presence of the miraculous tissue.

The tissue was removed from the water and laid on a cloth.

The miraculous tissue exposed at St. Hyacinth's Church in Legnica.

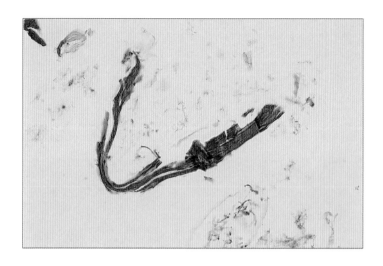

Myocardial fibers from the December 2013 Legnica miracle with clear evidence of fragmentation.

5

Legnica (2013)

Another surprise came from Poland. Only five years after the Sokółka event, a new episode took place, one very similar both in terms of how it happened and the scientific conclusions drawn from it. The meaning behind this insistence by Heaven on the same people and in the same land remains unknown. Could it be a prize or a warning? Was Poland receiving a heavenly caution to resist its advancing destructive secularism and avoid giving in to the flattery of modernism? After all, Poland had forged its resilience through a history of suffering, and it had not yet been fully corrupted by the "free" Western world. Alternatively, was the divine message some kind of call to conversion for Poles to make up for their shortcomings in the Faith, as well as their increasing neglect and corruption of religious values?

Legnica is a city of one hundred thousand people in Lower Silesia, in southwestern Poland. Interestingly, it is at the very opposite end of the country from Sokółka. It was part of Germany until World War II. After the war, Poland was torn apart and then joined back together a tad smaller and moved a few hundred kilometers westward, to please Stalin and the powers that had won the world conflict. This forced relocation imposed huge sacrifices on millions of German and Polish people. Thus,

A Cardiologist Examines Jesus

German Liegnitz became Polish Legnica. In Legnica, our focus is on a working-class neighborhood, not far from the city center, and its elegant neo-Gothic-style parish church of St. Hyacinth. On Christmas Day in 2013, the first morning Mass was being celebrated. There, the same event that happened in Sokółka five years earlier took place again: a consecrated host accidentally fell on the ground, more precisely on a carpet, within the sacred space of the sanctuary. It was a host that had just been dipped in the consecrated wine and became dirty upon touching the ground. The priest then decided, like in Sokółka, to follow the procedure we already know, and he put the host in a container, a metal chalice, with simple tap water for it to dissolve. The chalice was then kept in the tabernacle for a few days. On January 5, 2014, another priest, the eldest in the community, checked the sacred vessel and noticed that a crescent-shaped portion of the host, about 0.5 by 1.5 centimeters in size, had detached from the rest of the unleavened bread and was turning red. Some very clear photographs showing the different stages of the phenomenon can be seen on the parish website. Msgr. Stefan Cichy, the bishop of Legnica at the time, was informed, and he requested that the observations be continued. After two weeks, the colored portion of the host was still present on the surface of the water, while the rest had completely dissolved. At that stage, the bishop set up a committee of four experts to monitor the events.

With the bishop's permission, the committee began some scientific investigations. On January 26, 2014, some microsamples of the material were taken and initially analyzed at the nearby University of Wrocław. Later on, they were sent for further testing at the University of Szczecin.

On February 10, 2014, the resistant and mysterious dark red biological material was removed from the water and laid on a corporal cloth, onto which it is still attached. Initially, it looked like a raised red button almost shaped like a heart, although it shrunk a few millimeters in size by drying out in the following weeks and eventually took on its current appearance that has since remained unchanged.

In the official report, released by the diocese, we can read a summary of the scientific findings:

> The Department of Forensic Medicine could draw the following conclusions: "Histopathological images showed tissue fragments containing fragmented portions of striated muscle. The image to which the examined tissue was overall most similar to … was that of cardiac muscle … displaying changes that often accompany a state of agony." DNA tests confirmed that the tissue is of human origin.

In January 2016, Bishop Zbigniew Kiernikowski, who had succeeded Msgr. Cichy, presented the case report to the Congregation for the Doctrine of the Faith at the Vatican. Finally, on April 10, 2016, he published a statement declaring that the eucharistic event that happened at St. Hyacinth possesses the qualities of a miracle. He requested that Fr. Andrzej Ziombra set up a suitable location for the exposition of the relic and its veneration by the faithful in the same church. Moreover, he asked that future visitors be given adequate information and that regular catechesis meetings take place as well. Finally, a logbook was set up to record any graces received by the faithful, as commonly done for any other miraculous events. In the summer of 2016, the monstrance containing the relic was solemnly moved to a Divine Mercy chapel in a side nave within the same church of St. Hyacinth. Many pilgrims currently visit the church from the entire surrounding region, and it is still common practice for the parish priest to spend some time with visitors at the end of Mass to explain what happened in 2013.

A reference text, edited by the Diocese of Legnica, was made available in 2017. It includes original testimonies as well as a rich collection of photographs.

Besides these official documents, I shall now discuss some extra details about the scientific investigations I was personally made aware of by Dr. Barbara Engel, the head of cardiology at the Legnica hospital. She was also one of the members of the scientific committee instituted by Msgr. Cichy.

Fifteen specimens were taken from the host fragment and, precisely to avoid the controversies that took place in Sokółka, sampling procedures took place in the presence of witnesses and were photographically documented step-by-step. Some control samples were also set up with non-consecrated hosts, wine, and tap water. These were carefully prepared by using host wafers taken from the same production batch as that of the soon-to-be-examined consecrated host in question. Initial testing was commissioned to the Institute of Forensic Medicine in nearby Wrocław and revealed the following:

1. The material was degraded due to significant autolysis and from remaining in water for a prolonged period of time. Still, the histological structure seen under the microscope was best in keeping with striated muscle tissue. Unfortunately, the considerable tissue degradation prevented definitive immunohistochemical confirmation of this hypothesis.

2. The tissue was not made of bacteria. The bacteria that were present only represented a negligible local contamination. In particular, there were no bacteria

known to produce coloring substances, like *Serratia marcescens*.

3. There was no significant fungal contamination: Grocott's silver stain, specific for fungi, yeasts, algae, and spores, indeed yielded a negative result.
4. No DNA amplifications were obtained by PCR technology.
5. The turning of a bread host into the tissue that was examined was deemed to be scientifically inexplicable.

Not fully satisfied by the incomplete Wroclaw results, the scientific committee turned to the University of Szczecin—which had made itself available for further testing—and asked for a second opinion after a few months. The same microscope slides prepared in Wroclaw, the Wroclaw report, and a leftover paraffin-preserved fragment of original material were forwarded to Szczecin. Different histopathological analytical methods were used there, and another DNA detection attempt was made. In summary, the following was demonstrated:

1. A microscope examination under ultraviolet light, with an orange filter, finally allowed the recognition of the myocardial origin of the muscle tissue, with clear signs of fragmentation. Those microscopic images were very similar to the Sokółka ones.
2. At the University of Szczecin, too, testing with specific immunohistochemical markers yielded a negative result.
3. Surprisingly, fragments of nuclear and mitochondrial DNA were found that were sufficient to prove the human origin of the tissue beyond doubt. The researchers and the diocese kept further details on these DNA tests strictly confidential due to concerns about misunderstandings and inappropriate sensationalism.

As in Sokółka, despite the macroscopic aspect of the relic looking like a blood clot, no blood cells were found, and the possible presence of ABO blood group antigens was not tested for. Still, we know that even in the absence of blood cells, that test still could have been theoretically performed (as was done in Lanciano), since ABO antigens are not just confined to red blood cells, but rather, they are also present on other types of body cells.

Bibliography

Sanktuarium sw Jacka. 2019. Sanktuarium sw Jacka w Legnicy. Website. Accessed July 12, 2021. https://www.jacek-legnica-sanktuarium.pl/info/en.

English version of the St. Hyacinth Parish website about the eucharistic event with photographs and the official public statement by the bishop on April 10, 2016.

Kandra, Greg. 2016. "Miracolo eucaristico in Polonia approvato dal vescovo." Aleteia. Website. Accessed June 27, 2020. https://it.aleteia.org/2016/04/19/miracolo-eucaristico-in-polonia-approvato-dal-vescovo/?utm_campaign=NL_it&utm_source=daily_newsletter&utm_medium=mail&utm_content=NL_it-Apr%2019,%202016%2010:36%20am.

Summary report of the April 19, 2016, events by Italian news agency Aleteia.

Cenci, Federico. 2016. "Polonia: un'ostia presenta 'le caratteristiche di un miracolo eucaristico.'" Zenit. Website. Accessed July 12, 2021. https://it.zenit.org/2016/04/20/polonia-unostia-presenta-le-caratteristiche-di-un-miracolo-eucaristico/.

Summary report of the April 20, 2016, events by Italian news agency Zenit.

Legnica Dami TV. 2016. "O cudzie coraz głośniej." You-Tube. Accessed July 12, 2021. https://www.youtube.com/watch?v=Vms6tomfSvU.

Video summary of the press conference for the presentation of the miracle.

Kiernikowski, Zbigniew. 2017. *Bóg przemówił w Legnicy.* Kraków: Wydawnictwo M.

Official summary report of the Legnica events issued by the diocese and published in 2017. Its medical and scientific research section is very accurate, although very succinct.

6

Possible Eucharistic Miracles Inexplicably Opposed by Church Authorities: Campoalegre (2006) and Buffalo (2018)

I already mentioned that Mexican Fr. Raymundo Reyna Este-ban, as a young priest in the Dominican Republic, had already witnessed a likely miraculous event before the Tixtla miracle took place: a consecrated host, that had appeared to be bleed-ing, was nonetheless destroyed by letting it dissolve in water, as precisely requested by the local bishop. This was certainly a key backstory for understanding Fr. Rayito's "holy" enthusiasm and lack of "prudence" when, years later, he immediately showed the bleeding Tixtla host to the six hundred witnesses who were at-tending Mass. That way, the new and yet-to-be-recognized Tixtla miracle—a second miraculous event in Fr. Rayito's life—was certainly spared from being censored. Instead, it was protected from the excessive prudence that—we must admit—is often present among Church authorities, a prudence that Fr. Rayito had sadly already experienced.

The 2017 Australian documentary *The Blood of Christ* that I already mentioned also included a report on another credible South American miraculous event. This took place in the poor parish church of Our Lady of the Divine Love in Campoalegre, central Colombia, in the Neiva Diocese. There, during Holy Week in 2006, a sister of the Rome-based Daughters of Our Lady of the Divine Love found that a consecrated host had apparently bled while stored in a small cylindrical metal pyx. Fr. José Fidel Medina Salinas, the parish priest at the time—now living at his order's Rome headquarters—confirmed to me the accuracy of what was reported in the Australian documentary. He told me that Msgr. Ramón Darío Molina Jaramillo, bishop of Neiva at the time, was prudent but generally in favor of the authenticity of the event and suggested preserving the host with great reverence in a tabernacle. There were no objections to a scientific study and, only a few days after the event, a doctor friend of the parish priest had already confirmed that the liquid present on the host was blood.

Soon after, as is always the case in South America, Dr. Ricardo Castañón Gómez was involved. In the summer of 2006, Dr. Castañón had already sampled the relic and started investigating. Fr. Fidel told me that those investigations yielded very interesting results, including unprecedented findings compared to other eucharistic miracles. Unfortunately, however, none of the results have ever been disclosed to the public. Moreover, Dr. Castañón has never published any document on Campoalegre, nor has he ever spoken about it at any public conference. I suppose that is because he has never been given formal permission to do so.

Still, we know that Mike Willesee and his Australian Channel Seven team were in Campoalegre sometime between 2015 and 2016. There, they interviewed Fr. Juan Ricardo Yangua Lapouble, who had succeeded Fr. Fidel as parish priest at Our Lady of the Divine Love. In addition, they also video-recorded the moment in which a fragment of the still well-preserved 2006 bloodstained host was sampled to undergo new investigations. In his documentary, Willesee then went on to "stab us" with an outrageous revelation. In 2012, Msgr. Froilán Tiberio Casas Ortiz had become the new bishop of Neiva, replacing Msgr. Molina. For some reason, the new bishop had been hostile toward the presumed eucharistic miracle—to the point that he had gone to Campoalegre in person and destroyed the host himself, in front of his dumbstruck parish priest, and then buried it in the garden. Later on, Willesee tried to contact the Neiva Diocese asking for explanations, without success. I also wrote a letter asking for the same information in August 2020 but never received any reply.

We further know that the Australian team investigated the fragment taken by Willesee in Campoalegre, thereby obtaining an inexplicable result, which, precisely for this reason, was compatible with other truly miraculous events. Without getting into the details, the documentary mentioned the presence of white blood cells—and thus blood—with recognizable DNA that, even with the best technology available in recent times, still defies all common identification tests (I shall discuss this type of recurrent outcome and its meaning more extensively in a later chapter).

What happened in Campoalegre was an unprecedented event: a possible miracle that no longer exists, on which there is scientific documentation that has outlived it. Still, the results in these documents have not been revealed, or have only been roughly disclosed with regards to the Australian investigations. Who knows if, one day, Church authorities will once again reopen a file on Campoalegre to reconsider the event, starting from the existing scientific data. As a Catholic, I hope that light will be shed on this disconcerting case, and that an act of justice and reparation will be done for a possible wicked abuse.

A Cardiologist Examines Jesus

In mid-November 2018, at St. Vincent de Paul Church in Springbrook, in New York State's Buffalo Diocese, a consecrated host was inadvertently dropped on the floor during Mass. A deacon implemented the usual procedure we are familiar with: he put the host in a water-filled glass container with a metal lid and locked the vessel in a tabernacle. Only a few days later, on November 30, Fr. Karl Loeb, the parish priest, along with an assistant, rechecked the container: the water had almost completely evaporated, although a crescent-shaped portion of the incompletely dissolved white host at the bottom had turned bright red. The color of the new substance then turned brownish a few days later. There are adequate quality photographs of the host that are available online as documentary evidence of what happened. The parish priest immediately informed the local bishop, Msgr. Richard Malone, and his auxiliary bishop, Edward Grosz. The answer was disconcerting: as the host had already dissolved (a clearly false premise, directly contradicted by the available photographs), Jesus could no longer have been present, and thus it was necessary to destroy what was left. It was mostly Bishop Malone who pushed in that direction, as Auxiliary Bishop Grosz later spoke about these facts with unease. Bound to his vow of obedience to his bishop, Fr. Karl then destroyed with great reluctance what potentially could have been a eucharistic miracle.

However, what Bishop Malone had underestimated was the response by the U.S. Catholic community. The episode did not remain hidden: in December 2018, the powerful EWTN Catholic television network dedicated its authoritative program *The World Over* to what had just happened in Buffalo. The broadcast included an interview with Lisa Benzer, a St. Vincent de Paul's parishioner and an eyewitness.

It is astonishing to read hundreds and hundreds of online comments by Catholic faithful on this report, many of them, of course, from Catholics in the Buffalo Diocese. These were like a single chorus of disapproval and bewilderment. "Why didn't the bishop consent to carry out some simple investigation?" "Why did he deprive us of a possible source of grace?" The common theme driving the scandal was the refusal to carry out any scientific tests: Perhaps it could have been a natural contamination, but why prohibit investigations that could have ascertained it?

Why would a bishop want to destroy a possible eucharistic miracle? Shouldn't a holy bishop instead rejoice and hope that the possibility of a genuine miraculous event in his diocese could reawaken the lukewarm faith of his flock? This is not easy to answer. On some occasions, a bishop who knows his sheep and his land well can, or must, keep a healthy level of skepticism toward "excessive" spiritual phenomena reeking of heresy. Still, neither the Campoalegre nor the Buffalo events would seem to fit in this suspicious category for any particular reason.

Toward the end of 2018, the Buffalo Diocese was caught up in a storm, with Msgr. Malone busy defending himself from the accusation of having covered up countless incidences of sexual abuse. Because of that, in November 2019, Malone had to tender his resignation. Perhaps it was feared that a eucharistic miracle could have made the diocese even more visible to the media, which, in turn, would have cast even more spotlights on the legal proceedings that the diocese was sadly trying to conceal?

As far as the South American case, Mike Willesee instead hypothesized an ideological prejudice: the bishop was afraid that a eucharistic miracle could have brought "controversies" into the Church. Into the Catholic Church? Controversies that could have been disruptive to ecumenical dialogue? Let's not hide this away from each other, dear reader. Here we are entering a hazy territory, where a lack of faith can even turn into hatred against the most sacred gifts we have, and ultimately against faith itself.

Bibliography

7NEWS Spotlight. 2019. *Science's Search for Jesus: 7NEWS Spotlight*. Documentary. YouTube. Accessed June 12, 2021. https://www.youtube.com/watch?v=mWmdXqIhjSs .
Documentary by Mike Willesee from the Sunday Night series broadcast on April 9, 2017, on the Australian Channel 7. The report on Campoalegre and the images of the relic being sampled are from 14:37 to 18:17.

Arroyo, Raymond. 2018. "A Eucharistic Miracle in Buffalo?—The World Over, Television Program." EWTN. YouTube. Accessed September 29, 2020. https://www.youtube.com/watch?v=X22I-fz8x9U.

7

Why I Disregarded Betania (Venezuela, 1991)

On December 8, 1991, at a farm named Finca Betania, 65 kilometers south of Caracas, part of a host being consecrated by a priest was said to have bled during Mass. The fact was witnessed by thousands of faithful, and the host is still preserved and exposed at a nearby monastery. The local bishop, Msgr. Pio Bello Ricardo, immediately began an inquest that also included a scientific investigation assigned to the Department of Forensic Medicine of Caracas. Very early on, already in February 1992, he recognized the eucharistic miracle as authentic.

Nevertheless, I disregarded this episode for two reasons, even if initially it was actually part of my research project.

To begin with, no account of the Caracas investigations—not even in the form of a summary or excerpt—is available as a printed publication, at least to my knowledge. Online pieces of news are shallow and imprecise. At present, traveling to Venezuela in person to investigate the facts firsthand would not be prudent due to obvious political reasons.

But, above all, I personally have many doubts regarding the spiritual integrity of the Venezuelan woman around whom the "Betania phenomenon" has been growing. After doing my own research about the story and Maria Esperanza Bianchini's "charisma," I cannot fathom in my conscience how a true eucharistic miracle could have happened in the context of the mediocre, equivocal—and at times unorthodox—spirituality of that seer.

With all sincerity, I can only express my embarrassment when faced with this miraculous event. I suspect its supernatural origin, but I withhold my judgment.

8

The Passion Cloths

I believe a brief detour to a different topic — although one that is
somewhat complementary to that of eucharistic miracles — is now
warranted. The Passion cloths are ancient fabrics the Church has
venerated for centuries as relics, as having both come into contact
with the Body of the Redeemer and been soaked in His Blood.
Their authenticity is certainly not a dogma of the Faith, especially
after the controversial carbon-14 dating tests to which they were
subjected. Still, I find it unforgivable to forget or to belittle the
tradition that has handed down these cloths to us with love and
devotion, and I find it dishonest and shallow to shut my eyes to the
surprising results of the science that has studied them extensively.

The link with eucharistic miracles is obvious: it is the search
for biological traces that would hypothetically belong to the
same man. Discovering consistent elements among the cloths
or between a cloth and a eucharistic relic would reciprocally
strengthen the authoritativeness of each scientific finding.

If just about everyone knows — at least on a superficial level —
about the Shroud of Turin, few, even among Catholics, know
about the Sudarium[74] of Oviedo. But when it comes down to

---

[74] *Sudarium* is the Latin word for sweat cloth.

the Holy Tunic of Argenteuil, almost nobody knows about its existence. Still, it will be necessary for us to dwell on these cloths for a moment—especially on the last two, which are less well known—in order to deepen our understanding of eucharistic miracles. The Passion cloths will indeed come to our aid almost like "witnesses" to give us greater insight into the topics of the next few chapters, especially those on the blood and the DNA.

The Shroud of Turin

As everyone knows, the Shroud of Turin is the sheet that would have wrapped Jesus' Body in the tomb. I have no fear in revealing to the reader my firm conviction regarding the authenticity of the Shroud: the sheet not just *would have* but *did* wrap Christ. I can say this based on an enormous amount of compelling scientific data. After all, this was the opinion of the Catholic Church itself up until the carbon-14 dating of 1988.

The Shroud is a relic like no other. It possesses an "intrinsic" hardcore authenticity. To make myself clear, I shall begin by saying that the Shroud is perfect in all its details: a clear example of this is that its human image is a three-dimensionally encoded photographic negative showing off a realism that would transcend any art style. It is much more genuine than even the most daring attempts at reproducing it that possibly could have been conceived by the mind of a single incredibly brilliant AD 1300 medieval forger. This is because its image is accurate in all its anatomical and pathophysiological details. The linen cloth also contains traces of true human blood, as well as mineral and plant environmental elements that we have just begun analyzing in the last forty years. These prove a degree of complexity that could not possibly fit with the trivial manufacturing of a forgery. In other words, it is a unicum, a "one and only" find on Earth, an object that should not exist. This is because, up to this day, we still cannot fathom how the Shroud's image could have been generated, let alone how someone could find a way to reproduce it. In this regard, I should point out the clumsy and scientifically laughable failed attempts by Italian chemist Luigi Garlaschelli.

Hence, the Shroud is keeping ahead of the best science we challenge it with. It is an object that daringly survived through the centuries, as if gifted with a life of its own. It survived iconoclasm; it moved away from Constantinople before the Turkish invasion; it escaped from France where it would not have survived the French Revolution; it survived fires and ordeals so that people in modern times could feel moved in front of the most majestic and sublime facial image that ever existed, after the famous photographs taken by Secondo Pia in 1898. The Shroud would truly remain inexplicable, impossible, unreproducible regardless of any radiocarbon dating result. The limitations of the carbon-14 dating performed in 1988 on the Sacred Linen were exceedingly gross. I sincerely recommend that any readers not fearing confrontation with an inconvenient and censored truth do their own honest research on this topic.

These limitations were due to the vague protocol used to sample the original fabric and the control samples. There were also the limitations related both to non-adherence to blind testing and to the fact that the tests were not simultaneously performed in the three designated laboratories where they were meant to be done. As was shown later on, the laboratories had a chance to talk to one another before releasing their results. Moreover, there was a very strong bias related to the area of the cloth that was chosen for sampling: the upper left corner. That is an area that is significantly different from the rest of the Shroud, as unarguably demonstrated by Raymond Rogers in 2005. This was evidenced by the presence of vanillin[75] in the growth knots of the flax fibers, the finding of a superficial layer of alizarin pigment, an acacia gum stain, and the presence of cotton blended into the original flax — all obviously more recent contaminants that would have skewed the result. Finally, there were obvious limitations in statistical analysis. The brief and uninformative 1989 article in *Nature* failed to hide the lack of homogeneity of the data[76] obtained from the Shroud. This was despite the appropriate recalibrations applied to the math and the supercilious rhetoric of the article, arguing that its results had to be "conclusive evidence." The actual data revealed instead that the Shroud's fragment, unlike other control samples, behaved anomalously, as if it was made up of two or three different fabrics at the same time.

Only in 2017 did the British Museum finally disclose all of the original raw data from the three laboratories involved in the dating project, after a specific legal inquiry. The statistical heterogeneity of the results has thus been demonstrated with even greater strength, along with the unreliability of the final carbon-14 dating. It should be noted that this review of the raw data was published in 2019 in *Archaeometry*, a prestigious

---

[75] Vanillin is the primary component of the vanilla bean.

[76] In statistics, data homogeneity is a concept that arises when describing the properties of a dataset. Homogeneous data tend to be "clustered" around one similar value. This means that, despite unavoidable experimental error, the experiment succeeded in measuring a single variable. In a heterogeneous dataset, instead, the experimental data is clustered around widely different values. If this happens to a great extent, the scientist should begin to wonder whether he or she is actually unknowingly measuring different concealed variables, rather than simply facing repeated gross experimental error.

scientific journal ironically published by the University of Oxford, one of the three centers that performed the initial 1988 carbon-14 dating.

Indeed, the reality was that a certain type of nonrandom and nonuniform but rather linear contamination had affected the analyzed Shroud fragment and introduced a clear systematic error[77] in the distribution of carbon-14 across its longitudinal axis (i.e., the axis of the entire Shroud front image, running from the feet toward the head). The fabric, beginning with the fragment analyzed in Oxford and moving on to the one tested in Zurich and the one dated in Tucson, seemed to get younger by about a century for every couple of centimeters when moving toward the right. This is an absurd anomaly that should have made any statistician with a little prudence withhold judgment and cancel the test.

What is the reason for this curious longitudinal trend? There are many hypotheses. The most credible, supported by many authoritative and independent findings, seems to be the one about the contamination by more recent fabric fibers added to strengthen or substitute missing parts of the cloth, clearly in increasing proportions in the sampled fragments when moving from left to right. Unfortunately, for the average person of our time, even if he or she is moved by sincere curiosity, after the carbon-14 test of 1988, the Shroud is irredeemably a "medieval fake" to be considered on a par with some bizarre archaeological oddity, a tamed and almost fully understood specimen, at most deserving of a documentary warning us against the excesses of

---

[77] Systematic error, by definition, is predictable and typically either constant or proportional to the true value. Once identified, it can easily be corrected.

human gullibility. I acknowledge, with profound bitterness, the ideological and technocratic "veil" covering, in our time, the most important Veil of all times. Even Roman Catholics are inevitably victims of this sham and are fooled all the more when they support a "pure," idealistic, and "disembodied" faith that prefers doing without blood-dripping relics and overly generous signs from Heaven. However, I have no doubt that the moment of truth shall return and the Shroud will win back its proper place and the status it deserves.

The Sudarium of Oviedo

The Sudarium is an ancient bloodstained linen cloth, 83 by 53 centimeters, that has been stored in Spain for at least a thousand years in Oviedo's cathedral. According to tradition, it is venerated as the cloth that would have been wrapped around Jesus' head after death, covering His battered face out of respect and drying His wounds. Like the Shroud, the Sudarium has also undergone carbon-14 dating. Four dating tests, carried out between 1990 and 2007, seemed to agree on a historical age around the year AD 700, even though one of the four results had to be rejected in order to obtain a statistically sound homogeneity test. It is well established that radiocarbon-14 dating is not always reliable. An ordinary example of this was the blind control sample used in the "impeccable" protocol employed for the dating of the Sudarium of Oviedo in 2007 by Beta Analytic in Miami: discouragingly enough, the linen cloth of an Egyptian priest mummy from Tannis, belonging to the twenty-first Egyptian dynasty between 1110 and 950 BC, did not turn out to be three thousand years old as expected. Instead, it was experimentally estimated to be only three hundred years old, in a timeframe between AD 1660 and 1960. Still, faced with four different dating results, out of which at least three were concordant, accepting the scientific verdict would seem to be common sense: the Sudarium of Oviedo could not belong to the first century AD, and thus it could not be anything other than one of the many fake relics that were certainly circulating in the Middle Ages. This had also been my own opinion, at least until I dug further into the more recent scientific literature.

Probing further into this matter would entail admitting that the Sudarium had to be crafted with a degree of sophistication and attention to detail that poorly fit with a simple forgery from the seventh and eighth centuries. Moreover, too many coincidences are in common with the Shroud of Turin (such as the same blood group), to the point that one might wonder if they had been made by the same "forger." But how would that be possible if the two cloths were from different ages (as suggested by carbon-14 dating) as well as different geographical origins?

Let's begin by analyzing the bloodstains. The blood is real blood, of human origin. After extensive research on the Sudarium in the last twenty years, it is now possible to reconstruct the details of the process that produced those bloodstains. To be brief, I shall dwell only on two types of stains: the so-called central and point-like ones.

The most important and larger ones are the central stains due to leakage of pulmonary edema[78] fluid from nose and mouth after death, which then spread onto moustache, beard, nose, and forehead. In the same context, fingerlike marks can be distinguished, compatible with the external pressure applied by two hands that

---

[78] Pulmonary edema is the accumulation of fluid in the tissue and air spaces of the lungs. It is most commonly due to heart failure, and it can cause severe breathing difficulty and death.

attempted to dab nose and mouth. It was possible to reconstruct the order in which the stains themselves were formed. The sequence begins with a head tilted 70 degrees forward and reclined rightward by 20 degrees, which was then positioned facing down on a hard surface, according to a sequence compatible with death on a cross followed by being taken down from it.

Let's now turn to the relationships with the Shroud of Turin: it should first be said that the stains on the Sudarium frankly do not outline a recognizable face, exception made for the profile of the right ear, which is not visible on the Shroud. Also, in terms of anthropometric comparisons,[79] the bloodstains on the Shroud of Turin need to be distinguished from its complete and mysterious facial image. It is actually correct to look for the direct overlap between the bloodstains on the Shroud and those on the Sudarium, given the common process that generated them: the staining of a cloth by contact after being wrapped around the head. But this is not the case for the image of the face on the Shroud which has to be three-dimensionally reconstructed before any possible concordant marks on the Sudarium can be verified. Indeed, the Spanish Sindonology Research Centre (EDICES) researchers established a good level of anatomical concordance in terms of the shape and length of the nose, nostrils, brow ridges, mouth, chin, and beard. In particular, the overlap in the forehead area is very striking where the central stain on the Sudarium closely follows the contour of both the right eyebrow (in its lower portion) and the hairline on the Shroud (in its upper portion). Moreover, even more surprisingly, the inner border of the central stain on the Sudarium coincides with the famous Ɛ-shaped epsilon stain

---

[79] Anthropometry is the scientific study of the measurements and proportions of the human body.

on the Shroud (or, like its mirror image, the 3-shaped stain on its photographic negative). Furthermore, a bloodstain located on the inner aspect of the left eyebrow displays a rather curious "behavior," worthy of a sophisticated and ironic word puzzle: its center is in Oviedo, while its contour is in Turin.

I would invite the reader to watch the online documentary and interview with Prof. César Barta, mentioned in my bibliography, which shows much clearer images than any other written description of these details, as well as the interview with Prof. Jorge Rodríguez, covering the three-dimensional reconstruction of the face of the Shroud.

The point-like stains are a grouping of small and well-demarcated spots. They are located at one end of the Sudarium, in an area that made contact with the back of the neck. The blood they are made of—unlike that of the central stains[80]—was fresh whole blood: the darker central color and the serous halos[81] around the stains' edges reflect what would be expected to happen with the shrinkage of blood clots—clots that originated from fresh blood oozing out of open wounds.[82] They are stains that, at first sight,

---

[80] The central stains are traces of pulmonary edema fluid. This frothy pinkish fluid is classically described as watery and bloodstained.

[81] Serous haloes would arise from contact with serous fluid. Serous fluids are all kinds of watery pale-yellowish bodily fluids that resemble serum. Serum, in turn, is the watery component of blood—rich in protein and mineral salts—which can be observed if blood is left to clot in a test tube: blood cells collect at the bottom, a clot forms on top of the blood cells, and the serum is the yellowish liquid floating on top of both.

[82] If blood were left to clot on a cloth, just like in a test tube, its cell component would clot in the center of the stain, whereas its watery serum component would form a surrounding halo by "wicking" outward along the fabric fibers.

already coincide with a similar image on the back of the neck of the man of the Shroud, traditionally attributed to the wounds inflicted by the crown of thorns. Using dedicated software, the Spanish researchers demonstrated that the exact overlapping of part of the Shroud's representation of the back of the neck, on the point-like stains of the Sudarium, results in the surprising spatial matching of a whopping six out of eight reference points if rotated by 19 degrees. This demonstration, too, is a reason for watching Barta's documentary, although this is not all: just like on the face of the Shroud, there are soil residues on the tip of the nose of the Sudarium image as well. This is likely to be the evidence of a fall on the ground without being able to land on outstretched hands. Interestingly enough, the soil residues are more compatible with Jerusalem's soil rather than with the soil in Oviedo. Scattered throughout the entire cloth there are traces of aloe and a substitute for myrrh. There are Mediterranean pollens, including a *Helichrysum* pollen granule, which is also the most widely detected pollen type on the Shroud. Moreover, the same pollen granule is coated in blood, thus proving its presence since the very first hour when the Sudarium was used, as opposed to a later addition. The finding about the pollen granule also confirmed the use of the same oils and balms on both the man of the Sudarium and the man of the Shroud, according to the recent resounding discovery by Dr. Marzia Boi. In conclusion, just as with the Shroud, the Sudarium's carbon-14 dating result needs to be questioned in the light of many other scientific findings supporting its authenticity. The Sudarium is an incredibly sophisticated relic, and a hypothetical forger who manufactured it in AD 700 would then need to demonstrate exceptional and inexplicable knowledge in pathophysiology, forensic medicine, transfusion medicine, anthropology, botany, and even geology.

The Holy Tunic of Argenteuil

Let's finally focus on a third and barely known, though authoritative, Passion relic: the fragments of what would be left of the seamless robe worn by Jesus on his ascent to Calvary. This is the same tunic for which soldiers were casting lots at the foot of the Cross, according to the Gospel narrative.

The Tunic of Argenteuil is now preserved at the Basilica of Saint-Denis in Argenteuil, 12 kilometers northwest of Paris. It is a garment made of sheep wool, 122 centimeters long and 90 centimeters wide at the level of the armpits. It is made up of twenty separate pieces, two of which are larger in size. Aging signs are quite obvious, and unfortunately most of the front part is missing. However, the overall make of the garment can still be appreciated, including a portion of the hem around the neck and just a hint of the missing sleeves. Just like the garment described in the Gospel of John, it is a single, uninterrupted, seamless fabric whose warp and weft are woven together in a plain weave,[83] compatible with the work of an ancient domestic loom. The wool is medium-quality, spun with a strong and uniform Z-twist, thus yielding a fine wavy fabric, ideal for inner garments. The yarn was treated with potassium alum (a dye fixative) and then dyed madder red, hence obtaining the uniform extant red-brownish coloring. This is also the color of the alizarin pigment already found in that left upper corner of the Shroud that underwent radiocarbon dating. All these fabric features are certainly already in keeping with a hypothetical origin from first-century Palestine.

---

[83] A plain weave is one in which the vertical warp threads are held steady on the loom, while the horizontal weft threads cross over and under each warp.

The presence of the Tunic of Argenteuil has been documented as far back as the year 1156. Tradition, however, takes us back even further to Charlemagne: the emperor would have received the precious garment directly from the Byzantine empress Irene, and he would have then gifted it to his daughter Théodrade, the abbess of the "Humilité-de-Notre-Dame" monastery in Argenteuil. In fact, a document stored at the National Library of Paris attests to the gift of a fragment of the Tunic from Argenteuil to the Abbey of St. Medard de Soissons around the year 840.

The historical events involving the Tunic are very troubled. The garment was hidden many times to survive plundering by the Normans and the Huguenots. It was lost and found again. However, the most dramatic moment was during the French Revolution in 1793, when Fr. Ozet, abbot and parish priest of Argenteuil, was forced to take extreme measures: he cut the seamless relic into pieces, distributing some to trusted parishioners and burying two major fragments in the bare earth of his rectory's garden. He then spent two years in the "people's prisons" and, immediately after being set free, tried to recover all the Tunic's fragments. He more or less put back together the back portion, but significant parts at the front were deemed lost for good.

The Tunic, too, could not escape carbon-14 dating. In October 2013, local authorities[84] and the bishop secretly arranged scientific investigations that included radiocarbon testing. The latter dated the Tunic back to AD 530–650. The analysis was performed by the Commissariat for Atomic Energy (CEA) of

---

[84] The tunic is classified as a "historical monument," and since 1905 it has belonged, with very secular pride, to the French nation rather than to the Church.

Paris-Saclay under no blinding conditions, as the researchers knew exactly what they were testing. As expected, the local newspapers quickly sold the news to the public: the ancient Holy Tunic of Argenteuil had to be a medieval fake to be stowed away in "the attic of history," together with many other "harmless wacky good things." Alas, modern man needs to break free from so much ancient heritage to gain a new and more mature awareness. Not convinced, Profs. Gérard Lucotte and André Marion, the two main independent researchers of the Tunic of Argenteuil, organized a second radiocarbon dating the following year under "blind" conditions, by Archéolabs in Grenoble: the result was AD 670–880.

Clearly, something is not right: the two dating results, actually obtained from the same fragment named "S2a," are not at all overlapping, even by extending the confidence interval by two standard deviations (that means to include 95.4 percent of all possible cases). Either the Tunic is from before AD 650 or it is from after AD 670 — one radiocarbon dating voiding the other! There is no need to say that, once again, these results reveal the intrinsic weakness of radiocarbon dating when applied to ancient fabrics. Prof. Lucotte attempted gaining further insights into the matter and pushed on with X-ray spectroscopy[85] to examine ten Tunic fibers that had undergone the standard preparation process for carbon-14 dating. It is actually well known that, prior to

---

[85] X-ray spectroscopy is a technique that detects and measures photons, or particles of light, that have wavelengths in the X-ray portion of the electromagnetic spectrum. When X-rays are shone on a given sample, the latter will absorb the light energy and then, in turn, emit its own spectrum of light. When interpreted, emission spectra will give information about the chemical composition of the specimen.

measuring the carbon-14 isotopes,[86] it is necessary to eliminate up to more than half of the original weight of the sample every now and then. This is done by washing away any organic contaminations through a three-fold "acid-base-acid" protocol sequence with specific alcohols and solvents. Most notably, however, any carbon present in the form of calcium carbonate[87] is also washed away to avoid skewing the result, as the fabric would have inevitably come into contact with it over the centuries. Prof. Lucotte was confident that wool could absorb much more water—and the calcium carbonate normally dissolved in it—than flax or cotton could. He proved his point with his spectroscopy approach: the interpretation of the sulfur[88] and calcium "spikes" in the spectrum emitted by the Tunic sample confirmed that, even after the usual preparatory "cleansing" procedures, one-third of the initial amount of calcium carbonate was still left in the sample, with an obvious and inappropriate "fabric-rejuvenating" skewing effect. Despite Dr. Lucotte's experiments, it remains difficult, if

[86] Isotopes are variants of a particular chemical element. These variants differ in number of neutron particles contained in their nuclei—thus, all isotopes of a given element have the same number of protons but different numbers of neutrons in each atom. Some naturally occurring isotope versions of an element, like carbon-14, have radioactive properties.

[87] Calcium carbonate is the limestone commonly dissolved in water. Of course, some of the carbon atoms in calcium carbonate will be naturally present carbon-14 radioactive isotopes. Thus, sample contamination by limestone will tend to "rejuvenate" the age of the specimen on carbon-14 dating.

[88] Prof. Lucotte was interested in the sulfur spike because the former is present in the protein keratin, which is the building block of wool hair. Hence, the sulfur spike could be used as a reliable reference as emitted by the actual material to be analyzed, rather than other contaminants.

not impossible, to clarify all the causes underpinning the differences in the Tunic's radiometric dating results. But perhaps it
is even more difficult for public opinion, as with the Shroud of
Turin, to set aside the already well-established "medieval fake"
reputation associated with this fascinating relic.

The scanning electron microscopy and X-ray spectroscopy
studies carried out by Prof. Lucotte on dusts, pollens, and algae
deposited on the Tunic are also very interesting: the biological
species he identified, except for later contaminations, are all
compatible with a Mediterranean origin, a warm and dry climate
and an arid and desert-like soil. However, the most scientifically
stimulating finding is that of the extremely abundant presence
of human blood on the Tunic (of the same blood group as that
on the Shroud and Sudarium). It is a recent discovery: the red-
brownish background color of the fabric hides bloodstains whose
presence can instead be felt by touch. Those who have had the
privilege of examining the Tunic recall feeling more rigid and
thicker patches in the fabric. Under the electron microscope,
even wool fibers not taken from those blood-rich patches were
still covered in red blood cells, often in groups of hundreds,
amassed in micro-clots. In other instances, the red blood cells
were lined up, as if drawing the course of capillaries. They were
red blood cells of smaller size compared to normal, between 5
and 6 microns, instead of the physiological 7 to 8 microns: this
could be easily explained by dehydration over the centuries.

Prof. André Marion, a nuclear physicist and engineer at
the Centre National de la Recherche Scientifique (CNRS),
studied the positioning of the bloodstains on the Tunic. He
concluded that the tortured man of the Tunic must have been
loaded mostly on his left shoulder by a full cross, as shown on
traditional iconography, and not just a horizontal beam as we

are sometimes led to believe. Furthermore, a similar and patient three-dimensional reconstruction of the bloodstains on the back image of the Shroud allowed Marion to demonstrate the nearly total overlapping of the Tunic's stains with the ones on the Shroud, a point that must be considered in favor of the respective authenticity of both relics.

Lastly, the Tunic contained not only red blood cells but also DNA-containing white blood cells and hair follicles. Once again, Prof. Lucotte, an unquestionable authority in genetics, a pioneer of molecular hybridization techniques, and the discoverer of the original Y chromosome haplotypes, extensively studied the DNA of the man of the Tunic in recent years. Remarkably, he derived an extremely accurate and impressive genetic identikit from it. We shall discuss this in detail in one of the upcoming chapters.

Bibliography

Damon, P., D. Donahue, B. Gore, et al. 1989. "Radiocarbon Dating of the Shroud of Turin." *Nature* 337: 611–615.
The official article about the Shroud's radiometric dating.

Marino, J., and M. Benford. 2000. "Evidence for the Skewing of the C-14 Dating of the Shroud of Turin Due to Repairs." *Worldwide Congress "Sindone 2000."* Orvieto, Italy.
Report by the Marino couple about the initial evidence on the theory of the invisible mend at the Orvieto congress.

Rogers, Raymond. 2005. "Studies on the Radiocarbon Sample from the Shroud of Turin." *Thermochimica Acta* 425 (1–2): 189–194.
Fruit of Rogers's courageous work, this book was published only a few weeks before he passed away due to an uncurable disease.

Van Haelst, Remi. 1997. "Radiocarbon Dating the Shroud: A Critical Statistical Analysis." Shroud.com. Website. Belgium. Accessed July 12, 2021. https://www.shroud.com/vanhels3.htm.

The Belgian chemist competently and carefully discusses the fallacies of the statistical analysis in the *Nature* article.

Brunati, Ernesto. 2005. "Altro che rammendi! La datazione della Sindone e' tutta un falso." Collegamento pro Sindone Internet. Accessed July 12, 2021. http://www.sindone.info/BRUNATI1.PDF.

The Italian engineer found evidence of malicious tampering with the radio-dated samples by reviewing statistical errors.

Rinaldi, Gian Marco. 2012. "La statistica della datazione della Sindone." Gian Marco Rinaldi. Accessed July 12, 2021. https://www.academia.edu/35904379/La_statistica_della_datazione_della_Sindone_2012_.

The writer and mathematician defends the official version of the radiometric dating by recognizing and attempting to integrate its statistical gaps.

Walsh, Bryan, and Larry Schwalbe. 2020. "An Instructive Inter-Laboratory Comparison: The 1988 Radiocarbon Dating of the Shroud of Turin." *Journal of Archaeological Science: Reports* 29: 340.

Walsh, Bryan. 1999. "The 1988 Shroud of Turin Radiocarbon Tests Reconsidered, Part I." Internet Archive WayBack Machine. Richmond, Virginia. Accessed July 12, 2021. http://web.archive.org/web/20040422010105/http://members.aol.com/turin99/radiocarbon-a.htm.

Part 1 of the statistical demonstration of the heterogeneity of the samples and of the linear relationship between dating and the location of the samples on the Shroud.

Riani, Marco, Giulio Fanti, Fabio Crosilla, and Anthony Atkinson. 2010. "Statistica robusta e radiodatazione della Sindone." *Sis-Magazine* 1 (1).

The article demonstrates the systematic and linear effect of a natural contamination on the 1988 radiometric dating with robust statistical techniques.

Casabianca, Tristan, Emanuela Marinelli, Giuseppe Pernagallo, and Benedetto Torrisi. 2019. "Radiocarbon Dating of the Turin Shroud: New Evidence from Raw Data." *Archaeometry* 61 (5), 1223–1231. Accessed July 12, 2021. https://doi.org/10.1111/arcm.12467.

The resounding article in which the raw results produced by the three laboratories involved in the Shroud's radiocarbon dating project were finally critically analyzed.

Fanti, Giulio, and Saverio Gaeta. 2013. *Il Mistero della Sindone: Le sorprendendti scoperte scientifiche sull'enigma del telo di Gesu.* 1st ed. Biblioteca Universale Rizzoli.

Book in support of the Shroud's authenticity with updated data.

Augé, Javier Briansó. 1997. *El Santo Sudario de la Catedral de Oviedo.* Graficas Summa.

Chiapusso, J. I. 2007. "Sudario de Oviedo y Palinogia." In *Oviedo, relicario de la cristianidad: Actas del II Congreso Internacional sobre el Sudario de Oviedo.* 1st ed., 125–135. Universidad de Oviedo.

A mine of information about the Sudarium of Oviedo is available in the records of the Second International Congress on the Shroud (April 2007).

Chiapusso, J. I. 2016. "Sudario de Oviedo y Palinogia." *Territorio Sociedad Poder* II:125–135.

Gil, César Barta. 2007. "Datación radiocarbónica del Sudario de Oviedo." In *Oviedo, relicario de la cristianidad: Actas del*

II Congreso Internacional sobre el Sudario de Oviedo. 1st ed., 137–155. Universidad de Oviedo.

Ortego, F. M. 2007. "Otros estudios de carácter quimico y biológico: datación del Lienzo." In *Oviedo, relicario de la cristianidad: Actas del II Congreso Internacional sobre el Sudario de Oviedo.* 1st ed., 159–166. Universidad de Oviedo.

Moreno, G. H., and M. O. Corsini. 2007. "Consideraciones geométricas sobre la formación central de manchas del Sudario de Oviedo." In *Oviedo, relicario de la cristianidad: Actas del II Congreso Internacional sobre el Sudario de Oviedo.* 1st ed., 237–265. Universidad de Oviedo.

Blanco, J. D. V. 2007. "Síntesis: Cómo se utilizó el Sudario de Oviedo?" In *Oviedo, relicario de la cristianidad: Actas del II Congreso Internacional sobre el Sudario de Oviedo.* 1st ed., 279–294, Universidad de Oviedo.

Gil, César Barta. 2007. "Aproximación del EDICES al estudio comparativo del Sudario de Oviedo: Síndone de Turin." In *Oviedo, relicario de la cristianidad: Actas del II Congreso Internacional sobre el Sudario de Oviedo.* 1st ed., 393–423. Universidad de Oviedo.

HMTelevision. 2016. "Entre profesionales: El Sudario de Oviedo 6/7." YouTube. Accessed July 12, 2021. https://www.youtube.com/watch?v=YFukUGbW_1Y.
Episode 6 of the Spanish documentary with an interview with Prof. César Barta Gil.

HMTelevision. 2016. "Entre profesionales: El Sudario de Oviedo y la Síndone 7/7." YouTube. Accessed July 12, 2021. https://www.youtube.com/watch?v=gRYbBpjT6MY&t=6s.
Episode 7 of the Spanish documentary with an interview with Prof. César Barta Gil.

Supercatolico. 2015. "Científicos demuestran el mismo origen del Sudario de Oviedo y la Sábana Santa." YouTube. Accessed July 12, 2021. https://www.youtube.com/watch?v=HdBJ0wm 2UXQ.

Interview with Prof. Jorge Manuel Rodríguez Almenar by Fr. Javier Alonso. Particularly significant at min. 15:55 with the images of the superimposition of the Sudarium's stains on the three-dimensional rendering of the face of the Shroud.

Marion, André, and Gérard Lucotte. 2006. *Le linceul de Turin et la tunique d'Argenteuil: Le point sur l'enquête.* 1st ed. Paris: Éditions des Presses de la Renaissance.

History of the Tunic of Argenteuil and the most recent findings by the most active French researchers in the field.

Lucotte, Gérard, and Philippe Bornet. 2007. *Sanguis Christi: Le sang du Christ. Une enquête sur la tunique d'Argenteuil.* Guy Trédaniel Éditeur.

The French geneticist tells everything he discovered about the Argenteuil relic.

Site officiel de la Sainte Tunique du Christ conservée à Argenteuil. 2020. Website. Accessed July 12, 2021. http://sainte-tunique.com/.

Official website of the Holy Tunic of Argenteuil. Historical and scientific reports are available on this website.

KTOTV. 2016. "Restauration de la Sainte Tunique d'Argenteuil." YouTube. Accessed July 12, 2021. https://www.youtube.com/watch?v=Uf2wGzhXmo8.

Report of the recent restoration of the Tunic by Claire Beugnot.

Gross, Philippe. 2016. "Installation Sainte Tunique." YouTube. Accessed July 12, 2021, https://www.youtube.com/watch?v=0dOXlfmt1Xw.

Images of the day of the installation of the Tunic on March 24, 2016.

KTOTV. 2016. "La Sainte Tunique d'Argenteuil." YouTube. Accessed July 12, 2021. https://www.youtube.com/watch?v=1azKaLj56to.

French Catholic TV interviews by historian Jean-Christian Petitfils with Fr. Guy-Emmanuel Cariot, parish priest of Argenteuil, and Bishop Stanislas Lalanne of Pontoise.

9

The Heart

We have reviewed only five eucharistic events, the only ones that underwent scientific testing with published reports in the last decades. A sample of five is a very small one, compared to the hundreds and hundreds of miraculous facts documented in sacred chronicles. Still, it can't be missed that heart muscle tissue was remarkably found in all of these five miracles. Even when the matter budding and growing out of consecrated bread looked like a blood clot — as in the latest cases in 2008 and 2013 in Poland — later analyses instead excluded the presence of blood but revealed the samples to be entirely made of heart muscle tissue. On January 7, 2009, even Prof. Sobaniec-Łotowska, in Sokółka, was convinced she had been taking microsamples of clotted blood but had to change her mind a few days later, faced with the evidence of her own histological analyses.

Why the Heart?

The U.S. Catholics Bishops recently reminded us that the whole Body, Blood, Soul, and Divinity of our Lord are mysteriously present in "any fragment of the consecrated host or in any drop of the Precious Blood."[89] In this time of growing religious illiteracy, I shall point out again that from a theological perspective, not only does the bread become the Body of Jesus, but also His Blood. Likewise, not only does the wine become the Blood, but also the whole Body of our Lord (as masterfully clarified by St. Thomas Aquinas in his *Summa theologica* III, q. 76, a. 1). This is due to the natural coexistence and union of both Body and Blood in the Person of Jesus Christ. Objections, mostly of Hussite origin,[90] about the "incompleteness" of Catholic Holy Communion — which the ordinary faithful often only receive in the visible species of bread — are thus meaningless. In the 2009 Tixtla investigations, we witnessed the identification of many human tissues in the consecrated host, including blood with its red and white blood cells along with myocardium, adipose cells, and, arguably, mesenchymal cells. Hence, the Tixtla miracle is a direct scientific confirmation of this theological principle, one that cannot be easily rejected.

But let's get back to the heart. Finding any human tissue in a consecrated host certainly represents a scientifically inexplicable fact. This is regardless of the tissue's histological classification:

[89] This explains why the breaking of the consecrated host during Mass does not compromise the presence of Christ as a whole in the smaller portions of the host that are distributed during Holy Communion. It also explains why blood and heart muscle tissue could be identified in the microscopic samples that were taken from the eucharistic miracles discussed in the previous chapters.

[90] The Utraquist heresy in Bohemia was a branch of the Hussite movement in what is now the Czech Republic. It insisted that Communion be distributed to the laity in both forms. Likewise, most Protestants deny the Real Presence altogether, despite insisting on receiving both bread and wine.

muscular tissue is no less "miraculous" than epithelial, connective, or nervous tissue when found in the unleavened bread of a host originally made with wheat flour and water. Hence, a fragment of skin, lung, or brain would be no less "baffling" than a fragment of heart. Still, Heaven's preference for the latter organ is clear.

Throughout all cultures and times, the heart has represented something beyond its function as the muscle-pump of the circulatory system. It was only rationally "downgraded" to this materialistic concept in 1628 with the publication of *De motu cordis* (*On the Motion of the Heart*) by William Harvey. Too often, for modern man, heart symbolism is reduced to a stylized emoticon, to the organ and site of feelings and emotions to be set against the much more important head, the seat of rationality and thought. I still recall Mrs. Washkansky's tenderly human and understandable reaction when, in December 1967, she disclosed her worry and anxiety about her husband no longer loving her when he would wake up after his heart transplant surgery with the heart of another person. I think we should distance ourselves from this symbolism, more suitable for Italian pop music songwriters who have much abused the rhyme between the Italian words for *heart* and *love* (*cuore* and *amore*) and delve deeper into this matter.

It is part of everyone's experience to feel the presence of a pulsating organ in a central and protected position in the middle of the chest, inside our sturdy, protective rib cage. The heart's unceasing motion is simply indispensable to life—its arrest immediately leads to death—and we feel its beat speed up when we are startled, not only due to physical effort but also due to the heart's close connection with our thoughts and emotions. So the heart easily lends itself to a more important symbolism, well understood by the ancients, that we also find in biblical tradition.

The heart thus symbolizes two essential and complementary aspects of man's inner life:

1. It represents the center of a human being. It is the intimate and privileged seat of a person's deepest will and intentions. It is the core on which an individual's unity and wholeness depend and into which flows the whole concrete being of mankind (partially paraphrasing Karl Rahner).

2. It is the interface between man's bodily and spiritual natures overcoming the Platonic dualism of body and soul. So the heart also becomes the seat of religiosity, a window opened on transcendence.

In the Bible, too, the word *heart*—appearing nearly a thousand times—only rarely means the physical organ beating in the chest. Instead, it generally stands for an inner human faculty, such as the ability to know, to discern, to memorize—or, more simply, it points to the person as a whole, the whole that can only be fully known by God. Let's delve further into this mystery of our fondness for the heart. The great Pope Pius XII, in his 1956 encyclical letter *Haurietis aquas*, dedicated to the devotion to the Sacred Heart of Jesus, regarded the heart of Christ as "the noblest part" of His human nature. He stated this despite acknowledging that all parts of the Body of Jesus Christ are hypostatically united[91] to the Person of the Word, and thus worthy of the same worship and devotion that the Second Person of the Holy Trinity deserves. Devotions to specific parts of Jesus'

---

[91] The hypostatic union refers to Christ's humanity and divinity in one *hypostasis* or person, in a single individual existence. It is the most basic theological formulation for the unity of the Second Person of the Trinity with His humanity.

Body have indeed emerged within Christianity throughout the centuries: the Sacred Heart, the Holy Face, the Lord's Wounds. Even if somewhat renewed in the widespread devotion fostered by St. Faustina to the Divine Mercy, the popular devotion to the Sacred Heart has unfortunately been nearly forgotten nowadays. Still, it is certainly worth commenting on it, as it used to be the backbone of a widespread spirituality understood by many ordinary people, confirmed by mystics, and supported by a powerful theological system. Because of that, depictions of the Sacred Heart are present in almost every church and, up until the recent past, could be found in every Catholic household. Its imagery truly sums up the mystery of the Redemption in a very effective and powerful way.

Let's actually dwell on its more popular representations, like the ones by Batoni[92] or Morgari,[93] thought to be insignificant and off-putting by art experts: Christ's peaceful visage, His loving and penetrating gaze on anyone looking at Him as He points to the center of His chest with His hands still bearing the Passion stigmata. In these depictions, His heart is pierced by a spear, crowned with thorns yet burning with love for humanity, behind a Cross. The devotion to the Sacred Heart is one with biblical origins and references in patristic literature. However, it really only gained momentum in the seventeenth century, with the apparitions to St. Margaret Mary Alacoque. The spirituality of the Sacred Heart exalts God's merciful love in a very concrete

---

[92] Pompeo Batoni was a 1700s Italian painter famous for his portraits (especially popular in Great Britain) as well as his representations of the Sacred Heart.

[93] Luigi Morgari was another late 1800s to early 1900s Italian painter, primarily of frescoes and religious themes such as the Sacred Heart.

way thanks to the image of the heart: it is a call for penance and atonement for sins. As foreseen by God's unfathomable plans, the Sacred Heart certainly helped save countless souls.

A Few Anatomical Notions

Muscle tissue is essential to animal life and can be organized into actual muscle organs to allow for mobility. Alternatively, it can also form finer muscular bundles or layers surrounding internal organs to support their normal functioning, such as with peristalsis[94] in the gut. There are three types of muscle tissue that are easily distinguishable from one another histologically:

1. *Striated skeletal muscle* makes up muscles under voluntary control. It is defined as striated because it is made up of strictly parallel actin and myosin myofibrils[95] displaying perpendicular clear and dark bands. Muscle cells, containing many myofibrils, fuse together, forming cylindrical muscle fibers by sharing their off-centered and peripherally located DNA-containing nuclei. This tissue is called skeletal because it makes up the muscles linking together the bones of the trunk, head, and limbs, permitting their reciprocal movements controlled by the central nervous system.

2. *Smooth muscle* is made up of single spindle-shaped cells with centrally located nuclei. No ordered striations can be recognized in the myofibrils within its cells.

---

[94] Peristalsis is a series of coordinated, wavelike muscle contractions propelling food in the digestive system.

[95] Actin and myosin are muscle-specific proteins that are part of the contractile apparatus of a muscle cell. Myofibrils are the contractile units within each muscle cell.

The tissue typically slowly and rhythmically contracts when stimulated by the autonomic nervous system.[96]

3. *Heart muscle tissue* displays somewhat intermediate features: it is striated, even if in a less regular and uniform way compared to skeletal muscle. Its cells are joined together but not fused. They remain distinct from one another, and their centrally located nuclei are not shared. Typically, heart muscle cells tend to bifurcate, issuing appendages they use to connect to other neighboring cells at their extremities. Altogether, they create a sort of "muscular net" with unique, sturdy, and well-recognizable joining elements, called intercalated discs, at contact points. The tissue contracts on its own, controlled by specialized pacemaker cells. These generate and spread an electrical signal throughout the heart by means of periodical self-excitation. However, their pacing activity is influenced by signals from the autonomic nervous system and circulating hormones such as adrenaline.

Heart Muscle Tissue

The unique striated cellular structure and the unmistakable overall framework of heart muscle tissue would make it relatively easy to recognize under a light microscope after adequate staining. The electron microscope can then zoom in further to identify unique subcellular details. Lastly, immunohistochemistry can detect specific proteins, either inside the cell or on its surface,

---

[96] The autonomic nervous system controls all involuntary bodily functions. Some of its components are in the central nervous system, and others are in the peripheral nervous system.

giving further molecular confirmation about the identity of the tissue. However, from the accounts of the eucharistic miracles we have been studying, we already know that these miraculous tissues seem to be self-preserving in a way that defies all scientific expectations: the relics were usually set in transparent, more or less permeable monstrances at room temperature and exposed to the devoted faithful. They were never sealed in sterile test tubes at minus 80 degrees! The worst conditions were those endured by the 1996 Buenos Aires tissue. It was preserved for one month in common tap water and then for years in distilled water. The latter would have actually ensured the osmotic destruction of any biological tissue in only a few days' time.

In all of the five cases we are considering, the identification of heart muscle tissue has always been achieved after careful study and thorough differential diagnosis.[97] Let's consider them one by one.

In Lanciano, despite the inability to stain cell nuclei and the absence of striations, the ancient tissue is clearly of mesodermal[98] origin and displays syncytial[99] junctions formed by cell fibers through bifurcations and reciprocal linkages, multiple

---

[97] Differential diagnosis is the systematic process of differentiating between two or more tissues sharing similar features to determine their pathological state. It is also used in the same way in medicine to differentiate between diseases with similar signs and symptoms and then identify the correct diagnosis.

[98] The mesoderm is a progenitor tissue layer in the embryo giving rise to all types of muscle tissue as well as other tissues.

[99] A syncytium is a tissue pattern with cells interconnected by specialized membranes with gap junctions, as seen in heart muscle cells and certain smooth muscle cells. This tissue structure allows for the passage of an electric signal leading to synchronized muscular contraction.

features typical of heart muscle tissue (as in the original report by Prof. Odoardo Linoli). But it is not just the microscopic appearance of the tissue from Lanciano that is suggestive of its cardiac nature: the whole macroscopic structure of the Flesh recalls a cross section of the whole heart, complete with details including arterial and venous blood vessels, the vagus nerve, and the endothelial layer lining the inner heart chamber. Prof. Linoli shared with Prof. Ruggero Bertelli from Siena his definitive and certain diagnosis: it was *human* heart tissue, as confirmed by the Uhlenhuth test.[100]

Around March 2000, the Buenos Aires study on the *muestra humeda* sample from the 1996 event was assigned to Dr. Robert Lawrence, the Californian forensic examiner at Delta Pathology Associates in Stockton who prepared the microscope slides. Dr. Lawrence described a degraded and difficult to recognize tissue, which he thought was skin. What caught his eye was the high degree of infiltration by white blood cells, an important feature of inflammation. In the following months and years, the same slides were shown to other professionals, and one of them advanced the hypothesis of muscle tissue. The extraordinary experience of Prof. Zugibe, chief of forensic medicine and cardiologist at Rockland County in New York, was finally required to make an authoritative diagnosis. Years later, even Dr. Lawrence agreed with Prof. Zugibe's diagnosis at a meeting in St. Francisco.

For the Tixtla miracle, too, the microscope slides prepared by two different laboratories in Mexico and Guatemala displayed a

---

[100] The Uhlenhuth test is an effective though currently obsolete immunological reaction that confirms the human origin of a blood sample. Prof. Linoli managed to apply the same test to the heart muscle tissue he was studying and obtained a positive result.

tissue difficult to identify. The cells were particularly degraded by self-destroying processes: striations and intercalated discs were missing, and the nuclei were not always central. Still, the overall structure of the elongated, mostly parallel, and frequently bifurcating cells directly joining up with neighboring fibers could not but recall the look of heart muscle. Dr. Eduardo Sánchez Lazo stated that immunohistochemical tests—unfortunately without specifying which ones—confirmed the cardiac nature of the tissue, and this finding was included in the final report by the Mexican laboratory. On the contrary, Dr. Carlos Parellada informed us that the Guatemalan slides did not react with the desmin and myosin[101] histochemical probes, and this was attributed to the poor state of the tissue. Finally, Columbian cardiologist Dr. Marco Blanquicett Anaya recognized the tissue structure of an infarcted and inflamed heart muscle tissue: in other words, cardiac tissue that would have suffered a heart attack.

In Sokółka, Prof. Stanisław Sulkowski and Prof. Maria Elżbieta Sobaniec-Łotowska at the University of Białystok concluded in their scientific report that the tissue they analyzed was of cardiac origin "or at least, among all other tissues of a living organism, heart muscle tissue was the one most similar to it." As they explained, its fibers showed centrally located nuclei. Moreover, remnants of intercalated discs and bundles of delicate myofibrils could be appreciated under the electron microscope.

Lastly, in regard to the Legnica miracle, the initial investigations carried out at the University of Wrocław immediately described a material resembling striated muscle tissue. However, the sample lacked reactivity to two immunohistochemical markers due to

---

[101] Desmin and myosin are proteins specific to the contractile apparatus of a muscle cell.

tissue degradation in the context of prolonged water exposure. As part of further testing at the University of Szczecin, the orange filter ultraviolet light microscope confirmed the cardiac nature of the muscle tissue with images that were very similar to the ones obtained in Sokółka. DNA testing finally confirmed the human origin.

Suffering Heart

Since it has been established that striated heart muscle tissue was identified in all five miracles we considered, a powerful diagnostic conclusion can now be drawn across the board, based on all the studies that were carried out, except for those by Prof. Linoli on the ancient miracle of Lanciano, which did not yield enough clinical information for this purpose. However, the exception made for Lanciano is quite understandable: demonstrating the cardiac nature of thirteen-hundred-year-old tissue stored in a monstrance without preservatives was an incredible feat in and of itself. Moreover, finer tissue analyses could not have been realistically performed on that miracle in 1970. Instead, the heart muscle tissues of Buenos Aires, Tixtla, Sokółka, and Legnica all revealed specific pathological signs suggestive of a common and narrow differential diagnosis: a limited number of medical and traumatic conditions that would give rise to the abnormal features seen in these tissues — all linked with extreme physical, emotional, and spiritual suffering in broader nonmedical terms. Amazingly, these signs of suffering could still be appreciated and distinguished from other less specific time-related signs of tissue degradation and autolysis. The latter were undoubtedly aggravated by exposure to poor or even adverse storage conditions — especially in Buenos Aires and Tixtla — during the prolonged time lags between the appearance of each tissue and its sampling.

A Cardiologist Examines Jesus

We know that the cardiac tissue identified in these four miracles came from a heart that was experiencing terrible suffering, gripped by wrenching spasms: a heart — at least in Buenos Aires and Tixtla — that was still in agony at the time of histological sampling.

By integrating the results of the four investigations, we can formulate a precise histopathological diagnosis based on two major common findings:

1. There were clear signs of fragmentation and segmentation of the heart muscle fibers, especially in the better-preserved Sokółka and Legnica tissues. Moreover, contraction band necrosis was also described in the cardiac fibers of the Sokółka miracle.

2. There was considerable infiltration by white blood cells in the tissues of Buenos Aires and Tixtla.

Let's try to understand this better. By *fragmentation*, we mean the clean break of a heart muscle cell crossways to its length, at any point, even repeatedly. We are instead more accurately talking about segmentation when referring to a detachment between cells at the location of the intercalated discs: the elements that tightly connect muscle fibers to one another, allowing their simultaneous contraction. Both types of injuries are part of — or better, are the final outcome of — a histopathological picture due to the spasmodic and excessive contraction of myofibrils. Associated with these types of injury is the severe tissue damage of contraction band necrosis, or CBN. This is characterized by thickened contraction bands spanning the short axis of heart muscle fibers, parallel to their intercalated discs. All these cellular changes are also associated with the arrival of white blood cells from circulating blood, first as a defensive reaction and then to demolish unrecoverable structures. This normally happens in a very well-documented time sequence that entails, from the first few minutes, the infiltration by polymorphonuclear leukocytes,[102] which are then replaced—already in day one—by monocytes and macrophages.[103]

The pathological picture we just described is that of stress-induced cardiomyopathy, which anatomical pathologists have identified, for many decades, in victims of plane crashes or murders after violent beating and in deaths by stroke or suffocation —hence, all those situations in which an otherwise previously healthy heart is exposed, for a few minutes, hours, or rarely, days, to an extremely strong physical stress, or even just an emotional one, such as the fear or certainty of imminent death. The mechanism, experimentally documented in animal studies, involves the exposure to high levels of catecholamines.[104] These can be both

---

[102] Polymorphonuclear leukocytes are a broad class of highly reactive white blood cells including neutrophils, basophils, and eosinophils, which play key roles in the immediate or innate nonspecific immune response to infectious or injurious triggers.

[103] Macrophages derive from monocytes. They are white blood cells capable of phagocytosis, the engulfing and "swallowing" of any debris and degraded structures.

[104] Catecholamines are a class of neurotransmitters and hormones with similar chemical structures. They have many effects on both the central and peripheral nervous systems as well as direct effects on many organs and bodily functions. Broadly speaking, they are involved in fight-or-flight reactions and also in physiological stress caused by disease or trauma. They have stimulatory neurologic effects (such as increased alertness and agitation) and other effects, such as increased heart rate and blood pressure, dilated pupils, increased blood sugar, and various changes in the degree of blood vessel constriction shunting blood flow away from nonessential organs. Examples of catecholamines include adrenaline (epinephrine), noradrenaline (norepinephrine), and dopamine.

endogenous[105] and locally released by the sympathetic nervous system[106] nerve endings directly stimulating the heart. Tissue injury is mediated by the influx of calcium[107] into heart muscle cells and the activation of toxic oxidative agents.

Stress-induced cardiomyopathy has been classified by cardiologists, in the last few years, within the context of the wider spectrum of the ever more frequently diagnosed *takotsubo* syndrome. This curious word, which literally means "fishing pot for trapping octopus," refers to traps shaped like clay pots still used by Japanese fishermen to capture the tasty cephalopods. The reason why this syndrome was named after these octopus traps is that quite often, in the early stage of the disease, the affected heart is shaped like one of them: the upper portion of the left ventricle is excessively contracting, appearing like a narrow neck. The lower part of the ventricle is instead bulging out and minimally beating, with the "tip," or apex, of the heart actually staying still, much like the bottom part of an ancient amphora vase.

[105] Endogenous catecholamines are produced by the adrenal glands located above the kidneys and are released into the systemic blood circulation, hence exerting their effects throughout the entire body.

[106] The sympathetic nervous system is the functional division of the autonomic nervous system that is responsible for physiological fight-or-flight responses.

[107] The influx of calcium into cells is generally an important signaling mechanism and can have devastating consequences if uncontrolled: it can cause uncontrolled muscle contraction (spasm) and uncontrolled excitatory neurotransmitter release (driving the fight-or-flight response out of control), and it can even trigger specific mechanisms initiating cellular self-destruction.

This *takotsubo* terminology prevailed because it was first used by Japanese doctors in 1990 to describe a group of patients affected by the condition: they were usually middle-aged women, with symptoms, blood tests, and ECG changes suggestive of a "heart attack," who, surprisingly, did not demonstrate evidence of obstruction of their coronary arteries. What all these patients instead had in common was the presence of a highly stress-inducing event, such as a death in the family, a fight, or a motor vehicle accident, in the preceding minutes or hours. Fortunately, after overcoming the acute phase, these patients usually regain normal heart contractility in the following weeks and recover well. However, in the first few hours and days, the situation can be serious and prone to complications such as heart failure with pulmonary edema, dangerous and potentially fatal abnormal heart rhythms, and even rupture of the overstretched heart muscle wall itself, resulting in a hemopericardium: in this condition, blood from the ruptured heart accumulates in a space between the heart muscle wall and the pericardium, a fibrous protective sac that encases the heart. The ongoing accumulation of blood eventually exerts a compressive effect on the heart itself, impairing its ability to pump blood. This is known as *cardiac tamponade*, a condition quickly leading to death, if not treated by decompression; this condition, rather than simple suffocation, was possibly the final cause of Christ's death on the Cross.

I shall only suggest another possible though less likely diagnosis, especially where, from the viewpoint of anatomical pathology, the internal structure of the muscle cells in the tissue is less well defined: a "classical heart attack" due to the obstruction of one of the main coronary blood vessels carrying blood to the heart itself. In this case, too, there would be infiltration by neutrophil leukocytes followed by monocytes and macrophages.

A Cardiologist Examines Jesus

The myocardial cells would undergo the so-called coagulative necrosis,[108] with loss of recognizable internal structures, but in a resting state, without evidence of contracture and without, or with minimal appearance of, necrosis with contraction bands, or CBN. CBN could, however, make an appearance whenever the infarcted tissue underwent reperfusion: the return of fresh blood supply due to either spontaneous or therapy-induced breakdown of arterial obstruction.

Let's go back to listening to Prof. Frederick Zugibe's words, which were recorded while he was looking at the 1996 Buenos Aires sample for the first time without knowing its origin:

> This cardiac muscle is inflamed; it has lost its striations and is infiltrated by leukocytes.... This person's heart has been wounded and has suffered a trauma. The blood flow has been compromised and part of the myocardium has undergone necrosis. It resembles what I see in road accidents, when the heart is subject to prolonged resuscitation maneuvers, or it resembles what I find when someone has received severe blows to the chest.

In the final March 2005 report, Prof. Zugibe then stated the following:

> The [microscope] slide consists of cardiac tissue that displays degenerative changes ... with loss of striations, nuclear pyknosis, aggregates of mixed inflammatory cells consisting of chronic inflammatory cells (macrophages),

---

[108] Coagulative necrosis is a particular type of necrosis. Different dead tissues take on different appearances depending on the original tissue type and the cause of tissue death. In coagulative necrosis, the resulting dead tissue looks like a blood clot.

which are the predominant cells, admixed with smaller numbers of acute inflammatory cells (white blood cells, primarily polymorphonuclear leukocytes).

These degenerative changes are consistent with a recent myocardial infarction of a few days' duration due to an obstruction of a coronary artery ... due to clot formation ... or to injury to the chest wall. The dating of the injury is derived from the findings of a predominance of chronic inflammatory cells, degenerative changes of the myocardium with loss of striations, pyknosis of the nuclei, etc.

Dr. Blanquicett Anaya—a Columbian cardiologist to whom Dr. Castañón had shown the Tixtla specimens in June 2014—also recognized the presence of red blood cells associated with inflammatory cells such as neutrophils, eosinophils, and a vacuolated cell with a macrophage look, together with nucleated fiber-like structures subject to autolysis: a picture suggestive of infarcted cardiac tissue, or tissue that withstood a significant physiological stress, in which a typical inflammatory response was underway.

In conclusion, I shall repeat that, regardless of the overall diagnosis, myocardial cell fragmentation and segmentation are unquestionable signs of the most acute and harrowing suffering, of spasms so rapid and violent that were able to break the muscle cells themselves. These are injuries that could only happen in an expiring heart, consuming whatever energy it had left before dying.

Alive?

Finally, a truly mind-blowing fact: except for the ancient and mysteriously mummified Lanciano relic, all of the other four tissues undoubtedly revealed living features despite the concurrent degradation and autolysis. Let's expand on this.

In a December 7, 2000, interview, Dr. Lawrence — who was studying the 1996 Buenos Aires sample — explained that he managed to fix onto a microscope slide white blood cells that were actually living and active at the time of sampling. Furthermore, he commented that he could not possibly explain how those leukocytes had survived for three years in water without dissolving, when their destruction would normally inevitably happen within a few minutes, or at most one hour, after being separated from the living organism they came from, or after its death. Four years later, Prof. Zugibe expressed the same concept after examining that slide. However, he also commented on the tissue infiltration by leukocytes, which "normally do not live in the heart, but leave the blood and head toward a site of trauma or a wound." Hence, he concluded that the "sample was alive at the time it was taken." Moreover, he also specified that after such a long time in water, not only would white blood cells disappear but also any other human cell would no longer be recognizable.

In Tixtla, a macrophage was even caught on a microscope slide performing its usual duties: swallowing cellular debris. The microscope slide preparation procedure interrupted the life of that macrophage, capturing forever its vital and dynamic look, and its cytoplasm was full of lipid vacuolations[109] that had just

---

[109] The cytoplasm is the fluid inside any cell. All internal cellular reactions take place in cytoplasm. The cell nucleus and many specific cellular organelles and various other cell structures are all suspended in cytoplasm. Vacuoles or vacuolations are storage bubbles found in cells. They can have various functions, although in macrophages they specifically contain engulfed debris bound to be chemically digested inside them.

been swallowed. It should be appreciated that an inflammatory reaction like the one we saw in the Buenos Aires and Tixtla tissues is proof of the concurrent presence of a complete organism that is still living with a functioning immune system, an organism capable of coordinating a complex cascade of events involving several populations of appropriately stimulated and activated immune system cells.

Thus, these miracles are not just about the appearance of heart muscle tissue "out of nothing," or separated from the body it originally belonged to. On the contrary, the miraculous tissue was living and functioning because it was mysteriously connected to a complete, invisible body. This is because white blood cells are not locally produced in an inflamed tissue but rather come from elsewhere, making their way to their destination by means of a functioning bloodstream and attracted by the inflammatory response. Leukocytes tell us about a whole organism that is alive and trying to repair one of its inflamed and injured tissues.

During the weeks following the 1992 Buenos Aires events, some initial investigations were carried out with a lot of goodwill and very few means by Dr. Adhelma Myrian Segovia de Sasot, a hematologist at J. M. Ramos Mejía Hospital in the same city. In a June 1992 report, the doctor describes, still fresh, that biological tissue that, now dry, constitutes the relic visible today in Santa Maria of Avenida La Plata. Its macroscopic aspect recalled a blood clot, but under low power magnification (x16) and without staining procedures, a layered structure was appreciated and carefully described, although not formally recognized in histological terms. Within the structure of that mysterious tissue, Dr. Segovia de Sasot once described an area that, in her exact Spanish words, "*parecía latir rítmicamente*" — "seemed to be rhythmically beating." Only one area, and only on one occasion:

no camera recorded the event, but she couldn't refrain from describing what her eyes had seen, despite its baffling unlikelihood. Why would a professional put her reputation at risk and threaten her own credibility as a hematologist by witnessing an absurd event, if not because, in spite of everything, that was simply and truly what she actually saw? The only cells that rhythmically move are muscle cells. In particular, the ability to rhythmically and automatically contract is unique to cardiac muscle cells. If we were to accept the written and autographed witnessing by Dr. Segovia de Sasot—who unfortunately passed away in the year 2000—we would then have to accept the evidence, a cumbersome evidence, that these cells, whether myocardial or not, were truly alive.

Prof. Linoli could draw the same amazing conclusion when studying the macroscopic appearance of the Flesh of Lanciano. The roundish relic still bears on its edges about fourteen nearly equally distanced puncture marks made by either pins or small nails, utilized in all likelihood at some point in the past to ensure the relic itself would remain attached to some supportive surface. Linoli thought that the "nailing procedure" had to have been carried out in the first few hours after the miracle took place, precisely to counteract the rigor mortis phenomenon, which would have otherwise crumpled the relic up onto itself. The current shape of the Flesh of Lanciano is a rounded one, with a wide central hollow. This is not by chance, but rather, it is the result of its own natural hollow heart structure compounded by the "centrifugal" rigor mortis–related stretching exerted by the nails along its contour. Such force would have contributed to the laceration of its nail-free central portion, creating an even wider central empty space. Based on this rigor mortis theory, Prof. Linoli suggested that the Flesh of Lanciano must then also have been alive at the time of its miraculous apparition in the eighth century.

In conclusion, we are facing a short-circuiting of human reason: scientific tools are unequivocally demonstrating a biological reality gifted with the elegant complexity of living tissues. Yet those rigorous tools utterly fail to establish where those tissues came from and why they continue to exist somewhat immune to natural decay, defying biological laws. How could a fragment of living heart appear in the midst of a piece of bread? And how would it self-preserve for many years in water, or even distilled water, only partly deteriorating "in slow motion" while still lending itself to medical and scientific testing years later? How would the survival of transient cell populations—such as leukocytes—and their vitality at the time of sampling be explained in the absence of nourishment and in hostile environments? It is a brainteaser without solution for a man of science.

The Faith the Catholic Church has always professed now comes to our rescue.

Eucharistic miracles tell us of a wounded Body, one that was tortured to death on a cross in the outskirts of Jerusalem on a Friday before Easter between the years AD 30 and 33. In their puzzling unlikelihood, these miracles discreetly but clearly reveal who is really present in the Eucharist to anyone making a genuine effort to understand them. They speak of a presence that mysteriously trumps the limits of time and space: one that is present in any tabernacle at any latitude or longitude around the world, one that is present today just as it was yesterday or as it will be tomorrow until the end of time. The wounded Body of the Eucharist is also one that is gloriously sitting at the right hand of the Father, even if simultaneously suffering the torment of a heinous death on Golgotha in an eternal present. As proud contemporary citizens of the digital and technological world, we are also given the opportunity to use extremely powerful scientific tools to sustain our faith in that living and suffering heart which will be in agony till the end of the world.

Postscript

At the most recent International Congress of Sindonology,[110] held in Pasco, Washington, in July 2017, an Italian cardiologist, Dr. Pietro Pescetelli, proposed a pathophysiological sequence that would have led to the death of Jesus of Nazareth absolutely in keeping with what was discussed in this chapter. The cardiologist, by integrating the "clinical" data that can be gleaned from the Passion Gospels with the "medico-legal" evidence derived from the Shroud, challenged the currently prevailing theory of death by suffocation of the Crucified One. The Gospels describe Jesus as conscious and lucid to the last, able to swallow, speak, and even shout out till the very end. Moreover, as confirmed by the Shroud, the Gospel of John describes both Blood and water flowing from Jesus' pierced side after His death.

Well, all this, according to Dr. Pescetelli, is compatible with Jesus' heart suffering from a catecholamines-related stress, one capable of mimicking a heart attack, even in the absence of clinically improbable obstructing coronary artery disease in a young thirty-year-old. This catecholamine-related physiological stress could have been severe to the point of actually causing the rupture of the ventricular wall of Jesus' heart. This would have led to the collecting of Blood in His heart's pericardium, leading to compressive pericardial tamponade and immediate death. After death, His accumulated Blood vertically stagnated in the

---

[110] Sindonology is the formal study of the Shroud of Turin.

pericardium around the heart for some hours: it underwent the expected sedimentation, with its cellular component depositing at the bottom and its transparent serum floating at the top. After the spear thrust by the centurion in the right sixth intercostal space, Blood and then watery serum separately poured out of Jesus' side, according to the narrative in the Gospel of John.

Bibliography

González-Crussí, Frank. 2009. *Carrying the Heart: Exploring the Worlds Within Us*. New York: Kaplan.
A pathologist self-questioning about the history, scientific reality, symbolism, and beliefs of bodily organs.

Fineschi, Vittorio, Manolis Michalodimitrakis, Stefano D'Errico, et al. 2010. "Insight into Stress-Induced Cardiomyopathy and Sudden Cardiac Death Due to Stress: A Forensic Cardio-Pathologist Point of View." *Forensic Science International* 194 (1–3): 1–8.

Nugent, Kenneth, Menfil Orellana-Barrios, and Dolores Buscemi. 2017. "Comprehensive Histological and Immuno-chemical Forensic Studies in Deaths Occurring in Custody." *International Scholarly Research Notices* 2017 (1): 1–7.

Wittstein, Ilan, David Thiemann, Joao Lima, et al. 2005. "Neurohumoral Features of Myocardial Stunning Due to Sudden Emotional Stress." *The New England Journal of Medicine* 352 (6): 539–548.

Nef, Holger, Helge Möllmann, Sawa Kostin, et al. 2007. "Tako-Tsubo Cardiomyopathy: Intraindividual Structural Analysis in the Acute Phase and After Functional Recovery." *European Heart Journal* 28 (20): 2456–2464.

Mitchell, Andrew, and François Marquis. 2017. "Can Takotsubo Cardiomyopathy Be Diagnosed by Autopsy? Report of a

Presumed Case Presenting as Cardiac Rupture." *BMC Clinical Pathology* 17 (4). https://doi.org/10.1186/s12907-017-0045-0.

Elsokkari, Ihab, Allan Cala, Sayek Khan, and Andrew Hill. 2013. "Takosubo Cardiomyopathy: Not Always Innocent or Predictable — A Unique Post Mortem Insight." *International Journal of Cardiology* 167 (2): e46–48.

Radiant Light Broadcasting. 2017. Shroud of Turin Conference 2017. Recording. YouTube. Accessed July 12, 2021. https://www.youtube.com/watch?v=KkfTGXs9DKw&list=PLNXqdetrAZYxTFDcR8h1NFfhBLQq3Rrzp.

Video report titled "Physical causes of Jesus' death" by Dr. Pietro Pescetelli at the 2017 Sindonology Conference (July 20, 2017).

United States Conference of Catholic Bishops. 2020. "The Real Presence of Jesus Christ in the Sacrament of the Eucharist: Basic Questions and Answers." Retrieved from United States Conference of Catholic Bishops. https://www.usccb.org/prayer-and-worship/the-mass/order-of-mass/liturgy-of-the-eucharist/the-real-presence-of-jesus-christ-in-the-sacrament-of-the-eucharist-basic-questions-and-answers.

10

Blood

Blood is heavily laden with symbolism, just like the heart and maybe even more so. This mysterious bodily fluid has fascinated people of every age. The bright red color of arterial blood, just like that of a burning fire, has been called the most beautiful in the world.

From ancient times, blood has been thought to be precious for the living. Its clotting property was awe-inspiring for our ancestors: they knew that blood would mysteriously and rapidly congeal only when required, only when outside the body, in order to prevent further bleeding. Quite clearly, blood has always meant life, while bleeding has always been associated with weakness and the danger of death.

Indeed, blood lost and shed on the ground has often been the harrowing evidence of a violent death and the ultimate sacrifice. The outpouring of animal or human blood would appease the deities of all ancient religions and was thought to be necessary to maintain peace and harmony in society. Anthropologists and historians of world religions filled entire libraries with writings on these topics. In both Judaism and Islam, blood is still the subject of specific food preparation rituals and precise rules on the slaughtering of animals. Only kosher or halal foods can be eaten: those made with the meat of animals that were slaughtered by full and rapid blood loss.

Let's go back to Christianity. The ancient devotion to the Most Precious Blood does still exist, although it is even more neglected by modern-day Catholics than the devotion to the Sacred Heart. Remarkably, St. Thomas Aquinas wrote about it in his hymn "Adoro te devote":

> Me immundum munda tuo sanguine
> Cujus una stilla salvum facere
> Totum mundum quit ab omni scelere.
>
> Purify me, unclean, with Your blood
> Of which just one drop can save
> the whole world from all sin.

The Eucharist has been a topic of endless discussions by theologians and mystics of all times. Sacrifice, violence, suffering, and death are the harsh, difficult, and off-putting foundations of its divine mystery. These directly clash against the principles of our secular culture on a very basic level. In the Catholic Mass, bread and wine truly become and do not just symbolize the Body and Blood of Christ. Hence, they speak an extremely jarring and selfless sacrificial language that is completely opposed to the selfishness and indulgence focused on self-satisfaction that is at the core of our society. The Blood poured out in the sacrificial offering of the Eucharist is that of an innocent victim whose Body is hanging on a Cross.

In this chapter, we shall discover how the results of scientific investigations carried out on blood specimens taken from eucharistic miracles lead back to this harsh language of selfless suffering. Indeed, real human blood was found in the tissues of Lanciano, Buenos Aires, and Tixtla.

Lanciano

In Lanciano, the tissue handed down as the Blood of the eucharistic miracle and preserved in a precious glass chalice looks divided into five clotted and dehydrated fragments, weighing 15.85 grams altogether. In 1970, Prof. Linoli took a 318-milligram sample of this "stony and claylike" substance to clarify its nature and the species of organism it came from. Microscope slides were prepared by microtome slicing and the usual hematoxylin and eosin stain. However, after twelve centuries, well-defined cellular elements such as red or white blood cells could not be recognized under light microscopy. Thus, Linoli proceeded to microchemical analyses.

Two reactions aimed at detecting hematin and hemochromogen crystals[111] yielded negative results, most likely due to overall sample degradation and denaturation. Still, the orthotolidine test, looking for oxidases,[112] was intensely positive, although it was a low-specificity result: it could have been positive due to the presence of actual blood, but a false positive result could have been obtained from other tissues rich in fermenting organisms, plant extracts or finely ground metals. The final and unarguable answer was given by paper chromatography.[113] The eluting

---

[111] Broadly speaking, these tests screen for the presence of the iron-containing heme pigment molecule present in hemoglobin, the oxygen-carrying protein present in red blood cells.

[112] The orthotolidine test is another way to test for the persistence of heme group peroxidase chemical activity. Peroxidase activity is the ability to speed up the breakdown of peroxide molecules.

[113] Chromatography is a laboratory technique used to separate the components of a mixture: The latter is dissolved in a fluid called the mobile phase, or eluting liquid, which carries it through a

liquid containing the analyzed material repeatedly reproduced the chromatographic band patterns that were generated by eluting known standard hemoglobin and alkaline hematin samples. The Uhlenhuth precipitin ring test confirmed that both the Blood and the Flesh of Lanciano belonged to the human species, and the absorption-elution test[114] determined the blood group of both the Blood and the Flesh.

Prof. Linoli's investigations could have ended there with complete success, but two more common blood tests were carried out. These were very basic blood tests that most people have at any routine medical checkup: an electrolyte panel and protein electrophoresis. The content of the electrolytes invariably present in biological fluids were quantified: calcium, chloride, phosphorus, magnesium, potassium, and sodium. As expected, extreme sample dehydration resulted in the loss of these elements to the surrounding environment over the centuries. However, test results were still qualitatively interesting: all common electrolytes normally present in blood were also present in the Lanciano specimen—supporting its blood identity—but at such low concentrations that no pathophysiological interpretation reflecting the health and clinical state of the organism of origin could be formulated. Calcium was the only exception: it was present in excess, most likely due to external contamination throughout the centuries.

---

structure holding another material called the stationary phase. The components, dragged by the mobile phase, separate from one another into distinct bands at different locations along the stationary medium.

[114] The absorption-elution test is another analytical technique to identify blood group–specific antigens. It is explained in more detail in the next chapter.

Protein electrophoresis results were instead quantitatively remarkable. The elution fluid obtained from the Blood sample was actually five times more concentrated than common fresh blood serum, and the relative proportions of common serum proteins were in keeping with a perfect physiological profile. The proportions are reported in the table below and are all substantially within normal ranges:

	Blood of Lanciano	Normal ranges
Albumin %	61.93	52–68
α-1 Globulin %	2.38	2.4–5.3
α-2 Globulin %	7.14	6.6–13.5
β Globulin %	7.14	8.5–14.5
γ Globulin %	21.42	10.7–21
Albumin/total globulin ratio	1.62	1.13–1.73

This seems to suggest that the man whose blood appeared in Lanciano had to be enjoying good health, at least from the perspective of the immune system and protein metabolism.

Buenos Aires

As we know, human blood was present in the ceramic container holding the May 1 host and on one of the two patens used on May 10, 1992. This was ascertained by both hematologist Dr.

A Cardiologist Examines Jesus

Segovia de Sasot and oncologist Dr. Botto. Dr. Botto was immediately summoned by the parish priest and took some reddish material from the wall of the container stained on May 1. Tests carried out at the El Buen Samaritano hospital demonstrated the presence of hemoglobin. Although there is no written evidence of this, hematologist Dr. Khoan confirmed that the specimen was blood, according to testimonies collected by Dr. Castañón. It is quite difficult to unravel Dr. Sasot's reports: three possibly incomplete reports that were reproduced as photocopy images in the appendix of Dr. Castañón's book on the Buenos Aires events. She examined both a sample from the May 1 ceramic container and another one from one of the May 10, 1992, patens. She observed her specimens at different stages, initially without knowing their origins.

In an October 29, 1995, report—quite likely related to the May 1, 1992, event—Dr. Sasot unequivocally demonstrated the material she had examined was blood due to the following:

- A May-Grunwald Giemsa stain microscope blood smear revealed numerous recognizable white blood cells, whose differential count could be determined. This revealed an excess of lymphocytes compared to the normal range. However, rather strangely, there were neither red blood cells nor platelets:[115] a very rare situation to come across in a test tube of blood, even after centrifugation, let alone in a live organism, where this would be incompatible with life.
- It contained sodium and potassium ions, although their precise concentrations were not stated.

---

[115] Platelets are cell fragments present in blood whose role is to help with clot formation.

- It contained the enzyme lactate dehydrogenase (LDH).[116]
- It contained proteins whose electrophoretic pattern could be obtained: a physiological pattern, except for a reduction in the γ-globulins[117] component.

Moreover, in another June 1992 report by Dr. Sasot on the "blood-like material" taken three days after its appearance on a paten — in one of the two May 10 evening events — a May-Grunwald Giemsa stain microscope blood smear was prepared that yielded a white blood cell differential count very similar, though not identical, to the one reported in 1995. Dr. Sasot ended her report by certifying that the examined sample was *human* blood. Despite their gross limitations and approximations, Dr. Sasot's reports were worth exploring further, as they revealed precious and surprising details after a more careful analysis.

In the following years, the biological material of the May 1, 1992, relic unfortunately underwent decay phenomena, and when California-based Forensic Analytical analyzed item no. 1-1 in 1999, the blood-detecting orthotolidine test turned out to be negative. By running the same test, Forensic Analytical also ruled out the presence of blood in item no. 1-2, the 1996 Buenos Aires relic.

Later on, however, microscope slides obtained from this sample revealed a "suffering" cardiac tissue, the subject of my previous chapter. That tissue was infiltrated by white blood cells even

---

[116] LDH stands for *lactate dehydrogenase*, a protein enzyme molecule located inside nearly all living cells that is involved in mediating energy producing chemical reactions.

[117] Gamma globulins, or γ-globulins, are the antibodies used by the immune system to fight infection.

in the absence of red blood cells, which normally make up the majority of cells present in whole blood.

Tixtla

Human blood and other tissues were unmistakably present in the Tixtla relic. The Bolivian Gene-Ex laboratory identified the presence of human hemoglobin in a relic microsample by immunochromatography. The very moment the test was run by Dr. Susana Pinell under blind conditions was even filmed and is available online. Hemoglobin is only present in red blood cells and in no other living cell. Hence, the presence of blood in the Tixtla miracle was fully and unarguably demonstrated.

Moreover, two other laboratories, Corporativo Médico Legal in Mexico and PatMed in Guatemala, analyzed other hematoxylin- and eosin-stained samples under the light microscope. No typically biconcave-shaped[118] and nuclei-free red blood cells could be distinguished more than three years after the miraculous event. However, acidophile clusters compatible with clumps of red blood cells undergoing autolysis were appreciated. These were possibly in keeping with previously fully formed blood clots.

Astonishingly, white blood cells were instead identified. This could not be scientifically explained, as these would be expected to dissolve within hours after death. Instead, they were present in different subpopulations: neutrophils, macrophages, and basophils.

---

[118] Red blood cells are typically round, flattened, and centrally dimpled on both sides.

Moreover, the Mexican scientists at Corporativo Médico Legal also managed to demonstrate the presence of white blood cell–specific myeloperoxidases[119] and glycophorin A,[120] a protein that is only present on the surface of human red blood cells. Lastly, blood could not be detected in the miracles of Sokółka and Legnica. Only the presence of myocardial tissue could be demonstrated in the Polish relics.

Lymphocytosis

Let's go back and take another look at Dr. Adhelma Myrian Segovia de Sasot's papers. We should pay attention to an important finding that was demonstrated twice in a row: that of lymphocytosis. Lymphocytosis is the elevation of the lymphocyte white cell count relative to other types of white blood cells, particularly neutrophils. The two differential white cell counts are reported below and apparently originated from two different miraculous events that took place a few days apart from each other in the same Buenos Aires parish. They are remarkably similar, as if the same test was repeated on the same person:

---

[119] Myeloperoxidases are enzymes that are only present in some white blood cells: the granulocytes of the myeloid series. For instance, myeloperoxidases have an important role in neutrophils' respiratory burst reaction to infective agents: this reaction produces and releases several highly reactive and toxic free radical species that chemically destroy the invader and can, to a lesser extent, cause some degree of toxic damage to host tissues as well.

[120] Glycophorin A is a protein specifically located on the membrane of red blood cells, determining their MN minor blood group.

A Cardiologist Examines Jesus

White blood cell differential	May 1, 1992, event	May 10, 1992, event	Normal ranges
Band neutrophils	2%	0%	0–3%
Segmented neutrophils	43%	49%	40–60%
Eosinophils	6%	3%	1–4%
Basophils	0%	0%	0.5–1%
Lymphocytes	48%	47%	20–40%
Monocytes	1%	1%	2–8%

Two people could not randomly have had such similar and equally altered differential white cell counts. In a precise moment, that essentially identical degree of lymphocytosis had to represent the "biological" signature of a single specific individual. Hence, Dr. Sasot presented two investigations, two microscope slides, and two different differential counts that, in all likelihood, came from the same blood. It was either blood from the same event that was examined twice, or it was blood from the same person who bled on two different occasions. Unfortunately, the first hypothesis cannot be ruled out, given the insufficient clarity of the available notes. However, if true, the second hypothesis would certainly strengthen the claim of intrinsic authenticity for both miracles, almost as if we had demonstrated that both samples belonged to the same rare blood group.

But what is the meaning of this excess of lymphocytes in the differential white cell count? We should recall that, among various other classes of white blood cells, B lymphocytes are specifically responsible for the production of antibodies, whereas T lymphocytes are capable of direct killing of foreign infectious invaders or host cells targeted for destruction. Two categories of T lymphocytes, helper T cells and natural killer cells, or NK cells, carry out these defensive actions in different ways. What should a doctor be thinking of when caring for a patient with lymphocytosis? In an otherwise well adult without any clear symptoms or signs of infection, this would not be an expected finding. If persistent, it could be suggestive of a potentially serious blood cancer, such as lymphoma or leukemia. However, transient episodes of lymphocytosis are commonly associated with viral or bacterial infections.

In the context of eucharistic miracles, it is worth considering a condition that was only recognized and studied in the last few years: transient stress lymphocytosis, or TSL. Case reports were first published on it in the 1980s. The condition was primarily diagnosed in patients that had been taken to resuscitation facilities or intensive care units with traumatic, hemorrhagic, cardiogenic, or septic shock.[121] These patients had significantly raised lymphocytes in the first few hours of their hospital admissions, followed

---

[121] The medical definition of shock is different from its meaning in common speech: regardless of its underlying cause, shock indicates a systemic inadequacy of blood supply to all peripheral body tissues and organs. If not promptly treated, it can easily transition into an irreversibly worsening phase, rapidly leading to death. Systemically inadequate blood supply can be commonly caused by trauma, excessive bleeding, or heart pump failure.

by a completely opposite and abnormally low lymphocyte count twenty-four to forty-eight hours later. The degree of lymphocytosis was proportional to the severity of traumatic injuries, the latter being formally expressed in terms of an Injury Severity Score, or ISS. The higher the ISS score, the higher the risk of death.

Both catecholamines produced by the organism itself and those pharmacologically administered seem to play a role in TSL, similar to their role in stress-induced cardiomyopathy. The differences between activation mechanisms and specific responses by different lymphocyte subclasses are currently being studied and compared between those seen in TSL and the more well-known ones, observed in viral or bacterial infections. However, it is already well established that the release of a large amount of catecholamines—adrenaline in particular—does lead to the release of natural killer (NK) lymphocytes[122] in the bloodstream. These NK cells, normally making up 5 to 15 percent of the entire lymphocyte family, increase their blood concentration up to ten times in TSL and cause lymphocytosis in response to significant stressful stimuli: these include physical but also psychological trauma or even the abuse of psychostimulant drugs such as MDMA, or "ecstasy."

NK cells are part of the initial immune response enacted by the organism in response to signals of an attack or a threat to bodily integrity. Their release is considered to be an innate nonspecific reaction before the involvement and activation of B lymphocytes, cytotoxic T lymphocytes, and helper T cells. The latter are all part of the much more sophisticated, highly specific, and potent, but delayed, adaptive immune response—one that

---

[122] Natural killer, or NK, lymphocytes are well recognizable on a molecular basis due to the presence of their specific CD56 receptors on their cell membranes.

relies on the specific complementarity between foreign antigens and the production of antibodies. However, when the organism is suddenly threatened by trauma or infective agents, NK cells intervene immediately to destroy cells that are either infected or damaged beyond repair. NK cells do not accurately discriminate between infected or damaged cells that belong to the organism or foreign infectious cells: they cannot fully tell self from nonself. They have a broad "license to kill" and also cause some degree of collateral damage to the host, with the purpose of keeping infection at bay in the early stages of the immune response.

The Buenos Aires lymphocyte count is unfortunately only a numerical value, without any precise morphological or immunophenotypic details. Hence, we will never know if that lymphocyte excess was truly and specifically mostly due to NK cells as opposed to another lymphocyte subclass. Therefore, no other finer diagnostic hypotheses can be formulated at this stage, and the Buenos Aires lymphocytosis cannot be used to unequivocally confirm a TSL diagnosis. However, it can still suggest these important medical insights to the forensic pathologist.

Hypogammaglobulinemia

Let's now focus on a second interesting finding, hidden between the lines in one of Dr. Sasot's reports. In October 1995, she wrote that the protein electrophoresis of the blood sample she analyzed yielded a "physiological" profile, except for a reduction in γ-globulins. What was that all about? Electrophoresis separates plasma[123] proteins into five or six groups, according to their molecular weights. This

---

[123] Blood plasma is the yellowish liquid component of blood that holds the blood cells of whole blood in suspension. It is the liquid part of the blood that carries cells and proteins throughout the body.

allows us to quantify the relative percentages of proteins belonging to each of these groups with respect to the total amount of protein present in the plasma sample.

We already came across an example of normal plasma protein electrophoresis when discussing the miracle of Lanciano. In that panel, blood proteins such as albumins and globulins were separated into their α-1, α-2, β, and γ subclasses. The γ-group globulins are precisely the circulating antibodies produced by the B lymphocyte–derived plasma cells. They are proteins capable of binding specific antigens exposed on foreign cells, such as bacteria, on a one-to-one basis. By doing so, the foreign body is tagged as an "enemy" and presented to T lymphocytes in charge of destroying it: it is the mechanism of so-called specific or adaptive immunity, whose activation is slower but whose precision is extremely high, in stark contrast with the innate immunity mediated by NK cells.

Hypogammaglobulinemia, or a low number of circulating antibodies, is therefore an immune-deficiency condition making the organism less capable of responding to infections. It is a pathologic condition with many potential causes: it may be congenital or inherited, such as the common variable immunodeficiency (CVID) of young adults, or acquired, as a consequence of blood, liver, or kidney diseases. Often it can be associated, just like lymphocytosis, with great stressors and weariness—for example, in cases of major trauma, massive bleeding, burns, or major strokes.

For many decades, we have seen cases demonstrating the frequent onset of a reduction in immunoglobulins—especially of the IgG γ-globulins subclass[124]—from day one after severe traumas

[124] IgG γ-globulins are the subclass of antibodies that is produced last, after antibodies of the IgM subclass have been made available.

and for about a week thereafter. It is a transient phenomenon, followed by rising amounts of IgG in the next few days and even an actual rebound peak for the IgM[125] subclass at the same time. Hypogammaglobulinemia obviously increases the risk of infections, especially of the upper airways, and is correlated with a higher in-hospital mortality. Common causes of this deficit are usually either due to loss of blood proteins[126] by various mechanisms, or their reduced production by plasma cells, or both.

In conclusion, lymphocytosis and hypogammaglobulinemia represent an uncommon association of abnormal laboratory tests. They may be attributed to a coincidence of two concurrent pathologies: a young adult with CVID who is suffering from a trivial cold, an adolescent with mononucleosis who is developing kidney complications, or two aspects of the same pathology, such as an elderly patient with chronic lymphocytic leukemia.

However, we shouldn't miss another diagnostic explanation that could perfectly solve our diagnostic dilemma: we could be dealing with the victim of a severe trauma, probably in a coma, or a patient recovering after a delicate surgery. We could be looking at someone who suffered severe burns or shock due to infection. In short, our blood findings would be suggestive of a frail patient, someone on the edge of life and death, in a resuscitation bay or in

---

IgG antibodies take longer to be produced but are more highly specific than IgM antibodies.

[125] IgM γ-globulins are another subclass of immunoglobulins that typically make the first attempt at binding new antigens with low specificity.

[126] Blood proteins can be lost because of bleeding or fluid shifts between the circulating blood and the fluid bathing all cells. These shifts are usually due to excessive permeability of the tiny capillary blood vessels in the peripheral tissues.

an intensive care bed. In this clinical scenario, the combination of lymphocytosis and hypogammaglobulinemia would suggest to the treating doctor that his patient must have survived a major trauma one or, at most, two days before. In this context, lymphocytosis and hypogammaglobulinemia would then be expected to be dynamic and transient: the lymphocytosis will most likely turn into a low lymphocyte count within twenty-four to forty-eight hours, whereas the hypogammaglobulinemia will be expected to normalize within a week.

The heart of the living and suffering man I described in the previous chapter was oppressed by spasms and painful agony. Similarly, we can see that same "suffering" when reflecting on the laboratory findings related to the 1992 Buenos Aires blood. These findings lead to clinical insights that are absolutely compatible with the pathophysiological picture handed down to us by the Passion Gospels: one man, in perfectly good health until the day before, who was then severely traumatized and worn out to exhaustion after losing a significant amount of blood.

A very careful reader must then be wondering: Why was there no finding of hypogammaglobulinemia in the blood of Lanciano? The serum γ-fraction, estimated as 21.42 percent, and all the α-1, α-2, β, and albumin fractions were all within normal ranges. Would it not be rational to expect the same pathophysiological features both in Lanciano and Buenos Aires if both miracles were authentic? The answer is not a trivial one. To begin with, it would be incorrect to compare one blood sample examined only a few days after its appearance with an ancient one that clotted many centuries prior to its testing. In Buenos Aires, Dr. Sasot could still employ the same laboratory techniques she would have used to analyze any other recently collected fresh blood specimen. That was possible because her sample was still somewhat fresh. Prof.

Linoli was instead faced with a very different challenge: due to the age of his specimen, he had to adapt his analytical techniques, essentially by dilution, to compensate for extreme sample conditions. Although Prof. Linoli's investigations were absolutely valid from a qualitative point of view, they were certainly less reliable from a quantitative perspective. It is qualitatively unquestionable that the miracle of Lanciano contains true human blood. However, no accurate clinical judgment on the state of health of the blood of Lanciano can be made at this stage in the absence of reliable quantitative data.

Still, there is more to this: we must always keep in mind that these tissues, if truly miraculous, enjoy properties that transcend the biological laws governing our mortal bodies. For instance, they are gifted with a degree of inexplicable incorruptibility: although undergoing common degradation phenomena, they seem to be doing this with a mysteriously slow, millennial inertia. If these tissues are truly miraculous, they can also behave as they please, to some extent. They do not need to ask permissions to breach natural laws. They lend themselves to our scientific investigations and talk to us in a language that is incredibly coherent with the Faith. They also offer many scientific clues to stimulate our theological reflection and desire to know God. Still, there is no reason to expect that everything about this original discipline of "experimental and applied bio-theology" must be understood or must be humanly understandable. We shall appreciate these principles in the next chapters: on the one hand we will find a comforting coherence in the identification of the same blood group in all miraculous tissues. On the other hand, however, DNA analyses have indeed put scientists' patience and rationality to the test. Let's then continue on our journey with humility.

Postscript

Just like for the heart, the Shroud of Turin has something to say about the blood too. The linen cloth of Turin is stained with blood. This was proved beyond any reasonable doubt by the 1980 studies carried out by Alan Adler and John Heller from the STURP Consortium. Later on, the presence of hydroxyproline and an excess of bilirubin in the Shroud's blood were also confirmed. Hydroxyproline, an amino acid present in the structure of collagen, only appears in blood after very intense muscular efforts or prolonged stretching periods.

Bilirubin is instead the degradation product of hemoglobin contained in red blood cells. Hyperbilirubinemia—an excess of bilirubin in the blood—can be due to many causes that are well known to any medical doctor. Very commonly, the finding of a raised bilirubin is combined with other laboratory tests to draw conclusions on the health and functioning of the liver. One of the causes leading to accumulation of bilirubin in the blood can indeed be major trauma. This is because trauma and bleeding cause red blood cells to leak out of vessels and into tissues where they are broken down, thereby releasing hemoglobin. This scenario can also be compounded by impairment of liver function in the context of post-traumatic syndrome.[127]

Besides the presence of bilirubin, a recent study even identified the presence of biliverdin on one stained Shroud fabric thread. Biliverdin is the *first* degradation product of hemoglobin. Its production is enzymatically enhanced over the course of tissue injury, especially with trauma. This enhanced breakdown

---

[127] Post-traumatic syndrome refers to the many abnormal multisystem pathophysiological changes that take place in the body after major trauma.

of hemoglobin to biliverdin is thought to be beneficial for the organism due to the potent antioxidant[128] healing effect of biliverdin itself. Dear reader, as you can see, even the Shroud's hydroxyproline, bilirubin, and biliverdin are telling us a story of battery, torture, humiliation, and extreme suffering.

Bibliography

Thommasen, Harvey, William Boyko, Julio Montaner, et al. 1986. "Absolute Lymphocytosis Associated with Nonsurgical Trauma." *American Journal of Clinical Pathology* 86 (4): 480–483.
Study demonstrating the frequent association of trauma and bleeding with hematologic alterations characterized by initial lymphocytosis followed by low lymphocyte blood count in the first twenty-four hours.

Teggatz, J. R., J. Parkin, and L. Peterson. 1987. "Transient Atypical Lymphocytosis in Patients with Emergency Medical Conditions." *Archives of Pathology & Laboratory Medicine* 111 (8): 712–714.

Pinkerton, P., B. McLellan, M. Quantz, and J. Robinson. 1989. "Acute Lymphocytosis After Trauma — Early Recognition of the High-Risk Patient?" *Journal of Trauma* 29 (6): 749–751.

Karandikar, Nitin, Erin Hotchkiss, Robert Mckenna, and Steven Kroft. 2002. "Transient Stress Lymphocytosis: An Immunophenotypic Characterization of the Most Common Cause of

---

[128] Antioxidants are substances that protect cells against free radicals. Free radicals are highly reactive, tissue-damaging chemical species that can be produced for many reasons, but traumatic tissue injury and inflammation are certainly well-known causes of free radical formation.

Newly Identified Adult Lymphocytosis in a Tertiary Hospital." *American Journal of Clinical Pathology* 117 (5): 819–825.

Benschop, Robert, Mario Rodriguez-Feuerhahn, and Manfred Schedlowski. 1996. "Catecholamine-Induced Leukocytosis: Early Observations, Current Research, and Future Directions." *Brain, Behavior, and Immunity* 10 (2): 77–91.

Bigler, Marc, Simon Egli, Cédric Hysek, et al. 2015. "Stress-Induced In Vivo Recruitment of Human Cytotoxic Natural Killer Cells Favors Subsets with Distinct Receptor Profiles and Associates with Increased Epinephrine Levels." *PLoS One* 23 (10).

Auer, L., and W. Petek. 1976. "Serum Globulin Changes in Patients with Craniocerebral Trauma." *Journal of Neurology, Neurosurgery, and Psychiatry* 39 (11): 1076–1080.

Faist, E., W. Ertel, C. Baker, and G. Heberer. 1989. "Terminal B-Cell Maturation and Immunoglobulin (Ig) Synthesis In Vitro in Patients with Major Injury." *Journal of Trauma* 29 (1): 2–9.

Wilson, N., Y. Wu, and J. Bastian. 1994. "Immunoglobulins and IgG Subclasses in Children Following Severe Head Injury." *Intensive Care Medicine* 20 (7): 508–510.
This research demonstrated that 50 percent of patients with an IgG and IgM deficit in the first week followed by an IgM increase by 383 percent on day seven.

Prucha, M., R. Zazula, I. Herold, et al. 2014. "Presence of Hypogammaglobulinemia in Patients with Severe Sepsis, Septic Shock, and SIRS Is Associated with Increased Mortality." *Journal of Infection* 68 (3): 297–299.

Liesz, Arthur, Stefan Roth, Markus Zorn, et al. 2015. "Acquired Immunoglobulin G Deficiency in Stroke Patients and Experimental Brain Ischemia." *Experimental Neurology* 271 (1): 46–52.

This research demonstrates a transient decrease in IgG in the first seven days, when hypogammaglobulinemia is more pronounced. This is more frequently associated with bacterial infections.

Da Rocha Mafra, Olivia, Elirez da Silva, Tania Santos Gian, et al. 2010. "Hydroxyproline Levels in Young Adults Undergoing Muscular Stretching and Neural Mobilization." *Journal of Medical Biochemistry* 29 (1): 39–43.

The study demonstrates that body stretching and neural activation increase urine hydroxyproline concentrations by more than double.

Labori, K., and M. Raeder. 2004. "Diagnostic Approach to the Patient with Jaundice following Trauma." *Scandinavian Journal of Surgery* 93 (3): 176–183.

Laude, Jean-Pierre, and Giulio Fanti. 2017. "Raman and Energy Dispersive Spectroscopy (EDS) Analyses of a Microsubstance Adhering to a Fiber of the Turin Shroud." *Applied Spectroscopy* 71 (10): 2313–2324.

11

AB Blood Group

All attempts to determine the ABO blood group of any tissue sample taken from eucharistic miracles consistently resulted in the identification of the AB group. Specifically, these attempts were made on samples from the Lanciano and Tixtla miracles. Likewise, the bloodstaining on the three most well-known Passion cloths—the Shroud of Turin, the Sudarium of Oviedo, and the Tunic of Argenteuil—is also of the AB type. Always the same group—and also the rarest one.

As we shall see, this is simply an amazing finding that strongly supports the reciprocal authenticity of these events.

A Brief School Refresher

Many readers may be familiar with the four blood groups of the main ABO classification system—namely, groups A, B, AB, and O. Either from our school days or from our own experience as blood donors, we might also remember which blood transfusion pairings are allowed: from A to A and AB, from B to B and AB. Type O blood can be given to people of any blood group as a "universal donor." People whose blood is of the AB type can receive blood of any kind but can only donate their own blood to people of the same blood group.

A Cardiologist Examines Jesus

So what exactly are these blood groups? Why do they exist? Science has given a precise answer to the first question, while it is still working out the answer to the second one.

Even in ancient times, people guessed that transfusing blood from a human or animal donor into people dying from massive bleeding could be useful. Unfortunately, nearly all attempts ended badly. It is said that Pope Innocent VIII—nearing death in 1492—was transfused with blood from three children: on the same day, both the pope and the three young people died while the doctor fled from Rome! In 1829, English gynecologist Dr. James Blundell saved a new mother by transfusing her with blood from her husband with a purpose-made syringe. His later clinical experience involved ten more transfusion attempts: it is fair to say that five of them were successful, while the rest led to deadly outcomes.

The turning point came between 1900 and 1901, when Dr. Karl Landsteiner, an Austrian doctor, identified three distinct blood types among his assistants. These could be mixed with one another without agglutination—that is, without the formation of solid red blood cell clumps settling and disintegrating at the bottom of a test tube. He understood that the same process would lead to disastrous and deadly consequences if taking place inside the bloodstream of a living organism in the event of an incompatible transfusion. He discovered the A, B, and O blood groups, which eventually led to his well-deserved Nobel Prize for medicine in 1930, and soon after, he also discovered the AB group. Hence, large amounts of blood could already be transfused to the wounded in field hospitals relatively safely in World War I. Later on, Dr. Landsteiner and Alexander Wiener discovered the Rh blood group in 1940. Its name came from the type of rhesus monkey in which the Rh factor was first found.

Today we know about more than thirty types of blood group classification systems that we call *minor*, as their impact on the safety of transfusions is much less severe in case of mismatch. However, the two major ABO and Rh classification systems are still to this day the most important ones for the purpose of crossmatching blood or any other type of blood product to be transfused. The same crossmatching principles also apply to the selection of solid organs or tissues to be transplanted: after all, blood *is* a tissue, and blood transfusions are effectively a type of tissue transplant.

What, then, are the chemical elements determining the ABO system blood types?

They are oligosaccharides, or short chains of chemically linked sugar molecules. These are exposed on the surface of all red blood cells in any person. They are abundantly present: a few hundred thousand molecules—at times even up to one to two million—on each red blood cell. Moreover, they are also present on the surfaces of other types of body cells and can be isolated in bodily secretions such as saliva, tears, and sweat. These chemicals are also potential antigens: if produced by the individual and exposed on his or her own body cells, they will be recognized by a person's immune system as belonging to *self*. Because of this, the immune system will not mount an antibody response against cells belonging to its own organism.

However, it is known that if an individual's red blood cells do not expose the A antigen—because, for example, the person's blood is of the B type—his or her immune system will inevitably develop anti-A antibodies that will be present throughout life. Why would this happen in everyone even without any direct foreign blood exposure? The answer is that everyone's immune system is bound to be exposed to antigens very similar to the

ABO ones. These are carried on common viruses and bacteria that all human beings come across in their first few months of life. These early "immunological encounters" with very similar antigens result in the development of antibodies that effectively cross-bind all ABO antigens of foreign blood groups. Hence, should a type B individual be mistakenly transfused with group A blood, he or she would unfortunately mount an immune reaction against the transfused red blood cells. However, the fatal outcome of such incompatibility would be primarily caused by mechanical agglutination, well before the development of a full inflammatory lymphocytic response.[129]

Mechanical agglutination is a simpler process with catastrophic consequences: it causes the clumping reaction I mentioned before, one that is even visible to the naked eye in a test tube. This happens because foreign red blood cells are chemically clasped together by the host's antibodies, which are already present in the bloodstream. The result is the formation of dangerous and bulky clumps of red blood cells. These large clumps precipitate, or settle, inside blood vessels, effectively blocking them just about everywhere in the body. Laboratories can today easily and rapidly determine ABO blood groups by agglutination testing. This only involves preparing a glass slide with two separate drops of the blood to be analyzed. A small amount of "anti-A" serum with anti-A antibodies is added to one of the two drops. Similarly, a small amount of "anti-B" serum with anti-B antibodies

---

[129] The standard lymphocytic response would be the more complex recruitment of white blood cells of the lymphocyte class for targeted destruction of any antibody-tagged material. Antibodies are not capable of destroying what they tag. The actual destruction requires the presence of lymphocytes that recognize tagging antibodies.

is then added to the other. If no reactions take place, the blood group will be O; if agglutination only occurs after addition of the anti-A serum, the blood group will be A; if the blood only reacts with anti-B, then the group will be B, and if it reacts with both serums, it will be AB.

It is also possible to cross-check and verify what antibodies are present in the serum of the analyzed blood by observing its reaction when mixed with red blood cells of a known group. Furthermore, today we also know about the precise chemical composition of the ABO antigens, their various possible variants (A1, A2, etc.), and the portions of DNA on chromosome 9 required for their synthesis. This knowledge allowed the development of alternative methods to determine the blood group of a tissue or individual besides standard agglutination testing.

I should say here that every person has two genes or two complementary pieces of DNA information determining his or her overall ABO blood group: the two genes are actually carried on two paired versions of chromosome 9, with one chromosome originating from the father and the other from the mother. Moreover, the A and B genes are dominant, whereas O is recessive. This means that, if a person's genes are AA, he or she is homozygous,[130] and obviously the blood group will be A. However, even the heterozygous AO pair—that is, the A gene from the father and O from the mother, or vice versa—will result in the A blood group. A child's blood group can only be O if he or

---

[130] Homozygous means carrying two *identical* maternal and paternal copies (or *alleles*) of a given gene, in this case the blood group–determining gene. Heterozygous instead means carrying *different* maternal and paternal variants of the same gene.

she inherited the O gene product from both parents. Likewise, a child can only be AB by inheriting the A antigen from one parent and the B antigen from the other. Altogether, the various versions of a gene are called *alleles*. For example, three alleles are obviously present in the ABO system—A, B, and O—but only two of them can "occupy" two available "places" on each of the two paired chromosomes inherited from each parent. The table below summarizes all the possible relationships between *genotypes* and *phenotypes*—that is, between the pairs of genes and how they are expressed:

Genotype	Phenotype
AA	A
AO	A
BB	B
BO	B
AB	AB
OO	O

Before the advent of our modern and sophisticated DNA sequencing techniques, knowledge of the ABO system had already been used to draw reliable conclusions on the paternity and maternity of individuals. While paternity and maternity could not be determined with certainty, it was still possible to definitively rule them out in some cases. For instance, an A group father and an O group mother cannot possibly have a B group child.

How Are the ABO Blood Groups Distributed in the Human Population?

In 1954, Arthur Mourant published an actual geographical atlas with systematically collected results from about half a million tests done all over the world. His findings were mostly about native populations, excluding western colonizers and migrations in the last few centuries. This trove of data became invaluable for anthropologists: blood groups told of a complex and intriguing human diversity, following an invisible and unalterable code unknown to man before 1900.

It is certainly worth pointing out that the blood group distribution transcends any racial distinction based on skin color or other anthropomorphic data. On a global scale, the most prevalent allele is O in 63 percent of the population, followed by A in 21 percent and B in 16 percent of all people. Mourant's data show that the O allele is always present in more than 50 percent of all world populations. At the time of his study, the O blood group made up 95 to 100 percent of the population in Central and South America, though it was still very common in the rest of the world. It was followed by the A group, which was most prevalent in Europe, western Russia, the Middle East, Japan, and Australia. The less prevalent B group was more represented in central Russia, central and eastern Asia, and India. Only in some African regions does the B group prevalence exceed that of the A group. Finally, the AB group is the least represented worldwide. It is only a tiny pie slice, rarely exceeding 5 percent in those populations in which both A and B are present.

In today's world population, the relative proportions of the ABO groups are those listed in the table below:

O	40–45%
A	35–40%
B	4–11%
AB	1–5%

The AB group is by far the rarest one. Only in some Asian populations does it reach and exceed 10 percent: these are populations in which the A and B groups are both relatively common at the expense of O. An example is that of Ainu Japanese inhabiting Hokkaido Island, in northern Japan. They hold an AB prevalence record of 17 to 18 percent, similar to some other specific regions of China, India, and Korea. In Europe, the AB prevalence reaches 10 percent in Hungarian Roma and is still relatively high in Poland (9 percent), but also in the Czech Republic and Finland. It is interesting to point out the 8 percent figure in modern-day Israel.

How Are Blood Groups Determined in Forensic Medicine?

For a long time, forensic medicine has been tackling the problem of determining the ABO group of traces of congealed, dehydrated, or decaying blood found at crime scenes. Forensic scientists are well aware that achieving this goal cannot precisely identify a culprit, especially when the blood type is a common one. Still, blood group identification can often definitively exclude suspects of completely different blood groups. However, the DNA identification techniques developed in the last ten to twenty years have certainly superseded the limitations of blood group determination: genetic profiles obtained by STR analysis allow for the identification of an individual with a degree of accuracy nearing 100 percent. This can be achieved just by testing a hair sample or the invisible trail of skin cells we all leave behind us. Still, for many long decades, Hercule Poirot and Miss Marple — who did not have access to DNA technologies — had to simply rely on blood group identification.

I should point out that red blood cells in old traces of dried blood tend to quickly decay and rupture. Thus, the common, simple, and rapid agglutination tests used for fresh blood cannot be employed in these circumstances. Nevertheless, it has been demonstrated that the ABO antigens can resist dehydration for a long period of time, possibly for many years. Even with trace amounts of blood, it is still possible to observe reactions between specific antibodies and the sample by using certain analytical methods. These methods are specifically designed for these challenging tests: they can "amplify" and reveal any trace amounts of detectable ABO antigens present in the samples. Because of this, they have been successfully used even on ancient tissues originating from mummies or tombs that are two to three thousand years old. Moreover, we mustn't forget that, besides being found on red blood cells, ABO antigens are also present in many other tissues such as bones, muscles, and teeth.

The Miracle of Lanciano

Of course, the 1970 scientific assessment assigned to Prof. Odoardo Linoli also involved determining the miracle's blood group. Linoli's analytical method and his results have been thoroughly documented and published. They are readily available, along with extensive photographic evidence.

In short, he used the absorption-elution method and could then state the following in his final report: "The delicate absorption-elution test allowed it to be objectively concluded with full certainty that both the Blood and the Flesh of the eucharistic miracle of Lanciano belong to the same AB blood group."

The Miracle of Tixtla

Dr. Castañón Gómez oversaw the 2009 clinical investigations on the host that had bled three years before. He sent off the samples he had taken himself to two different laboratories for the detection of blood components and obtained compatible results. The original letterhead reports with photographs are reproduced in the texts by Dr. Castañón cited in the bibliography. The final report issued by the Corporativo Médico Legal laboratory of Mexico City headed by Dr. Eduardo Sánchez Lazo declared the following: "Immunohistochemical testing allowed stating with full certainty and objectivity that [the blood] is of the AB group."

Similarly, in 2010, the Gene-Ex laboratory headed by Dr. Susana Pinell Prado di La Paz (Bolivia) also demonstrated that the blood samples were of the AB type. The result was once again achieved by immunohistochemical techniques performed after initial reconstitution of the dehydrated samples with saline solution. Furthermore, a unique and astonishing finding came from Dr. Pinell Prado's laboratory for the first time in the world so far: the blood was found to be Rh *negative*. Dr. Pinell personally told me about her 2010 results, reiterating that she had not been told about the origin of the sample she was analyzing. When I congratulated her for being the first person in the world to identify Christ's Rh blood group, she did not reply out of modesty. Her finding will certainly require further checks. However, if confirmed by future tests performed on samples from other eucharistic miracles or Passion relics, it would be a striking discovery. If the extremely rare AB Rh-negative blood were to be systematically identified in multiple miracles and relics, that would raise the bar much higher for anyone arguing against their authenticity: it would be an extremely unlikely random occurrence that such a rare blood group was found in multiple "fake" specimens. I shall remind the reader that 15 percent of all human beings are Rh negative. After doing the math, only 0.75 percent of all human beings are AB Rh negative: only about 1 in 133 people.

The Shroud of Turin

Only in 1980–1981 did scientists John Heller and Alan Adler from the STURP Consortium demonstrate the presence of blood on the Shroud. After this discovery, the blood was also confirmed to be of human origin. Turin-based Prof. Pierluigi Baima Bollone was the first pathologist who demonstrated that the Shroud's blood was of the AB type in 1982. He analyzed twelve fabric threads taken on October 9, 1978, by comparing fibers originating from bloodstained areas to others originating from a "neutral" area of the Shroud. The bloodstained areas were those of the so-called blood belt, a name due to blood oozing out of the centurion's spear wound on the right side and trickling onto the back.

Control samples were also prepared: four made from fabric fibers stained with fresh blood and one made from fabric fibers stained with ancient blood, originating from a 1200 BC Egyptian funerary urn. Each fresh blood control sample was stained with blood of a different ABO type. Prof. Baima Bollone observed a ++ reactivity against A antigens and a stronger +++ reactivity against B antigens on the Shroud's bloodstained fibers. On the contrary, no reactivity could be observed when examining the Shroud's fibers taken from the "neutral area" and the Egyptian fibers. Presumably, the latter had to be stained with type O blood. Of course, the other fresh blood control samples either displayed very strong or no reactivity depending on their particular blood types.

In the same study, Prof. Baima Bollone also provided the result of a reverse grouping analysis: the search for anti-A or anti-B antibodies in the Shroud's samples. The negative result for the presence of either antibody type was in keeping with the Shroud's blood being of the AB type, although such finding is methodologically weak because it is indistinguishable from a false negative. Only two years later, in 1984, Baima Bollone perfected his determination of the Shroud's blood group by employing the much more reliable immunofluorescence technique: exposing the rehydrated samples to serums containing a single kind of antibody. Lastly, he also improved his technique by employing anti-O antibodies in addition to anti-A and anti-B antibodies in order to actively detect the O "antigens."[131] This was in contrast to just presuming that O antigens had to be present whenever no reactivity was observed after exposure to both anti-A and anti-B antibodies. His new results were a full confirmation that the Shroud's blood group was AB. Of course, the fibers from the "neutral area" that were not bloodstained did not react with any of the three types of antibodies.

In 1998, Dr. Leoncio Garza-Valdes at the University of San Antonio (Texas) carried out a similar study on other fragments taken from the Shroud. As a matter of fact, his were a series

---

[131] Strictly speaking, O antigens are not true antigens for human beings, as their sugar chain molecules are incapable of eliciting an immune response. However, antibodies against them can still be artificially made for laboratory use.

of studies that were never authorized by the bishop of Turin. Instead, he still carried them out with "accomplices" who were in possession of "leftover" Shroud fragments originating from the 1988 sampling taken for the purpose of carbon-14 dating. In his book titled *The DNA of God?*, Garza-Valdes stated that by immunohistochemical analysis, the bloodstained sample at his disposal reacted to anti-B antibodies and did not react to anti-O antibodies: a result compatible with the B or AB blood groups. It is unclear why he never tested his sample with anti-A antibodies, but this—as we shall see in the next chapter—is in keeping with the thoughtlessness that he demonstrated in other studies as well.

Just as with all claims about the Shroud, the determination of its blood group also led to endless arguments between Shroud experts and skeptics. One initial objection stems from the certain biological contamination of the Shroud over the centuries: how many hands touched its edges, sewed and mended it? How many lips kissed it? How many eyes wept on it? How many insects, mites, and pollen granules settled in it? How many bacteria and fungi grew on it? It is known that ABO antigens are present on many animal and human tissues. Therefore, there could be ABO contaminations capable of causing false positive serological results, leading to an incorrect blood group determination for the blood that is nevertheless present on the Shroud. If this were the case, however, Prof. Baima Bollone would have obtained positive serological results not only for the bloodstained fibers but also for the non-bloodstained "neutral area" control sample Shroud fibers. Of course, one further objection could then be the fact that bacterial contamination would be expected to be greater precisely in bloodstained areas; this objection is far from decisive, but there is no easy refutation.

An additional objection could arise from the tendency of some serological tests, especially the more outdated ones, to yield false positive results. These could have over-detected the A, B, and AB groups compared to the O group. Indeed, this probably happened in a 1977 Israeli study on skeletons: their absorption-inhibition technique overestimated 51 percent of their bony specimens to be AB. Still, multiple test results with consistent findings are now converging from several studies done not only on the Shroud but also — as we shall see — on the Sudarium of Oviedo and the Tunic of Argenteuil. Over the years, the tests have become more sophisticated and have been carried out in different laboratories, with different methods and reagents. Hence, the overall risk of an incorrect blood group determination for these analyzed blood samples is becoming increasingly small.

The Sudarium of Oviedo

For this relic, too, in 1985, Prof. Baima Bollone was the first scientist who determined that its blood was of the AB type. Having seven threads originating from bloodstained areas, twelve more from the edges of the Sudarium, and other material on adhesive tape, he employed a similar technique to the one he used for the Shroud. Once again, Prof. Bollone managed to demonstrate that the Sudarium's blood belonged to the AB group with a high degree of probability.

In 1993, Dr. Villalaín Blanco and Dr. Heras Moreno presented their tests on the Sudarium's bloodstains and control samples at a national paleontology congress in Valencia. They obtained strong B antigen and weak A antigen positivity from the bloodstained fabric. However, they also obtained some B antigen positivity from the non-bloodstained fabric. Because of this, they measured the absolute quantity of anti-B antibodies present in the two samples, and this was statistically higher in the bloodstained areas. Hence, at last, they could conclude that the correct blood group was AB.

Again, later in 1993, Italian hematologist Dr. Carlo Goldoni presented his own results obtained with two methods that both indicated an AB blood type.

The Holy Tunic of Argenteuil

Prof. Gérard Lucotte, the outstanding French geneticist who is certainly the greatest expert of the Tunic of Argenteuil, wrote about two investigations aimed at determining the blood group of the many red blood cells present on the relic in his 2007 book *Sanguis Christi* (*The Blood of Christ*). First, a 1985 study by Dr. Saint-Prix suggested that the Tunic's blood was of the AB type, although its "classical" immuno-hematological technique was not fully explained. Then the feisty geneticist surprised his readers with something groundbreaking by nonchalantly hinting in a footnote (no. 127 on page 149) that in the 2000s, Prof. Lucotte used the versatile laboratory technique of flow cytometry for the purpose of blood group determination. Having access to an abundant number of whole red blood cells, he tagged them — whenever they had the appropriate surface antigens — with monoclonal anti-A and anti-B fluorescent antibodies. He then let these red blood cells flow, one by one, in front of a laser beam. The presence of fluorescent antibodies could be detected by a light detector that precisely quantified the cells. The result was a twofold peak distribution of cell density for both anti-A and anti-B tagged red blood cells: the unequivocal demonstration that the blood was of the AB type. This was not a result due to the presence of multiple types of red blood cells from the blood of multiple people, incorrectly yielding an AB result once mixed together. The reason—as we shall see in the next chapter—is that Prof. Lucotte also obtained a single genetic profile of all the white blood cells[132] present in his sampled material. Hence, he demonstrated that all the red blood cells he analyzed also belonged to one single person.

Why the AB Group?

Let's now turn to the more delicate question we can no longer put off: Why was our Lord's Blood of the AB type? Could there be any particular mysterious meaning hidden behind this blood group on which Dan Brown could write his next best seller? I think this should be immediately and firmly clarified: any blood group would have been acceptable. Every drop of His most precious Blood has an infinite value that completely goes beyond which types of antigens are present on the Lord's red blood cells. However, if, one day, new sophisticated biotechnologies led to discovering that Jesus' Blood was actually type A, it would certainly be a hard blow to the credibility of the eucharistic miracles of Lanciano and Tixtla, as well as that of the Passion relics. Still, Christianity's faith in the saving power of Christ's sacrifice would not be undermined in the slightest.

Having said that, it is nonetheless quite obvious that whether we believe or not, Jesus of Nazareth's blood group *is an interest of ours*, because we are interested in everything about that man. All the more so because we are talking about the Blood shed on the most important event in world history and—for believers—in the personal history of every human being. If, as people, we like

---

[132] Red blood cells do not contain any DNA, as they do not have nuclei. However, white blood cells certainly do, and their DNA is meant to be identical if belonging to the same person.

to get involved, to analyze, and to publish scientific articles on the Tutankhamun mummy's blood group (type A, A2 sub-type), why, then, shouldn't we also take an even greater interest in Jesus'?

Real Blood, of a real blood group, flowed through Jesus' veins. This is because Jesus Christ was a real man, and His blood group was the same as that of millions of other human beings who lived before and after Him: it was not some sort of unique or "alien" blood group.

Let's then dive into a few reflections on Jesus' AB blood type.

A Credible Blood Group

The AB blood group already existed two thousand years ago, and it existed in Palestine. There is no need to draw on evolutionary hypotheses claiming that the A and B groups were already present in a distant past a few million years ago to prove this. Instead, one can be confident that the AB group must have been around for at least two millennia by simply reflecting on the current widespread worldwide distribution of the three ABO alleles. The extent to which these alleles are so closely intertwined in the Eurasian and African populations today could not be explained unless the different ABO groups also coexisted in ancient populations. If one blood group were truly recent and had only "just" appeared, let's say, one thousand years ago, its spread wouldn't have reached large areas of the planet yet, or it would have barely reached them. Thus, the AB group is not a brand-new blood type originating from a new mutation, but rather, it simply appeared — as an unavoidable minority — whenever the A and B alleles first happened to be present in the same region. Furthermore, direct evidence of the presence of the A and B groups in Middle Eastern and Mediterranean regions more than one thousand years ago has already been found in ancient mummies.

A Cardiologist Examines Jesus

It is not redundant to stress that the presence of the AB group in Palestine two thousand years ago is historically credible. In fact, even in recent times, a distinguished English historian and academic, Charles Freeman, plunged into this debate by advancing his claim that the AB group "is the most recent in evolutionary terms" and could not have appeared earlier than the ninth century AD, when the type A Caucasian populations and the type B Asian population of Mongolian ethnicity could "mix" with one another. Against all scientific evidence, Freeman stubbornly emphasized Dr. Peter D'Adamo's[133] controversial theories, but his true objective was that of tarnishing the Shroud's authenticity, as—according to him—the latter was artfully crafted by Church authorities in the fourteenth century to stimulate popular piety. When serving his purpose to demonstrate the medieval origin of the Shroud, the Oxford academic did not even hesitate to accept D'Adamo's pseudoscientific theories.

To conclude, it is worth mentioning a study supporting the credibility of the AB group that could be considered as "definitive" or even "excessive." In 1977, the University of Tel Aviv published an analysis on sixty-eight skeletons of Jewish people buried in Jerusalem in the first century AD and in En Gedi—an oasis and rural community on the Dead Sea—in the fourth century AD. Out of the fifty-five femurs in which the ABO antigens were identified, seventeen individuals were type A, eight were type B, two were type O, and a whopping twenty-eight (51 percent of the total) were AB. Given the unusual blood group distribution, the authors hypothesized the existence of an

---

[133] Dr. Peter D'Adamo is an American naturopath and a proponent of his own blood group diet, which is not based on any scientific evidence.

ancient Mediterranean population featuring a high prevalence of the A and B alleles compared to the O allele. However, more realistically, the study overestimated the prevalence of the AB group. As suggested by a French study ten years later, had the more specific immunofluorescence method been available at the time, many AB individuals would have been reclassified into other blood groups. One curious bit of information: at the end of the Tel Aviv study, all the analyzed bones were respectfully returned to their original tombs rather than left in a museum. Good for the Israeli researchers!

A Rare Blood Group

Out of the four ABO groups, the AB one is undoubtedly the rarest. It does not propagate on its own, as the dominant A and B groups do or as the recessive O group does. This is because an AB person can only pass on either the A or the B allele to his or her offspring, while there is no such thing as an AB allele. Therefore, the existence of the AB group depends on the preexistence of the A and B groups. Hence, AB could never become the most prevalent group. At most, it could be a little more prevalent in populations where A and B are relatively more represented than O. In the real world, these conditions are only found in the Japanese Ainu population and in some other central or western Asian regions, where the AB prevalence reaches, but never exceeds, 20 percent. This is a very high percentage value when considering that the current estimate of the AB prevalence in the world population is no more than 5 percent of all living humans.

Rarity and preciousness are therefore inscribed in the AB group. If there were an aristocratic blood group, in a way, the AB group would be it. AB is well suited to be the most precious and royal blood type in the history of humanity.

A Cardiologist Examines Jesus

The rarity of the AB group, as we shall soon discuss, makes the statistical likelihood of the eucharistic miracles and sacred relics being "fake" exceedingly small. This is because all the miracles with a known blood group and all the relics we discussed are of the AB type, even those originating from vastly different historical times, when the concept of blood groups was yet to be discovered.

The AB "coincidence" makes a crassly improvised fraud highly unlikely: a sacrilegious sacristan or an unworthy priest piercing his finger to stain a host with blood to simulate a miracle would hardly randomly produce an AB specimen. The blood group can also be used as a discriminating factor when assessing holy images presumed to have wept tears or exuded blood. Antibody tests easily and rapidly identify blood groups from blood or even tear specimens. They are simple and relatively inexpensive, and they provide immediate answers, unlike DNA profiling. The subject of weeping images and statues is fortunately outside the scope of my discussion: it is a field where the enemy sows confusion and uncertainty. What should one think of a statue of the Virgin Mary that first weeps type B blood and then type O, while the group of the transparent tears and sweat from the same image is AB? Commenting on that case, a theologian suggested that "both Jesus and Mary could be of all of their children's blood types." I'm certainly not convinced.

Unfortunately, the specificity of the AB group could also be used the other way around: should a modern-day forger attempt crafting a fake eucharistic miracle, he or she would need to use AB blood. Alternatively, the forger should at least produce some kind of medical certificate proving the same point. That way his or her sham blood would be of the same "blood type found on the Holy Shroud and in the miracle of Lanciano." I am not exaggerating: this is what was being talked about in regard to a bloody host produced in Ostina (Florence) in May 2003. That was not a Church-recognized event, and discussing it would do nothing other than shore up the revelations of a heretical windbag psychic who does not deserve any further publicity.

A Complete Blood Group

Whether or not the AB group was the last to appear in the history of humanity, it is nonetheless the most complete one, as it encompasses all the others. Remarkably, the AB group does not "neglect" the O group, as the O antigen is *also* present in AB individuals. This is because the O antigen is actually a short sugar chain molecule to which only one extra sugar element needs to be added to form either the A or the B antigen. If we wanted to read more into the AB group with some abstract thinking, we could think of it as a metaphor of the New Man, of "the fulness of him who fills all in all" (Eph. 1:23). Similarly, it could be a metaphor of the New Adam, of the starting point and the destination, as "all things were created through him and for him" (Col. 1:16). In the second century, St. Irenaeus stated: "Christ has recapitulated in himself all the blood shed by all the righteous and by the prophets who existed from the beginnings" (*Adversus haereses* V, 14.1; cf. V, 14.2). In this theological perspective, it is certainly quite appropriate that Jesus' blood is of the AB type.

This echoes the doctrine of Blessed John Duns Scotus, a Scottish Franciscan theologian of the thirteenth century, who advanced the hypothesis that Jesus, the second Person of the Holy Trinity, would have made Himself incarnate even if Adam had not sinned to begin with. If that had been the case, the purpose of Jesus' Incarnation would have been to "recapitulate" in Himself the whole of creation. However, as a consequence of Original Sin, Christ's recapitulation also became redemptive for all people.

Distinct Paternal and Maternal Origins

The AB group is the only one made up of two mutually exclusive maternal and paternal counterparts. If the A allele is inherited from the father, then the B one must be inherited from the mother, and vice versa, with no other options allowed. For all other blood groups, it isn't possible to clearly tell apart the maternal and paternal contributions: the presence of a recessive O allele is always possible in group A or B parents and thus also in their offspring. Because of this, for instance, it wouldn't be possible to know which parent passed on which allele to an AO genotype son whose parents were both AO. Similarly, a group O son must have inherited two O alleles, although their maternal or paternal origins are indistinguishable.

Through this "biological watermark" we can then see the image of a double and distinct paternal and maternal inheritance that belonged to the man who was born of a woman by the work of the Holy Spirit. Jesus of Nazareth's blood group—whose paternal and maternal alleles were different—represents, in a certain way, the duality of his human and divine nature within the unity of His Person. In strictly biological terms, instead, the AB group speaks about our Savior's human nature, reminding us that He must have had a Father besides his Most Holy Mother.

What we are facing here is the heavenly mystery of the Incarnation: an unfathomable one from a scientific perspective. Jesus was not conceived by parthenogenesis—that is, He was not a clone of His Mother—but instead, His Incarnation also required a male gamete, one that was not produced by any man.

Still, despite its *divine origin*, this gamete had to be a completely normal and *human* one to ensure our Savior could be a true man indeed. Otherwise, apart from all theological considerations, if Jesus had been a clone of His Mother, He would have been female. Since birth, the Baby Jesus was indistinguishable from any one of the billions of children who were born before and after Him, all of them — except for Adam and Eve — sons and daughters of their mothers and fathers. Therefore, the AB group invites us to meditate on the mystery of Christ, true God and true man, as formulated in the dogma of the Council of Chalcedon.

A Universal Receiver Blood Type

From the perspective of transfusion compatibility, Jesus' Blood is not what we would expect. Generosity and the turning of itself into a gift unconditionally offered to all are features of the O group: the "universal donor," which is all the more universal if also Rh negative. The AB group is instead the "universal receiver" that can only "selfishly" donate itself to other AB group individuals.

Let's then broaden this blood transfusion metaphor: the Blood of Christ freed us from sin (Rev. 1:5) and death. Moreover, in the book of Revelation, those in the crowd of the saved wear white garments washed in the Blood of the Lamb (7:14). It could be said that only the "universal receiver" AB blood type could then act as a "universal solvent" in which any kind of blood of any and every human being could be mixed to be purified. The AB blood welcomes our own blood, without reacting against it. That way *our* blood dissolved in *His* can be elevated to His infinite preciousness. In the blood type that welcomes all others, we can also find a reference to the precious blood of the martyrs contributing to the completion of the sacrifice of the Passion that took place on Mount Golgotha. More generally, we can meditate on the physical suffering of every Christian that, if freely accepted and offered, can mysteriously complete the redemptive suffering of Christ (Col. 1:24).

A Statistical Bomb

It is now time to focus on the statistical finding of the not-so-coincidental presence of AB blood in the specimens we discussed. I shall remind the reader that no blood group determination tests were performed on the eucharistic miracles of Buenos Aires, Sokółka, and Legnica. In Buenos Aires, this was due to the paucity of sampled material and the greater priority given to DNA analysis. In Poland, instead, this was because the other tests that had already been performed were considered sufficient to prove the miraculous nature of the events. However, wherever the blood group was identified in Lanciano, in Tixtla, and on the three main Passion cloths, the same blood group was found—without exception.

There were five blood samples from different materials, from vastly different historical times, and from distant places. Four of them were handed down to us from historical times when blood groups were not even known to exist. Hence, forgers could not have possibly picked the appropriate blood types on purpose every single time. Still, all five samples, according to tests that were often repeated multiple times, with different techniques and in different laboratories, were of the AB type.

Could this be random chance? Let's apply a few simple statistical formulas.

I shall recall that 5 percent—one out of twenty—is today's mean probability of belonging to the AB group for any individual of any Caucasian ethnicity. There is no reason to believe that the same baseline probability would have been much different twenty centuries ago. If the random event of "belonging to the AB group" were to occur on two separate occasions, it would be trivial statistics to know that the overall probability of that would be calculated by multiplying the two probabilities together. That is 1/20 x 1/20, which equals 1 in 400, and so forth for any further events.

The probability of three AB events would then be 1/20 x 1/20 x 1/20, which is 1 in 8,000: this would be the chance that three medieval forgers independently manufactured three false relics such as the Shroud, the Sudarium, and the Tunic and stained them all with AB human blood. Not only that but three different forgers would have had to do this three times a few centuries apart and also a few thousand kilometers from each other. Then couple that with randomly choosing three living and consenting volunteers who just *all* randomly happened to be of the AB type. We should admit that 1 in 8,000 probabilities is not exactly a trivial coincidence but rather an occurrence that we perceive as very distant and unlikely. To put it in perspective, it is estimated that the chance of dying in a car accident over the course of the following twelve months in the United States is 1 in 7,700, which is very similar. Despite that chance, we all keep driving our cars without serious concerns about dying, as we perceive this possibility as very remote and unlikely, even though our friendly insurance agents keep reminding us about that risk as one that is directly related to our choice to drive. If we were certain about the randomness of the AB blood on those three forged relics, then we should be equally certain about our inevitable and upcoming death on the road within a year! Our logic would persuade us to give up promptly any travels except for walking, flying on airplanes, or catching trains.

Let's make a funnier and less morbid example: in the Italian Lotto game, the chance of scoring three numbers in a row, by only betting on three numbers once and on a single Lotto wheel, is estimated to be 1 in 11,748. This is, frankly, so rare that "hitting the jackpot" would be the stroke of luck of a lifetime, even though it would only be one and a half times less common than the chance of the three relics randomly bearing the same AB blood group. If we thought that was common, then it would be time to swing by the betting shop where lots of cash would indeed be waiting for us.

If we also considered the Lanciano relic to be fake, as crafted in the murky early Middle Ages, we should then multiply by twenty times that previous "thin air" probability: we would end up with 1 chance in 160,000. This wouldn't exactly be a common event: the probability of dying from a lightning strike over an entire lifetime—according to the same American figures—is estimated to be 1 in 79,746. That means it would be twice as easy to die by lightning strike than to admit that the independent recurrence of the AB group in our four medieval specimens is due to chance. Perhaps it would be prudent for our secularist and rationalist friends to install some lightning rods on their home rooftops.

By factoring in the 2006 Tixtla event, the probability of a random fivefold AB group coincidence reaches numbers we truly cannot even imagine: 1 in 3,200,000. Above a certain cognitive threshold, our perception of thousands, millions, and billions turns into some ocean-sized numerical blur floating over our heads, and we are unable to argue with it any further.

n number of consecutive events	Percentage probability	p probability of the event (total = 1)	One chance in ...
1	5	0.05	20
2	0.25	0.0025	400
3	0.0125	0.000125	8,000
4	0.000625	0.00000625	160,000
5	0.00003125	0.0000003125	3,200,000

If the DNA, as we shall see in the next chapter, is unable to yield such crushing numerical evidence — perhaps by divine will coupled with human prudence and modesty — we must, however, admit that the AB group makes for a rather cumbersome stumbling block for those attempting to dismantle the authenticity of the Passion cloths and these eucharistic events. This is why no one dares to face this statistical argument about the Shroud, the Sudarium, and the Tunic. Instead, those arguing against them too often challenge the identification of the AB group itself with rather shallow statements such as "All ancient fabrics are AB," "The AB group did not exist in Palestine two thousand years ago," and so forth. Lastly, the investigations on the eucharistic miracles are instead simply ignored. The reputation of the laboratories and researchers who analyzed them is undermined without giving the time of day to even consider their results.

On the other hand, what I still cannot understand is the excessively prudent and submissive attitude of religious authorities:

the finding of the blood group concordance is a real "statistical bomb" that the Catholic Church could detonate with greater confidence in its apologetic battle. Who knows if the reader, at this point in time, is experiencing some sort of cognitive dissonance: If the authenticity of these fabrics and tissues is proven with a confidence of 99.99996875 percent due to the blood group concordance, why, then, doesn't anyone talk about them?

These specimens were actually analyzed in the 1970s and 1980s, which was some time ago. We are now the second generation in the entire history of Christianity that is coming to terms with these powerful and unprecedented findings. Isn't it time to set aside our fathers' shyness?

Bibliography

Hosoi, Eiji. 2008. "Biological and Clinical Aspects of ABO Blood Group System." *Journal of Medical Investigation* 55 (3–4): 174–182.

Yamamoto, Fumi-ichiro, Henrik Clausen, Thayer White, John Marken, and Sen-itiroh Hakomori. 1990. "Molecular Genetic Basis of the Histo-Blood Group ABO System." *Nature* 345: 229–233.

The fundamental discovery of the differences in the genetic sequences of chromosome no. 9, underpinning the three different A, B, and O alleles.

Segurel, Laure, Emma Thompson, Timothée Flutre, et al. 2012. "The ABO Blood Group Is a Trans-species Polymorphism in Primates." *Proceedings of the National Academy of Sciences of the United States of America* 109 (45): 18493–18498.

Garratty, G. 2005. "Relationship of Blood Groups to Disease: Do Blood Group Antigens Have a Biological Role?" *Revista médica del Instituto Mexicano del Seguro Social* 43 (1): 113–121.

Mourant, A. E. 1954. *The Distribution of the Human Blood Groups.* Oxford: Blackwells.

You will find details in "Blood Groups and Human Groups: Collecting and Calibrating Genetic Data after World War II" by Jenny Bangham. The first large study of great historical importance on the distribution of human blood groups in the native populations of the whole world.

D'Adamo, Peter. 2019. "Blood Groups and the History of Peoples." Dadamo.com. Website. Accessed July 12, 2021. http://www.dadamo.com/txt/index.pl?1010.

Klys, M., B. Opolska-Bogusz, and B. Prochnicka. 1999. "A Serological and Histological Study of the Egyptian Mummy 'Iset Iri Hets' from the Ptolemaic Period III–I B.C." *Forensic Science International* 99 (3): 229–233.

Kitano, Takashi, Antoine Blancher, and Naruya Saitou. 2012. "The Functional A Allele Was Resurrected via Recombination in the Human ABO Blood Group Gene." *Molecular Biology and Evolution* 29 (7): 1791–1796.

Genetic study reinforcing the existence of only one ancestral A allele for the first human species from which the B and O were generated through mutations. It claims that the original A group was initially lost and then reappeared about three hundred years ago, thanks to the recombination of the B and O groups.

Allison, M., A. Hossaini, N. Castro, et al. 1976. "ABO Blood Groups in Peruvian Mummies I: An Evaluation of Techniques." *American Journal of Physical Anthropology* 44 (1): 55–61.

Proof of the existence of groups A, B, and AB in Peru in the pre-Columbian age with AI, AE, and MA serological techniques.

Allison, M., A. Hossaini, J. Munizaga, and R. Fung. 1978. "ABO Blood Groups in Chilean and Peruvian Mummies II: Results of Agglutination-Inhibition Technique." *American Journal of Physical Anthropology* 49 (1) 139–142.

The study shows that it is possible to find all ABO groups in the Peruvian mummies between 3000 BC and AD 1400 by using the AI method. Vice versa, in the Chilean mummies they found either A or O blood, but neither B nor AB.

Sharma, Shikha. 2010. "ABO Blood Grouping: Methods and Procedures." Biotech Articles. Accessed July 12, 2021. https://www.biotecharticles.com/Others-Article/ABO-Blood-Grouping-Methods-and-Procedures-473.html.

Hummel, Susanne, Diane Schmidt, Melanie Kahle, and Bernd Herrmann. 2002. "ABO Blood Group Genotyping of Ancient DNA by PCR-RFLP." *International Journal of Legal Medicine* 116 (6): 327–333.

Brilliant research study by Prof. Hummel's group. In 2002, they demonstrated that the blood types of human remains from the Bronze Age could be identified by directly sequencing parts of chromosome 9.

Linoli, Odoardo. 1992. *Ricerche istologiche, immunologiche e biochimiche sulla carne e sul sangue del miracolo eucaristico di Lanciano (VIII secolo)*. 1st ed. Italy: Edizioni S.M.E.L.

Research from 1971 integrated with data from 1981. The book includes the investigations on the determination of the blood type of the Flesh and Blood of Lanciano.

Castañón Gómez, Ricardo. 2014. *Crónica de un milagro eucarístico: Esplendor en Tixtla Chilpancingo, Mexico*. Grupo Internacional para la Paz.

Interesting book on the Tixtla events, including the demonstration of the blood group of the same relic.

Kearse, Kelly. 2012. "Blood on the Shroud of Turin: An Immunological Review." Shroud.com. Accessed July 12, 2021. https://www.shroud.com/pdfs/kearse.pdf.

Garza-Valdes, Leoncio. 1998. *The DNA of God?* New York: Bantam Doubleday Dell.

Lucotte, Gérard, and Philippe Bornet. 2007. *Sanguis Christi: Le sang du Christ. Une enquête sur la tunique d'Argenteuil.* Guy Trédaniel Éditeur.

Reference book on the Tunic of Argenteuil. Two types of tests are mentioned in regard to the blood group determination.

Crainic, K., M. Durigon, and R. Oriol. 1989. "ABO Tissue Antigens of Egyptian Mummies." *Forensic Science International* 43 (2): 113–124.

French study on fourteen mummies simultaneously comparing three different blood-grouping methods (AE, AM, and IHF) as well as immunofluorescence.

Micle, S., E. Kobilyansky, M. Nathan, et al. 1977. "ABO-Typing of Ancient Skeletons from Israel." *American Journal of Physical Anthropology* 47: 89–91.

12

The DNA

A Brief School Refresher

Every human cell contains all its genetic material, which is DNA, in its nucleus.[134] The DNA of the human species is divided into twenty-three pairs of chromosomes. It is an extremely long double-stranded helix filament made up of complementary chains of paired nucleotide building blocks. Every nucleotide is made up of the same sugar molecule, a phosphate group, and one of four possible bases, each containing nitrogen: adenine, thymine, guanine, and cytosine. These are abbreviated with their initials—A, T, G, and C—for the sake of simplicity. The sequence of these bases strictly defines the order in which amino acids must be assembled to synthesize each specific cell protein. This happens by means of a coded language, the genetic code, associating one nucleotide triplet to a single amino acid type. Each triplet is made up of three consecutive nitrogenous bases on the DNA filament. The code is redundant, meaning that there are multiple different triplets coding for the same amino

---

[134] Red blood cells lose their nuclei during their process of differentiation from bone marrow stem cells. Hence, mature red blood cells are an exception to this rule.

acid. Indeed, there are sixty-four possible triplet combinations: AAA, AAC, and so forth, all the way to TTT. Each one can only code for one of the twenty amino acids that exist in nature. The only exceptions are a limited number of noncoding triplets that act as "start" and "stop" transcription signals. The code is unambiguous and universal. It is the same one for all human, animal, plant, or bacterial cells living on Earth.

A gene is every portion of the DNA nucleotide filament that encodes the full amino acid sequence of an entire protein. There are about twenty- to twenty-two thousand genes in the human DNA: a number that is very similar to the number of genes in other species. An initial finding that researchers found rather disconcerting was that out of the three billion nucleotide pairs in the haploid human genome,[135] only 1.5 percent are actually part of gene sequences. The rest is labeled *junk DNA*, as its meaning and purpose is yet to be understood. To this day, vast stretches of human DNA do not appear to have any known roles and are made up of incredibly long and barren series of repeated sequences. However, forensic medicine relies on this repetitive DNA to identify people.

DNA is loaded with lots of mythological pseudoscience in the fantasies of common modern-day people. This pseudoscience portrays DNA as the molecule that contains the entire *essence* of each living being, as if it were the new seat of the soul: the soul

---

[135] *Genome* simply means the whole diploid human DNA, while *haploid* means one-half of the entire genome: more precisely, either the one-half inherited from the mother, or the other half inherited from the father. This is because all cells in the human body—except for haploid reproductive *gamete* cells—contain two sets of chromosomes and thus two sets of alleles—or gene variants—for each necessary gene.

of each person and the soul of a people. We say "It's in my DNA" when talking about anything we believe to be deep-seated and spontaneous about our behavior. "It's in the DNA of Italians" to be saints, poets, navigators, or — more trivially — to avoid overcooking their pasta.

DNA in Forensic Medicine

One very important ramification of our knowledge about the structure and function of DNA — coupled with the widespread availability of PCR technology and gel electrophoresis — is being able to identify every single human being living in the world with enormous and exclusive accuracy. This can be done with trace quantities of biological samples. The polymerase chain reaction (PCR) easily amplifies specific DNA segments by producing millions to billions of copies of them. PCR can be performed whenever these two conditions are in place:

1. Trace amounts of a given DNA sequence are present in a sample to be analyzed.
2. The nucleotide sequences at the beginning and the end of the searched DNA segment are known.

Hence, PCR has two purposes:

1. Determining whether certain specific DNA sequences are present in an unknown sample
2. Producing a very high number of copies of a sought-after DNA sequence that can then be used to run many other molecular tests (this eliminates any concerns about running out of available sample)

On the other hand, gel DNA electrophoresis — similar to protein electrophoresis — separates DNA fragments within a sample according to their molecular weight. This is directly proportional to the number of nucleotides they are made up of.

These fundamental DNA technologies lay out the foundations of STR analysis.

What are STRs? Just a bit more patience with these technical terms. We have just seen that, surprisingly, most human DNA is not made up of precious genes gifting us with blue eyes or boosting our IQs. Instead, it is largely made up of embarrassing and boring long stretches of short two- to five-nucleotide-long sequences that may be repeated, for instance, from five to fifty times in a row. These sequences are called Short Tandem Repeats, or STRs. For example, D7S820 STR is found at a certain location on chromosome 7, and it is a GATA (guanine-adenine-thymine-adenine) sequence that is repeated five to sixteen times, as in GATAGATAGATAGATAGATA and so on. It is clear that this is not a sequence that is part of a coding gene, and it would make no difference at all if it were repeated six, nine, or fourteen times in a particular person. This is a general rule: the DNA mutations and variations that forensic medicine is interested in are always "useless" from a transcriptional point of view. This is because they are neutral and have no impact on the health and fitness of individuals. They can thus be maintained in later generations, as they confer no evolutionary advantages or disadvantages.

Out of that great pool of DNA variability, forensic medicine laboratories across the world agreed to focus on about ten STRs, which they shared and catalogued toward the end of the 1990s.

Initially, Interpol was quite content with seven STRs per identity profile. Scotland Yard instead used to request ten STRs plus amelogenin. Later on, the FBI's Combined DNA Index System (also known as CODIS) prevailed as the international DNA profiling standard: it included thirteen STRs and amelogenin. Amelogenin is not an STR but rather a real gene coding for the amelogenin protein, which is involved in tooth enamel production. Like any other gene in a diploid genome, it is located as a pair of alleles on both the X and Y sex chromosomes. Its Y-chromosome allele version is 112 nucleotides long, whereas its other X-chromosome allele version is known to have undergone a 6-nucleotide deletion and thus it is only 106 bases long. This difference in length allows for the sex identification of an individual by means of DNA electrophoresis: one thick band weighing 106 bases if female or two thinner bands weighing 106 and 112 bases if male.

In the United States, millions of citizens who had contact with the criminal justice system have had their CODIS profiles added to an enormous federal database.

The CODIS System

STR name	Repeated sequence	Chromosome number	Number of tandem repeats
CSF1PO	AGAT	5	5–16
FGA	Begins with TTTC	4	12.2–51.2
TH01	AATG	11	3–14
TPOX	AATG	2	4–16
VWA	TCTA/ TCTG	12	10–25
D3S1358	TCTA/ TCTG	3	8–20

A Cardiologist Examines Jesus

STR name	Repeated sequence	Chromosome number	Number of tandem repeats
D5S818	AGAT	5	6–18
D7S820	GATA	7	5–16
D8S1179	TCTA/ TCTG	8	7–20
D13S317	TATC	13	5–17
D16S539	GATA	16	4–16
D18S51	AGAA	18	7–39.2
D21S11	Begins with TCTA	21	12–41.2

All these acronyms and numbers may look complicated, but the process of identifying a person using the CODIS system or any other similar ones is surprisingly easy to understand. For every type of STR sequence that is known to exist in humans, every person will have two paired STR alleles. One allele will be located on a paternal chromosome and the other on the respective maternal one. These alleles differ from one another only in terms of STR copy numbers. Hence, every person has two repeat numbers for each STR. That is all!

For instance, let's take the CSF1PO STR on chromosome 5: Mr. Redman happens to have 9 and 10 repeats, Mrs. White 8 and 15, Mr. Black 9 and 12, and so on. Undoubtedly, if only one

STR at a time were used, there would be huge overlap with many identical matches between people, especially relatives. Because of this, to avoid error, these identification systems have been expanded from seven to ten, then thirteen and now twenty STRs at the same time.[136] Increasing the number of STRs considered results in a skyrocketing increase in test power. This makes it possible to identify a particular person essentially without chance of error. One person could be identified out of ten thousand people, excluding blood relatives, with only four STRs: an impressive result, but still too imprecise to charge someone in court. However, with thirteen STRs taken altogether, the match probability is boosted high enough to represent reasonable certainty.

Bob Blackett, an American forensic laboratory scientist, calculated that only one man in 7.7 x 10 to the power of 15 would have a standard CODIS profile identical to his own. He calculated that by knowing the relative frequencies of his own thirteen STR allele pairs in the Caucasian population. It would take one million Earth-sized planets to find another man with a CODIS profile like that of Bob Blackett! Of course, this is assuming that each of those planets were inhabited by seven billion people, the current world population. We can then appreciate that a DNA test based on at least ten STRs would essentially represent an irrefutable piece of evidence in a court of law. For these very good reasons, STR profiling is also known as "DNA fingerprinting."

Mitochondrial DNA

So far, we have discussed the so-called *nuclear* DNA, the one contained in the cell nucleus and making up the bulk of the human

---

[136] Since January 1, 2017, the FBI announced the introduction of seven more STRs in the United States CODIS database.

genome. However, there is a very small amount of DNA that is scientifically quite important: mitochondrial DNA (mtDNA), contained in mitochondria. Mitochondria are small organelles within cells that produce the energy required for all vital cellular processes, very much like power stations. Interestingly, mitochondria generally store two to ten copies of their own DNA. MtDNA is used to synthesize some, but not all, components of a mitochondrion. In mtDNA, the DNA double helix is not organized into a chromosome, but rather, it forms a closed ring filament, like the DNA of the more "ancient" bacteria. MtDNA is made up of 16,569 nucleotide pairs, a minuscule number compared to the three billion nucleotide pairs of nuclear DNA. The nucleotide sequence of mtDNA and all its variants are very well known, along with the thirty-seven coding genes it contains. The simple and "exposed" structure of mtDNA makes it ten to twenty times more susceptible to single nucleotide mutations compared to the double helix construction of nuclear DNA. Still, in absolute terms, the entire mtDNA sequence is rather short, and there are relatively few existing mutations potentially affecting it.

What makes mtDNA unique, however, is its maternal inheritance: it can only be inherited from the mother, without any paternal contribution. This is because mtDNA is only found in the maternal gamete, and unlike what happens in the transmission of the nuclear genome, it does not undergo any recombination and remixing with its paternal equivalent. Instead, it is identically passed on from the mother to all her children, unchanged through generations. This feature is very useful in the study of the history of mankind. Like an incredible "time machine," it allows researchers to chase the origin of mankind and develop theories on how people migrated across the continents in the distant past. MtDNA is a versatile tool to shed light on the kinship relationships that are today binding different peoples and ethnicities. Indeed, an actual *matrilineal* human family tree can be reconstructed in hindsight, based on patterns of haplotype transmission. Haplotypes are nothing but patterns of random and inconsequential DNA mutations that are passed on like a signature, from mother to children, at least in terms of mtDNA.

In particular, there are three specific mtDNA regions — also known as hypervariable (HVR) regions — where these haplotypes are concentrated: HVR1 (from nucleotide 16024 to nucleotide 16383), HVR2 (from nucleotide 57 to nucleotide 372) and HVR3 (from nucleotide 438 to nucleotide 574). On average, there are seven to fifteen mutations in the mtDNA of any modern-day person. They have been disseminated by our mothers over the course of millennia. From the study of these point mutations, any one of us could be classified into a particular haplogroup: for example, the H, J, K, N1, T, U4, U5, V, X, and W haplogroups are most prevalent in Europe. A sample of 2,799 Italians turned out to be 40.2 percent H, 8.2 percent T2, and 8.1 percent J. Over the years, studies on mtDNA variants have been further refined: other sequences have been included that allow the identification of much more precise haplotype subgroups. The broad H haplogroup, for instance, was then differentiated into its H2a, H2a2a, or even H2a2a1 subgroups, and so on.

From a forensic point of view, unlike the CODIS system, mtDNA does not allow the identification of a single human being: indeed, unless new mutations were to arise, brothers, cousins, and all descendants of the same great-great-grandmother would share the same mtDNA. Thus, the investigative value of mtDNA is not about being able to definitively incriminate a suspect, but rather, it is about ruling out anyone whose mtDNA is different. It can also provide a reasonable estimate of the suspect's ethnicity.

Finally, it is important to appreciate that mtDNA is more resistant to degradation compared to nuclear DNA. Many copies are also present within the same cell—even up to ten thousand. These features make the study of mtDNA particularly useful to a forensic doctor working on trace amounts of biological specimens that are ancient or undergoing decay.

The DNA of the Y Male Chromosome

The features of Y-chromosome nuclear DNA—like those of mtDNA—are also very unique and elicit great scientific and medical interest because of their many ripple effects on paleo-anthropology and forensic medicine. As we all know, in the human species there are twenty-two pairs of non-sex chromosomes called autosomes, numbered 1–22, and one pair of X and Y sex chromosomes. An individual is either female if carrying the XX pair or male if carrying the XY pair. Therefore, it is the presence of either X or Y in the fertilizing sperm that determines the zygote's sex. Unlike the other twenty-two autosomal pairs, the X and Y chromosomes are structurally differently and carry different genes. Because of this, no major crossover recombination events can really take place in an XY male, apart from genes located on the extremities of the chromosome "arms."[137] As a

---

[137] During one of the stages of *meiosis*—the production of gamete cells with only one-half of the entire genome—chromosome pairs often exchange chromosome tips in a process called *crossing-over*. The purpose of this exchange is to increase genetic variability between individuals. The Y chromosome, however, can only engage with this process to a very limited extent, due to its shape that is "lacking an extremity." Therefore, its genes

consequence of this, the Y chromosome, especially in its mostly nonrecombinant middle portion, behaves as a "mirror image" of mtDNA: it is nearly exclusively passed on from father to son without changes from maternal genetic interference.

Thus, the Y chromosome offers many research advantages compared to mtDNA. Indeed, after more in-depth studies, like a sort of genetic "black box," it turned out to be a more powerful and precise tool to shed light on the origin of the human species. Even being one of the smallest chromosomes, Y is still made up of more than 59 million nucleotides compared to only 16,569 bases in each copy of mtDNA. This massively increased the number of available DNA variants that could be studied to trace different populations' haplogroups and sub-haplogroups with greater accuracy. Hence, in the future, we could zoom further into new point mutations or new Y chromosome–specific STRs. Currently, the most common Y haplogroup in Europe is R1b, along with R1a and other I sub-haplogroups. In Italy, in a pool of 6,145 men, the most common haplogroup is R1b (39 percent), followed by J2 (15.5 percent), and E1b1b (13.5 percent). It is worth noting the anomalously high prevalence of I2a1 on the island of Sardinia (37.5 percent) in stark contrast to its national prevalence of 3 percent in the rest of the country.

From a forensic perspective, the advantage of studying the Y chromosome whenever possible is that of accessing several precious bits of information. To begin with, the Y chromosome confirms the male sex, and if sufficient haplotypes are available, it can provide an idea about the ethnicity of a suspect. Moreover, as I was previously hinting at, the study of Y haplogroups

---

are quite unlikely to be exchanged with the X counterpart, especially those located closer to its middle.

is gaining momentum due to the discovery of more and more sub-variants: throughout an entire chromosome, there is a truly countless number of possible mutations that will allow further expansions of databases and future knowledge. This will lead to an increasingly more precise definition of the DNA profiles of human males, almost to the point of being able to identify one single man out of all others, possibly with no need to use the CODIS system.

Cloning Fantasies

It may be surprising, but there is a real and flourishing pseudo-scientific subgenre dedicated to the hypothetical possibility of cloning Jesus Christ. Many authors have unleashed their imagination, perhaps inspired by the preliminary results obtained from the analyses of the extremely short DNA fragments found in the Shroud's blood in the 1990s. Should you attempt an online search by entering both *clone* and *Jesus* as keywords, the Amazon virtual bookshop would flood you with a large number of novels, narratives, and trilogies. Their typical plot involves some evil scientists getting their hands on a blood sample, usually from either the Shroud of Turin or the tip of the Holy Lance. They then manage to extract Jesus' full genome and use it to clone a new human being. Usually this "new Jesus" is then brought into the world thirty years later, when society is on the brink of collapse, a nuclear war is about to start, poverty and disease are rampant, and an environmental catastrophe is impending. Will this new man with unusual powers manage to salvage the world once again? Should we even doubt this?

Let's briefly touch on cloning. In short, this is the development of a new living being whose DNA is identical to that of an adult donor, as if the clone were an identical homozygous twin. The process involves transferring the nucleus of an adult donor cell into an egg of the same species whose own nucleus has been removed. If this cell then turns into an embryo that manages to implant itself into a uterus, and if it still continues to develop and grow and reaches birth, then a clone has been made. Everyone will have heard about Dolly the sheep, which, in 1996, became the first cloned mammal to be born by these means. However, it is probably not clear to everyone that these are experimental techniques with an extremely high failure rate: Dolly was "made" after 277 attempts.

Moreover, cloned animals are known to be frailer and live shorter lives because they are born with DNA that has already undergone aging; this DNA is "closer to the expiration date" because it is already affected by environmental mutations and physiological telomere shortening.[138] There are many other unknown reasons for the shorter life spans of clones that are likely related to issues with the physiology of embryonic development. Artificial cloning inevitably simplifies or eliminates delicate protective and crucial control mechanisms that would otherwise be present in nature. It is like installing the engine of a Ferrari in a tiny Fiat 500: the economy car will run faster, but never as fast as the original Ferrari and certainly without the same safety standards. Then there are other popular cloning "myths" that ought to be busted: first of all, an animal — or, God forbid, a human being — that was produced through cloning would still be *another* being. A clone would never simply be a "body cast"

[138] Telomeres are repetitive nucleotide sequences located at the ends of chromosomes. They shorten with every round of replication involved in cell reproduction. It is known that telomere shortening is associated with aging, mortality, and aging-related diseases.

into which the soul, conscience, and intelligence of the cloned individual would migrate. No creature could just keep on living for eternity by jumping from clone to clone.

A clone is effectively the equivalent of an identical twin, although gifted with its own life and absolutely distinct from its donor, just as a son is distinct from his parents. The bottom line is that should this elusive Jesus clone even be born—assuming he would even make it to thirty in good health—he would not be different from any other member of the *Homo sapiens* species at all: he could not walk on water. Indeed, we could not even assume that his face would actually look like that of the Savior: "Copy Cat," the first domesticated cat cloned, after eighty attempts, in 2001 in Texas, did not actually turn out to look like Rainbow, the cat she was a clone of. Neither her fur color nor her character was similar. A California-based biotechnology company, Genetic Savings & Clone, Inc., had sponsored the project hoping to launch a pet cloning business charging $50,000 as the modest price for each cloned puppy or kitten. Unsurprisingly, it had to close down in 2006 due to lack of requests.

Ron Wyatt's Expeditions

On the occasion of the third Italian edition and the first English edition of my book, I thought it would be worthwhile adding a section on the mysterious investigations carried out by Ronald Eldon Wyatt, an amateur Seventh-day Adventist archaeologist. In the last few years, many Italian readers have been asking me for clarification in regard to this dubious though fascinating researcher and his theories. I imagine that my Anglophone readers would probably have an even higher level of curiosity about him.

I cannot help feeling sympathy for this Tennessee nurse who truly made the "Indiana Jones" legend come true, more than any other explorer or archaeologist. In his self-financed travels, he managed to discover all that was yet to be discovered, without any connection to the world of mainstream archeology: the site of Noah's Ark, the exact place where the Jewish people crossed the Red Sea, the ruins of Sodom and Gomorrah, and the true Mount Sinai. Ron Wyatt's discoveries have been marked by signs and heavenly visions along his way. They encouraged him to persevere in his excavations in moments of hardship.

However, the climax of Wyatt's career as an archeologist was in the early 1980s: he claimed to have found the true place where Jesus was crucified and, in the ground six meters beneath it, a cave containing the furnishings of Solomon's Temple. These, along with the Ark of the Covenant, would have been stored in the cave by the prophet Jeremiah in an attempt to salvage them from the destruction about to be wrought by Nebuchadnezzar. Ron Wyatt found a crack in the rock, caused by the earthquake that took place at the time of the Crucifixion, as described by the Gospels. The crack turned out to connect the hole dug in the ground, where the Cross was planted, with the underlying cave, where the Ark of the Covenant was stored. The Savior's Blood would have dripped down through this passage and into the Mercy Seat, the top of the Ark. Hence, Ron courageously collected a few fragments of blood crusted on the rock and sent them off for testing. Dear reader, please don't bother requesting Wyatt's photographic evidence of the Ark of the Covenant and the Tablets of the Law stored inside it. All you will get are some miraculously blurred images. But fear not: with a little patience, all these discoveries will be clearly and unequivocally shown to us—when the world is ready.

There are online video and audio recordings of a few conferences where Ron Wyatt spoke about the blood he collected. In a moved and quivering voice, he explained how the blood was still alive after two thousand years: in an Israeli laboratory, it had regained its original look and physiological functions after simple rehydration. The baffled Israeli researchers also documented the presence of only twenty-four human chromosomes in the blood sample, presumably by performing a karyotype analysis on the white blood cells: a haploid genome, made up of twenty-three chromosomes — including an X sex chromosome, as one would expect to find in a female egg gamete — plus a single paternal Y chromosome. This story about the twenty-four chromosomes — twenty-two autosomes, plus X and Y sex chromosomes — outlived Ron Wyatt, who died in 1999, and it became popularly known and "accredited" as a "believable" demonstration of the Virgin Birth of Christ: a miraculous conception that would have merely entailed a divine intervention to introduce the Y chromosome required to justify the Savior's male sex.

Once again, dear reader, please don't expect to receive any written or filmed evidence of these sensational laboratory tests: if authoritative, they would and should have been published in a first-class scientific journal. Ron Wyatt must be taken the way he looks, wearing a plaid shirt under a vest with plenty of pockets as the most authentic impersonation of Indiana Jones.

I do hate always being an annoying buzzkill, but I must remind the reader that no human being belonging to the *Homo sapiens* species has ever lived or will ever manage to live with only half of his or her human genome. Yes, indeed it is true that in the last few years scientists created some haploid human embryonal stem cell lines — each containing twenty-three chromosomes, twenty-two autosomes, plus an X chromosome — which could survive and differentiate into specialized body tissue cells. However, it is hardly imaginable that a full human embryo could develop from a haploid stem cell. A diploid genome, made of forty-six chromosomes, is indispensable for the life of a normal human being. The main issue preventing the viability of a haploid embryo is the imprinting phenomenon: many genes are only active either in the paternal or the maternal chromosomes, with their respective maternal and paternal counterparts silenced by DNA methylation.

We are aware of some serious genetic medical conditions in which imprinting plays a fundamental role. For example, Prader-Willi syndrome is due to the deletion of a functional fragment of paternal chromosome 15. However, the deletion is not compensated by the corresponding imprinted and silenced genes otherwise present on the maternal version of the same chromosome. Unfortunately, this leads to a syndrome characterized by intellectual disability, severe obesity, hypogonadism, low muscle tone, and short stature. If the lack of a small portion of chromosome 15 is responsible for such drastic changes, let's not imagine what sort of consequences the lack of the entire paternal genome except for chromosome Y could lead to. This would not be a genetic condition compatible with life.

The Jesus described by Ron Wyatt would not be a true man. He would be a hologram living miraculously by fully violating any natural law. If Jesus really only had twenty-four chromosomes, He would not have truly taken on our human nature. This would have had devastating theological and spiritual consequences for all believers, and I think I should not add much more to this.

One last observation: Ron Wyatt's Jesus, by virtue of only having a single copy of chromosome 9, could be of any blood group *except* for the AB type.

Dear reader, I hope you, too, understand that the books that have already been written on Jesus' DNA do not really shed any light on the matter. Let's then go through the actual findings that have thus far emerged from the scientific study of the eucharistic miracles and the Passion cloths.

The DNA of the Eucharistic Miracles

Due to obvious historical reasons, we shall not look into the miracle of Lanciano. DNA analysis techniques were simply not available at the time of the 1970 scientific assessment, nor when the 1981 supplemental analyses were carried out. Moreover, no one would have known which DNA variants they should have been looking for.

Even in Sokółka, the 2009 investigations focused on tissue histopathology. Profs. Sobaniec-Łotowska and Sulkowski didn't find it necessary to attempt any trials of DNA profiling. There was possibly only a small amount of sample, and the resounding demonstration of the presence of heart muscle tissue was thought to be sufficient for having the miracle recognized by the Białystok Curia.

We shall then pay attention to the investigations on the miracles of Buenos Aires, Tixtla, and Legnica.

Buenos Aires

Let's go back to St. Mary's Parish. On October 5, 1999, Dr. Castañón was sampling two specimens while being videotaped by Ron Tesoriero: Sample no. 1-1 was taken from the small blood crust from May 1992. Sample no. 1-2 was taken from the August 1996 material preserved in distilled water.

Both sterile and sealed test tubes were sent off to Forensic Analytical in Hayward, California, near San Francisco. The laboratory was chosen because of its reputation and its expertise in analyzing very small samples. There, only Dr. Vanora Kean knew about the origin of the samples, while none of her colleagues did. On December 9, 1999, Dr. Kean advised Dr. Castañón that "minimal quantities of human DNA" were present in both samples no. 1-1 and no. 1-2, as a preliminary finding. Investigations continued on, but the result was disappointing. The DNA extraction, quantification, PCR, and gel electrophoresis methods that were employed are fully explained in the final May 1, 2000, reports by Forensic Analytical. They are cited in the appendix sections of both Dr. Castañón's and Ron Tesoriero's books. Nine of the most common STR polymorphisms—all belonging to the CODIS system—along with the two amelogenin genes were searched for in vain: none of them could be identified, and no PCR amplification products were obtained.

Still, at least in regard to sample no. 1-2, the presence of good-quality high-molecular-weight DNA was detected. Faced with such an equivocal result, the researchers could not suggest any definitive conclusion. They could only hypothesize that the tissue sample could have been of nonhuman origin. As they stated, "[It] may contain good quality non-human DNA."

Tixtla

As we already know, the local curia entrusted the scientific investigations of the Tixtla miracle to Dr. Castañón. Many tests were carried out since 2009, including a DNA study that was repeated twice in two different laboratories: by Dr. Sánchez Lazo at Corporativo Médico Legal in Mexico and by biologist Eyda de Campollo—affiliated with Mariano Gálvez University—at the Guatemalan Instituto de Investigaciones Químicas, Biológicas, Biomédicas y Biofísicas, I2QB3. Indeed, both samples, preserved in paraffin and sent to these two different laboratories, yielded the same negative result. According to the Mexican report, the presence of genetic material was detected. However, no known coding gene sequences could be identified, and no useful DNA profiling marker sequences could be amplified by PCR. Similarly, the November 9, 2012, Guatemalan report specified that no complete genetic profile could be identified, due to the poor DNA conditions: the DNA was totally degraded and fragmented. The study included fifteen STRs and the amelogenins, but no result was reported, not even a partial one: in all likelihood, nothing could be really amplified or recognized.

Was the overall picture emerging from the Buenos Aires and Tixtla investigations a disappointing one? The analyzed biologic material was always and invariably described as poorly or very badly preserved: it had spent years at room temperature, without any preservative agent. Have we then at the very least missed out on a historical opportunity by failing to identify the genetic profile of the tissues in those eucharistic miracles? How could it be possible that we couldn't even amplify one single STR polymorphism? Could it be that this very feature—the complete absence of any DNA profiling result—was actually suggestive of a hidden yet surprising meaning?

Dr. Castañón, who seemed to be knowledgeable about this, was not at all disappointed when he found out about these DNA results. He and his partners had investigated quite a few other cases in the previous twenty to thirty years. They still keep information on many of these cases strictly confidential, as they have not yet been fully studied or have not yet been formally recognized by Church authorities. Dr. Castañón is unquestionably one of the most authoritative figures in the world for any matter in this extremely specialized research field. Indeed, drawing on his experience, he claimed that the inability to obtain the DNA profile of an allegedly miraculous specimen is currently a "confirmation" of its authenticity and its supernatural origin. Paradoxically, the bad news coming from genetic laboratories was actually a reason for satisfaction for Dr. Castañón's investigators. They used the term *control variable* to describe this. So far, every time a genetic profile could be identified in their samples, it was due to involuntary contamination, usually by someone who had touched the relics. Alternatively, they had not been dealing with a miracle but, rather, with a scam. It is as if the Tixtla and Buenos Aires miracles actually consisted in the stoic impassibility of non-falsifiable heavenly signs: relics that could not be forced to reveal something they didn't want to, or possibly something *they could not*, no matter what kinds of experimental conditions they were subjected to. Just like defeated hounds, both fluorescent genetic probes and PCR primers came back to the scientists empty-handed: after scanning all those DNA filaments looking for their binding sites, they still could not find those typical "signatures" invariably present in all human DNA.

Between 2015 and 2016—as shown in the documentary *The Blood of Christ: Proving the Existence of God*—Mike Willesee took further samples from the Tixtla relic for genetic analyses. That documentary, whose final form wasn't controlled by Willesee, ended with a tacky ideological scam by stating that female human DNA was found precisely in the Tixtla tissue. For more in-depth information, I dedicated my postscript paragraph at the end of chapter 3 to clarifying this sad story. The fine details of the true results emerging from the analyses carried out at the Victorian Institute of Forensic Medicine are not available to the public. However, it is obvious that if any genetic profile result—or even a partial one—had been identified, aside from that of the female DNA misattributed to the Tixtla miracle, the

Australian documentary would have had to give an account of such discovery with great emphasis.

Around 2016, to overcome the problem of a possible contamination of the DNA of the "miraculous" cells with that of skin cells belonging to people who touched the relics, Mike Willesee turned to the Menarini Silicon Biosystems laboratory in Bologna, Italy. The Italian laboratory had developed DEPArray technology, a cutting-edge technological solution that had originally been conceived to study cancerous tissues, although currently it is also being successfully applied to forensic medicine. DEPArray can identify and separately analyze every single cell in a "complex" and potentially contaminated biological sample. Each cell can then be individually recognized, typified, and literally placed inside an electrophoretic matrix. That way, free from any contaminations, the DNA of a single cell can be analyzed to obtain its genetic profile. Dr. Francesca Fontana, at Menarini Silicon Biosystems, could then use this technique to study three tissue samples taken from three different and allegedly miraculous South American relics, including a fragment of the Tixtla host. An overall summary of the results can actually be gleaned from Mike Willesee's posthumous autobiography, rather than from the vague Australian documentary, which did not disclose any precise data: all three samples contained human blood, with good-quality DNA-containing white blood cells. DNA was selectively extracted from the nuclei of single white blood cells and, once again, against all expectations, the genetic material did not allow for the identification of any STR polymorphism.

New Research on Mitochondrial DNA

As we know, mtDNA—extremely short compared to nuclear DNA and present in many copies in every single cell—is more easily found in ancient or degraded specimens. Through direct correspondence with Dr. Castañón, I know that he was at least looking into studying this type of DNA. In the summer of 2016, he was trying to connect with an important European laboratory with the aim of searching for the presence of mtDNA in his samples.

Similarly, Ron Tesoriero dedicated all of chapter 23 of his book *Unseen* to the potential profiling of mtDNA. This was after he acknowledged the failure of nuclear DNA testing on the Buenos Aires miracle, as well as on the blood taken from a sacred image in Bolivia in the 1990s, which he had extensively studied. The Australian lawyer could not help revealing his temptation to also study the relics of the Virgin Mary and her mother St. Anne, with the purpose of finding some sensational correlation. Needless to say, those relics smell fishy and are likely to be medieval forgeries or pious legends: St. Anne's tomb in Apt (southern France), or one of the many "hairs" of the Virgin, like those kept in Messina or Palmi (Italy). I cannot hide my own bewilderment when hearing about these projects, perhaps more suitable for Indiana Jones's next adventure or Dan Brown's next novel: they certainly wouldn't serve the purpose of respectfully gaining any further insights into the events we are discussing. Still, recent discoveries compel us to consider Ron Tesoriero's study proposals as not pseudoscientific at all:

1. In 2001, an mtDNA profile was successfully obtained from the alleged body of St. Luke the Evangelist, buried in Padua. The haplogroup pre-HV — genetically similar to those found today in Syria and Turkey — was isolated from a tooth, and this is quite in keeping with the evangelist being born in Antioch in the first years of the first century AD.

2. Recently, in December 2016, geneticist Gérard Lucotte published an amazing result from the study of a hair bulb that was thought to belong to Mary Magdalene, whose relics are said to be kept at St. Maximin's Abbey in Provence (France). Besides the female sex — obtained from the nuclear DNA amelogenins — he determined the entire HVR1 sequence of the mtDNA, thereby characterizing nine mutations, which identified the K haplogroup and, more precisely, the K1a1b1a sub-haplogroup. This is precisely the sub-haplogroup that is still to this day most frequent in Ashkenazi Jews, as it is the identity of one of the four mythical "founding mothers" of the Ashkenazi. Twenty percent of all the Jews of the Western Diaspora living today are the descendants of a great-great-K1a1b1a-grandmother who lived between two and three thousand years ago.

It must be admitted that genetics does have the power to make stories that sounded like pious legends or ancient fables suddenly believable and rational.

Legnica

Just as I was writing this chapter, I received the news about the results of the DNA analysis from the second and very recent Polish miracle. I had a personal conversation with Dr. Barbara Engel, head of cardiology at the local hospital and involved in the investigations, and with Fr. Krzysztof Wisniewski, spiritual father of the local seminary and appointed by the diocese as a theologian expert for the St. Hyacinth dossier. I received confirmation that both nuclear and mtDNA were found in the heart muscle tissue of Legnica. Despite its poor condition, due to heavy fragmentation, there was still enough DNA to demonstrate the human nature of the tissue. In the second series of confirmatory tests — performed at the University of Szczecin — two portions of nuclear DNA could actually be isolated and amplified: two fragments which, as explained, were part of a personal identification system. Quite likely, these must have been STRs, almost certainly belonging to the CODIS system. However, researchers and Church authorities in Legnica have kept their utmost reserve since the discovery. The fear — as it was hinted to me — had been that of placing an excessive weight on the genetic findings alone, leading to shallow sensationalism at the expense of the deeper spiritual meaning that should instead arise from the 2013 event. Still, two DNA amplifications were sufficient to establish beyond doubt that the heart muscle tissue belonged to the human species, and that should be enough. Finding only two sequences, as opposed to the ten to twenty that are routinely looked for, was in keeping — as already made clear — with the poor quality of the original tissue specimen: had many more sequences been found, that would have led to the suspicion of contamination with good-quality foreign DNA.

MtDNA was also identified. This could perhaps give rise to a hypothesis on the ethnic origin of the heart of Legnica, though up until now no nucleotide sequence, no mutations, and, of course, no haplogroup classification have been made known.

What does this mean? The reader must be wondering: "But how? You had just convinced us that it was to be expected — and almost inevitable — that no known sequences should be found in the DNA of eucharistic miracles, and now these people have found both nuclear DNA and mtDNA?" Dear reader, welcome to an unknown territory, a new continent yet to be explored. I can only describe what happened, what could be seen and measured. Later on, we shall try and draw some tentative, hypothetical, and by no means definitive conclusions. Meanwhile, let's look for other clues in another category of curious and anomalous objects: the Passion cloths.

The Shroud of Turin

After demonstrating the presence of blood on the linen cloth in the 1980s, a few researchers attempted looking for traces of DNA in the following decade. Although heavily degraded human cells were found, it is difficult — if not impossible — to find anything genetically meaningful to identify the DNA profile of the man of the Shroud. This is also due to certain contamination from much physical contact with the Shroud's keepers and pilgrims throughout the centuries. Just as an example, the Chambéry nuns mended the Shroud's burns in 1532. We can actually only refer to two studies in the scientific literature, both done in the mid-1990s. It is a shame we "burnt off" those tiny precious blood samples taken from the Shroud so soon, at a time when DNA PCR technology was still in its early days.

In 1995, a group of forensic medicine researchers headed by Prof. Marcello Canale, at the University of Genoa, attempted applying the new PCR techniques to the DNA on the Shroud and the Sudarium of Oviedo for the first time. For just a short while, in the summer of 1995, there was a flashing rumor about reasonable similarity found between the genetic profiles of the blood of the two relics. That wasn't the case: the interview with Prof. Canale published in the Italian tabloid *Who* in July 1995 was simply distorted for the sake of sensationalism. This was uncovered just a few months later when the Genoese researchers' scientific article was published in a minor Italian sindonology magazine no longer available. I owe first author Dr. Lucia Casarino for finding one very precious copy for me.

The Genoese researchers—pioneers in this promising scientific field—looked for the presence of four STRs and the amelogenin sequences in a few bloodstained threads taken from the areas of both feet on the posterior Shroud image. They also looked for the same sequences in some loose and unstained threads taken from other sites closer to the edges. The samples had already been taken at the time of the 1978 sampling. At the same time, they performed the same tests on some fibers from the Sudarium of Oviedo. Out of the four STRs they had been looking for, two are still being used currently as part of the CODIS system and all the most common laboratory kits. The other two, FES/FPS and F13A1, are no longer important in common practice.

Unfortunately, the researchers gave a very scanty explanation of their results. They only published the original image of the amplification report of the TH01 and FES/FPS STR analysis: the mere printout produced by the PCR laboratory instrument, with the tersest explanation. No details about the VWA, F13A1, and amelogenins results were discussed. In their extremely brief discussion, they explained that in both samples—from both the Shroud and the Sudarium—and in both types of fibers—the clean and bloodstained ones—different DNA contaminations could be detected. This was apparent because of the overlapping of more than two alleles for the same STR. Likewise, as I can deduce myself, contamination by female individuals would have also been obvious, due to the unbalanced ratio between X and Y amelogenins. The Genoese researchers, however, did not mention that very clearly; actually, they didn't mention amelogenins in their discussion at all. By integrating this data with the explanations given in another study by the same researchers, done at around the same time, I could nonetheless interpret the bands on their gel electrophoresis image and quantify the number of repeats for each STR as listed in the table below:

STR	bp (base pairs)	STR repeats
TH01	between 162 and 174	7, 9.3 (and perhaps 10)
FES/FPS	between 212 and 234	9, 10 (most prevalent), 11, 12, 13, 14
Amelogenins?	107	X

The other scientific work I already mentioned is the one by Dr. Leoncio Garza-Valdes, published in 1998. Garza-Valdes had some small blood particles from the area of the left hand that were sampled in 1978 by Alan Adler, and a few extra ones that were taken from the region of the back of the head by by Prof. Giovanni Riggi di Numana, the Italian chemist involved in cutting the sample for 1988 carbon-14 analysis. Luckily, on this occasion Garza-Valdes did not work by himself but, rather, sought Dr. Victor Tryon's cooperation. At the time, Dr. Tryon was an expert of emerging DNA technologies at the University of San Antonio (Texas). On Tryon's advice, an initial attempt was made to first try to clone the beta-globin gene, which is known to be particularly easy to find in ancient DNA. It was Nancy Tryon, Victor Tryon's wife, who demonstrated—without knowing the origin of the sample—the presence of the beta-globin gene on the Shroud, and she also managed to obtain the sequence of its first 268 consecutive base pairs. Garza-Valdes proudly reported the whole sequence on page 121 of his book and used this finding—with a good nose for marketing—to motivate his catchy book title. Thanks to this success, Garza-Valdes could ask Riggi for further blood samples that demonstrated the presence of both X and Y amelogenins: a crucial result to demonstrate the male sex of the sampled DNA. Garza-Valdes's book is geared toward the general public and provides no further technical details about the specific laboratory techniques that were used, nor does it dwell on the issue of potential sample contamination.

In a 2004 interview, the authoritative researcher Raymond Rogers mentioned a new and more recent study on the Shroud's bloodstains assigned to Prof. Andrew Merriwether at Binghamton University in New York. The study did not yield any results, since the blood was thought to be too ancient, the DNA too fragmented, and the risk of contamination extremely high. This conclusion was confirmed to me in person by Dr. Merriwether. The study, however, did not lead to any written publication.

In 2015, the Shroud's DNA was brought back as a topic of discussion, although this time under a new and completely different spotlight. Up until then, the focus had been on identifying the DNA of the man of the Shroud and trying to distinguish it from that of many other biological contaminants present on the relic. However, in that year, the focus actually shifted to studying the DNA of biological contaminants themselves: countless human, animal, and plant DNA traces left on the cloth over the centuries. A new article by first author Dr. Gianni Barcaccia, a geneticist at the University of Padua (Italy), was deservedly published in the prestigious journal *Nature*. The Italian scientists systematically studied all the DNA fragments of plant origin and the animal and human mitochondrial DNA traces found in five dust samples. These were collected in 1978 and 1988 by suctioning the gap space between the Shroud and the Holland Canvas behind it. The Holland Canvas is the supporting fabric the Shroud has been sewn onto for centuries. The identified nucleotide sequences were systematically compared with the most updated databases, and the results were surprising.

In terms of plant DNA, this work integrated other historical studies, such as those by Max Frei, Uri Baruch, and the more recent ones by Gérard Lucotte. In the latter, Prof. Lucotte had already recognized the presence of pollens on the Shroud, using both light and electron microscopy. Nineteen distinct plant species typical of European forests were identified by Barcaccia's team, the most common one being spruce, although Mediterranean plants such as clover, ryegrass, and plantain as well as other edible ones like chicory, hops, pickle, and grapes were present. The origin of these plant species is consistently European, Middle Eastern, or North African, except for the North American *Robinia*, which was successfully imported to the Old World in the last few centuries, and some Asian pear and plum tree species that spread throughout Europe and Mediterranean regions at the time of Marco Polo. Only two animal DNA traces were found: one brief sequence of *Lanius meridionalis koenigi* (a passerine bird nesting in southern Europe, northern Africa, and the Near Eastern regions) and a mysterious trace compatible with a seaworm from the northern Pacific. No traces of mammalian animals or pets were identified.

Let's now turn to the human contaminant DNA. As expected, abundant human traces were left on the Shroud by all those who touched it, kissed it, or wept on it. Ninety-three mtDNA sequences were amplified and thirty-eight different mtDNA profiles were recognized by analyzing the mtDNA locations that most commonly carry individual variations. Such profiles were those of different people who belonged to haplogroups present in Europe, northern and eastern Africa, the Middle East, and, surprisingly, India. The authors of the study suggested considering the traces sampled from the back of the linen as more ancient and meaningful for the purpose of determining the possible journey of the relic throughout history. This was in comparison to those traces taken from the linen edges, the areas that were manipulated in recent times for the purpose of taking samples in the 1980s. From all these results, human DNA contaminations appeared to derive from four geographical regions, with some overlaps:

- the Middle East, given the H13, H33, and R0a haplogroups
- southeast Europe and Turkey, given the H1a, H2a, and H13 haplogroups
- western Europe, including France and Italy, given the H1j and H3 haplogroups
- India, given the M56 and R8 haplogroups

The unexpected finding of the Indian haplogroups led the authors to hypothesize—as an alternative to the contact between the Shroud and Indian pilgrims—the weaving of the Shroud's flax fabric itself in the South Asian subcontinent. The authors diplomatically considered this large quantity of results as compatible with both the "rational" hypothesis of the medieval origin of the Shroud—as suggested by the unreliable carbon-14 dating—and the "traditional" hypothesis claiming that the Shroud was truly the burial linen of Christ. Indeed, the "traditional" hypothesis would suggest that the linen came from Jerusalem, perhaps transited through Edessa and Constantinople before reaching France and then Turin.

A Cardiologist Examines Jesus

I believe that paying a toll to the *political correctness* of "lay science" by acknowledging the carbon-14 dating results is an unavoidable requirement for publishing a study in *Nature*. Wind can certainly carry pollen or eastern plant fragments to Lirey, Chambéry, and Turin. Similarly, throngs of North African, Ethiopian, Middle Eastern, or even Indian Christians could come to Europe as pilgrims after 1353, to touch the newly manufactured Shroud. However, an impartial observer could not miss recognizing the Mediterranean and Middle Eastern "center of gravity" toward which not only the Shroud's plant DNA contaminants, but also, and even more so, the human ones gravitate. This center of gravity is much more compatible with the traditional origin of the relic.

The Sudarium of Oviedo

In 1995, in addition to the twelve Shroud fibers, Prof. Canale's Genoese researchers received seven threads that had been taken officially from the Sudarium of Oviedo in 1985. Blood had already been identified on three of them. The Genoese study, as already discussed in regard to the Shroud, was ambitiously aimed at comparing both sacred relics. In 1995, researchers already knew that the blood on both the Shroud and the Sudarium belonged to the AB group. If compatible genetic profiles had been found in both the Shroud and the Sudarium, that would have massively boosted the likelihood of both relics' authenticity, to the point that the accuracy of their carbon-14 dating results would have been called into question. In the study's conclusions that we already know, Prof. Canale's team combined the results from both the Sudarium and the Shroud: the search for four STRs and amelogenins revealed signs of contamination in all samples taken from both fabrics. This was evidenced by overlapping DNAs from multiple people, including male and female contaminations. For the Sudarium, too, the researchers again only presented the raw data as the image of a single DNA electrophoresis gel, showing band patterns for the TH01 and FES/FPS STRs, with no other comments. From that image, I could obtain the data in the table below:

STR	bp (base pairs)	STR allelic bands
TH01	154 to 170	-5, 6, 7, 8, 9-
FES/FPS	220 to 230	11, 12, 13
Amelogenins?	105	X

As a reminder, I shall repeat that only one or two allele electrophoretic bands would be seen on the gel if the sampled DNA only belonged to a single person. If two bands, these would have to be of equal intensity. Here, instead, five allele bands were seen for the TH01 STR and three for the FES/FPS STR. As for the Shroud, no data on the VWA and F13A1 polymorphisms or the amelogenins was presented: I could only guess that the 105 bp band may have been related to amelogenins, although this remains unclear in the absence of any explanatory note.

Further discussions about the Sudarium's DNA took place again in April 2007, on the occasion of the International Conference on the Sudarium of Oviedo, which took place in the same Spanish city. It was Dr. Antonio Alonso, a biologist and geneticist, who spoke about it. He revealed the results of the investigations he oversaw in Madrid in 1994 and 2005. In May 1994, at the request of the Oviedo Cathedral chapter, a total of twelve fabric threads were taken from the Sudarium using sterile technique. Three threads were taken from each of the two most bloodstained areas of the cloth. Similarly — as control samples — three threads were also taken from each of two areas that were not bloodstained, although they bordered the former bloodstained ones. All these samples are still supposedly stored at minus 80 degrees Celsius at the National Institute of Toxicology in Madrid. In 1994, the Spanish researchers made an initial DNA extraction attempt from two threads — a bloodstained one and a control one — without success. Dr. Alonso then wisely decided to buy some time by letting the samples rest in his freezer and await further advances in DNA analysis techniques.

Two more fabric threads were sacrificed in 2005: again, one bloodstained and one not. Once again, no nuclear DNA could be isolated. However, traces of degraded but *human* mtDNA were found in the bloodstained thread. Dr. Alonso was able to replicate multiple 100-140 bp mtDNA fragments with overlapping extremities, despite these being incomplete on their own. Like in a word puzzle, he could then reconstruct the entire HV1 mtDNA sequence from base number 16,024 to base number 16,365.

Dr. Alonso was very prudent: he could not rule out that the mtDNA trace he isolated from the bloodstained thread could have been a contaminant. Thus, he decided not to publish the mtDNA sequence for a series of very good reasons:

• He did not wish to create inappropriate sensationalism regarding such a delicate matter.
• He preferred awaiting further confirmatory results from other Sudarium material, possibly obtained with more

advanced DNA analytical techniques that might be made available in the future.

• He did not wish to create any references that could sway or corrupt the independence and genuineness of future studies on the Sudarium or other relics.

At the same time, he confirmed molds and fungi on the fabric threads by demonstrating the presence of *Arachnomyces minimus* mtDNA on the control thread. Still, he could not replicate the mtDNA of the flax plant whose fibers make up the Sudarium fabric itself, a point he noted to highlight the difficulty and unpredictability of these studies.

The Holy Tunic of Argenteuil

According to Prof. Gérard Lucotte—the geneticist who studied it more than anyone else in the last thirty years—the Tunic is literally covered in blood. Besides the many red blood cells—often exceptionally well preserved, but not containing DNA by definition—other cells were identified on the relic that became promising targets for DNA studies: white blood cells, fragments of skin cells, and hair bulbs. Indeed, Prof. Lucotte already had access to the relic in 1986. At the time, he focused on a portion of the fabric that was particularly stained with organic fluids. He took some samples from it and determined the following:

• There were traces of DNA on the Tunic. Some were of high molecular weight and thus possibly in keeping with recent contamination, while others were more fragmented, as would be expected with ancient DNA.

• A good amount of the ancient DNA was of human origin: for example, it contained the gene sequence for human albumin, a common blood protein.

• A typical Y-chromosome sequence was found: hence, it was the DNA of a male individual.

Prof. Lucotte also prudently preserved his leftover samples in a freezer for the following years. As we already know, PCR techniques capable of amplifying minimal DNA quantities did not became available to scientists until the 1990s. These techniques dramatically simplified DNA analyses and increased their diagnostic potential. Around 2000, Lucotte searched for the amelogenin genes in part of his leftover material and obtained two homogeneous bands of 106 and 112 base pairs respectively, a further confirmation of the male sex of the person who wore the Tunic. The two bands of equal intensity ruled out any feminine contaminations. In more recent times—because of his great expertise in the study of the Y-chromosome genetic variants—Prof. Lucotte could demonstrate that the Y-chromosome DNA he isolated belonged to the J2 haplogroup. This is a resounding finding, as the J2 haplogroup is strongly suggestive of a Middle Eastern origin and is absolutely compatible with the Jewish origin of the man of the Tunic. Indeed, still today, about 40 percent of Jewish males—both Sephardi and Ashkenazi—share the J haplogroup in its J1 and J2 subgroups. In particular, 25 percent of all modern-day Jews belong to the J2 subgroup.

Moreover, in regard to ethnic origin, Lucotte obtained an even more powerful result. He demonstrated the heterozygous nature[139] of his Tunic blood samples for a genetically inheritable disease that is only present in people of Mediterranean descent, especially Sephardi Jews, Armenians, Turks, and Arabs: familial Mediterranean fever (FMF). FMF, as known since 1997, is due

---

[139] Reminder: *heterozygous* means carrying different allelic variants for the same gene.

to a mutation of the gene coding for the synthesis of the pyrin protein,[140] which is located on chromosome 16. Those who are homozygous suffer from recurrent crises involving fever and abdominal and joint pains. The man of the Tunic was not affected by FMF; he was a healthy heterozygous carrier of the M694V FMF mutation on only one of his copies of chromosome 16. A 2000 study by Lucotte himself demonstrated that the prevalence of the mutated FMF gene in a sample of 702 contemporary Jews was 10.9 percent in Sephardi Jews, 9.2 percent in eastern Jews, but only 0.8 percent in Ashkenazi Jews.

We are now ready for the grand finale, with a mighty bang. Between 2000 and 2005—just in time for the results to be published in the 2006 and 2007 volumes cited in the bibliography—Prof. Lucotte successfully identified seventeen STR markers and the amelogenin sequences twice, with two different laboratory kits. Of the seventeen STRs, thirteen belonged to the CODIS system, whereas the remaining four did not. The two kits detected thirteen and eleven STRs respectively, of which ten were found by both. When detected, the alleles were only either one or two, therefore confirming that the DNA could only originate from a single person, without contaminations by other people. Both kits yielded consistently overlapping results, without exceptions. Those STRs that were not detected—such as CSF1PO—or that were only detected by one of the two kits correspond to longer, and therefore more fragile, DNA fragments. The difficulty in

---

[140] Pyrin, or marenostrin, is produced in certain white blood cells that play a key role in inflammation. Its protein structure allows it to interact with other molecules involved in the inflammatory response.

detecting them is clear evidence of the ancient nature of the examined DNA. These were the results:

	STRs	"Identifiler" kit	"PowerPlex 16" kit
	Amelogenins	X, Y	X, Y
	CSF1PO	–	–
	FGA	25, 25	25, 25
	TH01	6, 7	6, 7
	TPOX	8, 11	–
C	VWA	17, 17	17, 17
O	D3S1358	15, 18	15, 18
D	D5S818	11, 12	11, 12
I	D7S820	10, 12	10, 12
S	D8S1179	15, 15	15, 15
	D13S317	8, 11	8, 11
	D16S539	8, 13	–
	D18S51	15, 15	15, 15
	D21S11	30, 31.2	30, 31.2

STRs	"Identifiler" kit	"PowerPlex 16" kit
D2S1338	–	–
D19S433	14, 14	–
PentaE	–	–
PentaD	–	13, 14

A geneticist could not help shivering. These are data that un-equivocally identify — in a unique and unrepeatable way — the person who wore and bled on the Tunic of Argenteuil. If we cross-checked the distribution frequencies of the alleles in this profile with the ones in today's Caucasian United States population, we would find that the probability of any man in that group randomly having the genetic profile of the Tunic of Argenteuil would be 3.21 to the negative power of 22. In other words, one man in every three thousand billions of billions — 3 followed by 21 zeros — would randomly have the same genetic profile as the one reported in the table above.

As larger and larger databases of STR profiles have been compiled with the intent of mapping the distribution of these polymorphisms in world populations, slight variations in profile frequencies have been noted between different ethnic groups. Therefore, a clue about the "wanted" man's geographical origin is also hidden in his CODIS profile. A website affiliated with the Center for Research in Advanced Computing Systems[141]

[141] The link to the PopAffiliator 2 website is http://cracs.fc.up.pt/~nf/popaffiliator2/ (unfortunately not available in July 2021).

provides an updated algorithm that, by entering an appropriate number of STR alleles, generates a hypothesis on the ethnic origin of the proposed DNA profile. If we enter all of the thirteen known alleles of the man of the Tunic — even if just thirteen out of the sixteen that are requested — the algorithm will reveal to us that the origin of the Tunic's DNA is 85.3 percent Eurasian, 11.5 percent Asian, and, quite unlikely, 3.1 percent African or Sub-Saharan.

Prof. Lucotte admitted he truly put his heart into his personal search for the Holy Grail, demonstrating that the same nuclear DNA profile could potentially be found in the other major Passion relics. He made contact with the Sudarium researchers, though I believe without much success. He could instead examine dusts and fragments of the Shroud of Turin and managed to enter the inner circle of the most active sindonologists. In the last few years, he produced many original studies on dusts, pollens, and cells present on the Shroud. Still, so far, he is yet to find his Holy Grail.

When DNA Puts Miracle Forgers in an Awkward Spot

Please allow me a brief digression off the topic of eucharistic miracles just to stress the enormous potential that genetic analyses have in unmasking forgeries within the unfortunately fertile ground of fake miraculous phenomena. I shall just hint at a few events, listing them chronologically.

In May 1994, in Assemini, near Cagliari (Sardinia) in Italy, blood tears flowed from a statuette in the Sarras family's home kitchen. After years of controversies and resistance, the Sarras couple consented to a DNA test that ruthlessly demonstrated that the blood on the statue belonged to "the lady of the house," with whom it also shared the genetically inherited Mediterranean anemia blood disorder, which has an increased prevalence in Sardinia.

Let's just leave it to the family's lawyer to say that "if the Virgin had meant to appear in some way, she could have used the tears or blood of the person closest to her."

In August 1994, nineteen-year-old painter Cinzia Zambrella, from the Italian Basilicata region, noted tears of blood flowing from a portrait of St. Padre Pio she had painted herself and hung in her own bedroom a year before. The portrait was then taken to the local church of Sts. Cosmas and Damian in Bernalda, where it is still kept. The blood then underwent analyses that proved its human nature. Interestingly enough, St. Padre Pio's convent in San Giovanni Rotondo was also involved, as it generously provided a relic with the blood of the great saint for comparison. Further genetic tests certified that the blood on the portrait was not that of St. Padre Pio.

Let's now turn to the most controversial tear-shedding phenomenon that, in the last few years, has had the greatest impact on the Catholic world, or at least in Italy: Civitavecchia. There, in February 1995, tears of blood flowed from the face of a statue of the Virgin Mary purchased in Medjugorje and kept in the Gregori family's garden. Soon after, Prof. Angelo Fiori from the Policlinico Gemelli hospital and Prof. Giancarlo Umani Ronchi from Sapienza University in Rome established that the tears were made of the blood of a human male (there were always some theologians ready to explain why the blood could have been genetically male). The professors also identified five nuclear DNA polymorphisms. Later on, Criminalpol police experts also identified the mtDNA haplogroup (these data are still kept confidential). Only five STRs and a mtDNA haplogroup were technically not a complete personal identification profile, although altogether they still did account for a rather high discriminating power: Criminalpol Dr. Aldo Spinella estimated it to be one in fifty thousand, according to the FBI database. There would only be one Italian male in fifty thousand who randomly shared the same result.

Judge Massimo Michelozzi asked Fabio Gregori and his male blood relatives neighbors to undergo genetic testing to rule out a forgery, but they refused and successfully appealed to the High Court instead. Their refusal stemmed from the fear of the possibility of a false positive result, which in terms of probability, I should repeat, would have been in the order of one person versus the size of the entire population of Civitavecchia: a very low probability that should not have been greatly feared by someone who had not actually committed the hypothetical fraud. I don't wish to venture any further into this hornet's nest, but I do wish to point out that the second theological committee on the Civitavecchia events, which was chaired by Cardinal Ruini, stated in 2005 that the facts "are not consistent with a supernatural cause," a formal opinion by Church authorities that still applies to this day. My personal opinion in regard to the specific issue of genetic testing is that the Gregori family, even if possibly ill-advised, lacked in generosity and did not look good in the eyes of the public. Moreover, their refusal also ended up increasing the haziness around the entire event.

Julia Kim — also known as Julia Youn, her maiden surname — is a Korean woman whose life, since 1985, has been showered by an uninterrupted sequence of mystical experiences: visions and private messages associated with phenomena seen by bystanders. Communion wafers have been raining down in her presence, statues have been moving around, blood has been flowing from sacred images, and perfumes have been smelled. However, what

the Naju seer is most well-known for is a particularly excessive and—please allow me to say—frankly disgusting type of
eucharistic miracle: communion hosts—who knows if validly
consecrated—transform themselves in her mouth into fresh flesh
and blood, which Julia swallows with disarming ease (without
perhaps first showing what's in her mouth to those who are present around her, or better, to the lens of a photographer's camera).
All of Julia Kim's spirituality has been repeatedly condemned by
the Catholic Church hierarchy—for a series of good theological
reasons on which I will not dwell—to the point that whoever
follows her is subject to excommunication.

My reason for mentioning Julia is that in the autumn of
2006, nine blood samples collected between 1995 and 2006
were actually analyzed twice at the Humanpass Inc. laboratory in Seoul. These were samples of blood taken from sacred
images or hosts that had bled or "rained down." Alternatively,
the blood was directly collected in the seer's bedroom or even
gifted to her by Jesus Himself in a handkerchief and so forth.
Well, nine complete and impeccable reports were obtained that
unanimously stated beyond all doubt that the blood was human, genetically male, and belonging to the same person. For
future reference—before this could be deleted from the Korean
website najumary.or.kr—I transcribed the genetic profile that
was obtained, which is substantiated by credible photographic
evidence:

Amelogenins	X, Y
CSF1PO	9, 11
FGA	23, 24

TH01	7, 9
TPOX	11, 11
VWA	17, 18
D3S1358	15, 15
D5S818	12, 12
D7S820	9 11
D8S1179	11, 13
D13S317	10, 11
D16S539	11, 11
D18S51	14, 16
D21S11	30, 30
D2S1338	19, 19
D19S433	15, 15.2

I would like to remind the possibly baffled reader that, according to popular wisdom, there is no such thing as a perfect crime. To the same reader, I should also point out that if we entered this genetic profile into the algorithm I mentioned in the previous section on the Tunic of Argenteuil, we would obtain the following ethnicity results:

Population region	Probability
Asia	74.3%
Sub-Saharan Africa	13.1%
Eurasia	12.6%

Julia Kim didn't want to tell us, but we just discovered that her Jesus was, in all likelihood, Korean!

Let's end this roundup on a less distressing and more colorful note: in March 2006, at St. Lucy's Church in Forlì, Italy, some elderly faithful found out that the statue of the Virgin of Lourdes had blood on her face. Two years later, a judge condemned the former church keeper, sixty-year-old Neapolitan Vincenzo Di Costanzo. Of course, it was the DNA test that caught him out. Di Costanzo hadn't had an easy life and was hoping that the "miracle" would draw pilgrims, tips, and donations. Still, he pathetically tried to defend himself by saying: "Only God knows why my blood was there! You see, doctor, I am diabetic and inject myself with insulin every day. I lose blood everywhere!" His punishment was light: only a fine of 300 euros, although he ended up paying 6,000 euros after his DNA testing costs were added on.

A Few Concluding Reflections

In conclusion: what was Jesus of Nazareth's DNA really like during His life on Earth? Would it be possible to advance a few very cautious hypotheses? We are about to tiptoe into an uncharted land where I shall most respectfully try to integrate the recent scientific results with the truths of the Faith, handed down by generations of faithful people before us.

I shall propose two firm reference points about Jesus' DNA:

1. It was "normal" DNA, in every way similar and indistinguishable from that of any other male of the species *Homo sapiens.*

2. It inherited half of its chromosomes from His Mother, Mary.

Christ's Incarnation has represented a heavenly mystery for Christians of all times. At the time that the Nicene Creed's words "was incarnate of the Virgin Mary, and became man" are merely spoken, the modern Mass demands bowing the head, or the upper body. The old Tridentine Mass even involved kneeling at that point.

Jesus could have miraculously appeared, as an already mature adult, on the streets of Palestine in AD 30. Instead, it was obviously an integral part of God's saving plan that His coming was to take place in a woman's womb, in order for him to fully share our human nature, including life as an embryo and a fetus, birth, and growing up in a family with a father and a mother. True God, but also true man. Two natures, human and divine, in a single Person is what the dogma painstakingly taught in the first centuries of Church history.

It must be because of the legacy of the Catholic catechism that I inherited, but I cannot help finding the theories about an "odd" Jesus, with chromosomal anomalies and a questionable sexual identity, as frankly disgusting. How could the One through whom "all things were made" be satisfied with an *anomalous* body when coming down from the heavens to live with other human beings in the fullness of time? Rather meaningfully, the Gospels never describe Christ's physical aspect, either to exalt or belittle it. The first few generations of Christians—Justin, Tertullian, Clement of Alexandria—seemed to advance the idea of an "awkward" or even "deformed" Jesus, which was perhaps due to Isaiah's prophecy on the Servant of YHWH who "had no form or comeliness" (Isa. 53:2). Later on, the fourth century's great Early Church Fathers—Ephrem the Syrian, Gregory of Nyssa, John Chrysostom—spoke instead about Christ as "the fairest of the sons of men" (Ps. 45:2). Overall, I think it would be common sense to believe Jesus' physical appearance must have been very normal and indistinguishable from that of any other average Jewish man of the first century.

Here I would like to add a theological observation: Jesus was both the Victim and the High Priest in the supreme sacrifice that brought about the salvation of mankind. According to the Jewish ritual, the validity of a sacrifice required that both roles be undertaken by subjects of unblemished physical makeup. Not only did the animals, particularly the Passover lamb, have to be "spotless" to be sacrificed (as in Deut. 15:21 or Lev. 22:20), but also the *cohen*, the priest. He had to be a descendant of Aaron, who was originally authorized to offer the sacrifice in the Temple, and he could not have the smallest physical flaw: he could not be limping, or be short in stature, or have any deformity of his genitalia. This is just to mention a few of the traditional rabbinic norms.

If authentic, the Shroud reveals us a rather fit and almost athletic male physical makeup, despite its signs of suffering. If authentic, the Tunic of Argenteuil tells us—through the DNA of the large amount of blood it is covered in—of a man with a normal chromosomal makeup that was fully indistinguishable from those of his fellow citizens. This is to the point of even sharing with them the pathological familial Mediterranean fever gene, as a healthy heterozygous carrier.

Son of His Mother

It must again be a bias of mine, related to my Catholic upbringing, but it seems very logical to me that if the Incarnation of the second Person of the Holy Trinity had to take place in the womb of the Virgin Mary, it would have happened through an egg cell that was available at that time in the Mother's body, thereby fully respecting her female nature and fertile physiology. On the day of the Annunciation, the Virgin consented to her whole self becoming the "handmaid of the Lord" without reservation, like a real mother and not just like a surrogate one. The dogma of the Immaculate Conception of Mary—that is, Mary having been spared from Original Sin since the time she was herself conceived in her mother Anne's womb—allows Catholics an enviable degree of freedom of thought. It is that freedom that allows them to find it entirely natural that the Virgin Mary materially and physically engaged in the conception and knitting together of her Son in her womb.

I shall remind the readers who are not too keen on fine theological details: Christ took on the burden of all sins committed by all people of the past, present, and future. However, He absolutely lived free from sin since birth, or actually since the time He was conceived, and for His entire life as a man. This was an unavoidable and even indispensable theological condition that was required to ensure the efficacy of His sacrifice. It is apparent that Mary's participation in the conception of her Son then becomes a real dilemma for non-Catholic Christians who do not believe in her Immaculate Conception: the necessarily pure and "foreign" Body of Jesus would have inevitably been corrupted by Mary's human nature, as she would have passed on to Him the sin of Adam and Eve that we all share. However, in more practical terms and also according to Catholic sensitivity, even the simple growing up of the Son—in His Body and Soul—at such very close contact with His Mother—as if the Virgin had partaken in a nine-month-long Eucharist—required that Mary had to be preserved from Original Sin. This would still be the case independently of the Son's conception through her full participation in His Incarnation in her womb. Otherwise, her pregnancy would have been equivalent to the profanation of the Eucharist by an unbaptized person or by a Catholic living in mortal sin receiving Holy Communion.

Therefore, I think it would be sensible to believe that Jesus of Nazareth had to be physically similar to His Mother, just as all children in this world look similar to their mothers. It wouldn't seem reasonable that the Holy Family would have had to put up with an embarrassment—with their relatives and the people in their village—due to their Son randomly looking entirely different, as if He had been given to them by a prankster God.

Many Byzantine authors from the eighth and ninth centuries talk about the tradition handed down to them regarding a strong similarity between Christ and His Mother. For example, in the synodal letter addressed to Emperor Theophilus in 836 and written by the three patriarchs Christopher of Alexandria, Job of Antioch, and Basil of Jerusalem, Christ's physical appearance was accurately described according to the apostles' accounts. The letter stated that His "face was the color of wheat, similar to that of his mother." Another description was given by Epiphanius the Monk, who wrote: "With His face not rounded, but rather elongated instead, like that of His Mother, whom, after all, He resembled in everything." In the fourteenth century, Nicephorus Callistus Xanthopulus continued the descriptions given by his predecessors by writing: "His face was neither round nor oval shaped and was very similar, especially in its lower portion, to that of His Mother.... Lastly, He resembled His divine virgin Mother in everything."

At this stage, I would very much like to call in for help the great Italian poet Dante Alighieri as a witness to faith and sound reasoning. At verse 86, in canto 32 of *Paradiso*, the poet has made it up to the Empyrean, or Highest Heaven, and is finally allowed to simultaneously see all the blessed, laid out to form an immaculate rose in their Beatific Vision of the Holy Trinity. The highest and most prominent petal is for the Queen, and Dante is allowed to cast his eyes on Mary's face:

> But now look at the face which to the Christ
> is most resemblant; for its light alone
> can make thee ready to behold the Christ.

The similarity with the Son is not just in regard to His splendor and beatitude. It is also exquisitely physical. In order to add some theological authority to these reflections, I am quite happy to cite a passage by John of Damascus, one of the Eastern Church Fathers, who lived in the eighth century and put the dogma of Mary Mother of God in the following terms:

In a properly true and real sense we believe the holy Virgin to be the Mother of God. In fact, just as the One who was born from her is the true God, the true Mother of God is the one who generated the true God, the God who made himself incarnate within her. And when we say that God was born from her, we certainly do not mean to say that the divinity of the Word began to exist when made within her. Instead, we say this because the same God-Word—who was generated by the Father before all ages outside of time and who has been with the Father and the Holy Spirit without any beginning—in the last few days, and for our redemption, found a dwelling place in her womb and, without undergoing any change, He became incarnate in Her and was born from her. Therefore, the Holy Virgin did not generate a simple man, but rather the true God. And not just the true God, but also the Incarnate God. God the Son, however, did not bring His body from heaven, passing through her as if she were a channel, but rather, He took up his body—consubstantial with ours—from her, by giving it sustenance through His Person.

The Holy Spirit's DNA

What about the paternal DNA? What sort of difficulty could the Creator of the universe ever experience in miraculously providing a male gamete of adequate chromosomal content to fertilize one of the Virgin's egg cells at the right place and time? From a scientific point of view, the paternal chromosomal contribution is absolutely required for the birth of a healthy child, and all the more so for a male to be born. The paternal genome is necessary to define the healthy, physiological, and overwhelming difference between the Son's Body and soul and those of His Mother.

The Tunic of Argenteuil—if genuine—reveals pairs of numbers for each of its detected STR alleles. Each number in each pair indicates how many times the STR sequence is repeated in each allele version of that STR. Without any other reference, it is impossible to distinguish between the paternal or maternal origin of each number in each pair. However, the paternal origin is revealed whenever the numbers in each pair are identical. This is the case for the FGA, VWA, D8S1179, or D19S433 STRs. Because the Mother and the Son are homozygous for these particular

STRs, we could then begin to sketch out an initial paternal, but also maternal, "genetic profile." I am convinced that should we be able to obtain a complete CODIS profile of this DNA — forgive my terminology — of the "Holy Spirit," we would probably find it pretty average or simply adequate. It certainly wouldn't be that of an "alien" or "superman."

Finally, we also learned from the Tunic studies that the specific J2 haplogroup was unequivocally, mysteriously, but specifically detected in the paternal Y chromosome. We know that this haplogroup is suggestive of a Jewish ethnicity and that it is still shared by millions of men even today.

An Overview on the DNA of the Eucharistic Miracles

Let's now ask ourselves why no known nuclear STR polymorphisms could ever be found in the eucharistic miracles we've studied thus far, except for the partial and recent exception of Legnica. I think there are three possible explanations that could hold true at the same time:

1. The very poor DNA quality

The Buenos Aires and Tixtla DNAs were truly suboptimally, if not very poorly, preserved. Actually, they had not been preserved at all. As with all other eucharistic miracles, no storage or preservation techniques were used to protect them from environmental, physical, or biological contaminants. This is understandable: a miracle is not a "crime scene," and relics are not meant to be preserved in liquid nitrogen, because they are presents from God. Their spontaneous self-preservation, if present, is itself part of their miraculous nature.

In particular, I shall recall that the worst storage conditions were those in Buenos Aires: the 1996 tissue was preserved — who knows why — in distilled water, which is essentially a cellular poison. Furthermore, all the reports we came across described "suffering" tissues, whose DNA was fragmented and degraded. Therefore, quite simply, no valid STRs could be found because, if initially present, they were then either ruined or made illegible by decay. If we were patient enough, perhaps we could be luckier at the "next" eucharistic miracle, and the genetics laboratory might finally give us some satisfaction. The weak Legnica results seemed to be heading in that direction. The finding of only two STR amplifications — out of a batch of at least ten to twenty that were being looked for — was considered by the researchers as an expected result. It was a finding compatible with the poor quality of the original sample. If more STR amplifications had been detected, a degree of suspicion for contamination would have been raised.

2. God hiding Himself

As naïve "good Catholics," we might wonder why these miracles did not just equip themselves with some more resistant DNA to face our scrutiny if they were truly real.

Would that really come at an extra cost? I already mentioned Dr. Castañón's reflections in which he considers the consistent lack of DNA results — or presence of inconclusive ones — as an actual paradoxical marker of a miracle's supernatural authenticity.

What if this property was then actually a miracle in itself? After all, the Eucharist is God's willful and miraculous hiding of Himself under the species of bread and wine. In these eucharistic miracles, the concealment of God's DNA identity profile could not have been otherwise simulated by any human forger. Hence, could this silent DNA be a miracle hidden within the miracles? It could actually be a discreet and loving heavenly "signature" safeguarding human faith and freedom from an overwhelming light: an excess that would be otherwise unsustainable for human beings. As "men of little faith," we can stand the coincidence of the AB group in both the Lanciano and Tixtla miracles. This is because we can at least cast some doubts on the accuracy of the blood grouping results, or simply because the world's spotlights are focused elsewhere. This is even if this "coincidence" is rather powerful on its own and even more so if also factoring in the matching blood groups of the three alleged Passion cloths. However, a firm DNA finding would not go unnoticed, and we could not possibly ignore it as modern-day people living in the allure and borderline idolatry of the famous double helix. Could this, then, be a reason for God to deliberately weaken His miraculous manifestation? What about the Legnica DNA results? Could God have made a partial exception to the hiding of His DNA identity by relying on the researchers' discretion?

3. The DNA of glorified bodies

Catholic theology has already strived to define—as it could—some features that our glorified bodies will enjoy at the time of the resurrection of the flesh. Some clues come straight from the Gospels regarding the Resurrection, in which Jesus is shown to enter through locked doors into the room where the apostles were. At times He either hides or reveals Himself, like on the road to Emmaus or to Mary Magdalene in the garden. He lets Himself be touched and *is alive*, even though He still bears some open wounds of His Passion. He can eat and ascend to Heaven. He is the first fruit of the destiny we are all called to. Clearly, I am not just referring to the immortality of the soul but also to the actual physical resurrection of the body, to which the soul will be reunited at the time of the Last Judgment, according to Catholic doctrine.

It will not be a mere resuscitation of our current body, as happened to Lazarus, Jairus's daughter, or the son of the widow of Nain in the Gospels. Instead, it will be the resurrection of a "glorified" body with new and supernatural biological features. It will be a wonderful body that will not age and die again. It will be immune to any disease and free of any imperfection. Perhaps it will be like the body our ancestors Adam and Eve rejoiced in, in the garden of Eden, before sinning. Not only that but our glorified body may be an even more wondrous one. This is because the scars of our personal struggles that led to our overcoming of sin with the help of divine grace will also be glorified.[142]

Theological reflection also tried to describe some other features of the glorified body. These are *impassibility*: the inability to feel pain or immunity from any harm; *splendor*: the light that will radiate from everyone as an expression of the happiness of one's soul; *agility*: an instantaneous freedom of movement no longer subject to physical laws; *subtlety*: the perfect dependence of the body on the soul; and again *immortality*, *integrity*, *beauty*. I shall recommend the book *L'Eden, la resurrezione e la terra dei viventi* (*Eden, the Resurrection and the Land of the Living*), by

---

[142] *Kintsugi* is a Japanese word for "golden joinery." It is the Japanese art of repairing broken pottery by mending the areas of breakage with lacquer dusted or mixed with a precious metal, such as gold, silver, or platinum. In philosophical terms, it means treating breakage and repair as part of the history of an object, rather than something to disguise. The same principle can also be seen through the lens of the Catholic Faith: the wounds in our bodies and souls, often caused by sin, will not only be repaired in our glorified selves but also made beautiful.

Gianluca Marletta, to those wishing to deepen their knowledge about this topic.

Very well, then: What will the DNA of this body be like? We may suppose that it will also enjoy a marvelous perfection; it will be free of disease-causing genes, or genes that confer less than perfect traits, while maintaining overabundant individual variations and definite kinship with the relatives of previous and following generations. Alternatively, if it were to maintain its current nucleotide sequence, it will be gifted with control mechanisms capable of cancelling out any harmful effects that were causing disease, aging, and dying down here on Earth. I am dwelling on these idle considerations because nothing can prevent us from imagining what a "glorified DNA" could be like, in this unexplored territory. Quite possibly, it may be freed from all that useless repeated "junk DNA" the human species had never dared to eliminate of its own initiative, lest it may lose any small and possibly neighboring necessary sequences. If those redundant or disease-causing sequences were to be eliminated, then all STR polymorphisms would also disappear from the "glorified DNA." From a transcriptional point of view, STRs are indeed meaningless, as they do not lead to the production of any protein product. This is even if we find them useful as DNA profiling markers in forensic medicine. This neat and simple hypothesis could then explain why the DNA of a resurrected and glorified body would be refractory to common genetic identification tests. After all, it is certain that not even the pettiest crime will ever be committed in Heaven, and the FBI's DNA identification services will no longer be required.

Would it then make more sense to look for actually "useful" protein-coding genes in our relics' DNA? This may possibly be the case, although we are already aware of an exception to this "rule": the consistently negative results obtained from all attempts made at identifying the amelogenin genes in the eucharistic miracles. Amelogenin genes indeed produce essential proteins for enamel formation and are certainly far from being "useless repeats," unless we were happy to live without functional teeth.

Are the DNA and—More in General— the Biological Tissues of the Passion Cloths Different from Those of the Eucharistic Miracles?

It is difficult to provide definitive answers to this question by only relying on the few and partial experimental findings available. Truly, in this mysterious and uncharted territory, some results have even been prudently censored. However, Catholic theology does come to our aid on this topic by reminding us that Christ's presence in the world is threefold. The first type of presence is the *historical* one: that of Jesus' life in first-century Palestine. Up until His death on the Cross, Jesus' Body and Blood were those of a common mortal human being. Theoretically, we could then use our modern scientific instruments to try to analyze any traces of His mortal remains on the Passion relics and, after two thousand years, still hope to find some biologically rational results. It would then be a rational expectation to obtain some partial or incomplete genetic results—or completely spurious ones, due to DNA contaminations—from relics such as the Shroud of Turin and the Sudarium of Oviedo. Likewise, it would also be just as rational to glean solid and convincing results such as those obtained from the Tunic of Argenteuil.

The other two types of presence are instead hidden from our senses, exceptions made for miracles and apparitions. They are Jesus' *sacramental* presence in the Eucharist and His *natural* presence in Heaven. The latter is His presence in the fullness of His resurrected and glorified Body, sitting at the right hand of God the Father. We can then expect eucharistic miracles to manifest Jesus' *sacramental* presence, which is necessarily different from the other two types. Which biological features should we then expect to find in the tissues of eucharistic miracles? Miracles are, by definition, bewildering and otherwise inexplicable phenomena in which the Divine breaks into this world of ours. Miracles can ultimately do whatever they wish and override all the laws of biology, physics, and chemistry as they please.

Alternatively, we could also try to think about these apparent "violations" of natural laws in a different way: perhaps miracles actually point to a fulfilment of these laws beyond the constraints of our space-time universe. Because of this, our most sophisticated scientific instruments could actually be completely useless and inadequate for their study by our ordinary means. Still, miracles are not trying to fool human beings: if they happen, it is because they want to remind us about something important, often something quite dramatic and urgent.

Broadly speaking, I believe we could glean two complementary principles from the scientific investigations that we discussed. On one hand, there is a language of truth and consistency emerging from scientific findings in regard to what the eucharistic sacrament means or *is*. As a Roman Catholic, I feel sustained and comforted by what science has so far been able to tell me about the Lanciano, Buenos Aires, Tixtla, and Polish events. The scientific study of the tissues originating from these miracles does not involve embarrassing surprises or theologically equivocal findings. Instead, the concepts of a living and agonizing heart, a "suffering" blood, and a consistent blood group can only be uplifting for the believer.

On the other hand, these miraculous tissues can still maintain an unyielding and noble detachment from worldly reality: they can survive in very poor or adverse storage conditions and display incomplete or "silent" histological or immunohistochemical features that seem to be hovering between life and death. Almost mockingly, their DNA seems to escape from the molecular probes used in common identification tests. What would this "sacramental" DNA then have in common with the "historical" DNA originating from the leftover traces of Christ's mortal remains? Would it always be the same, one test after another? Would it perhaps be able to change, hide itself, or even play with our curiosity?

Our forefathers had already asked themselves a similar question when wondering about the destiny of the Blood that Christ shed during His Passion. St. Thomas Aquinas stated that the Blood that was shed is an integral part of Christ's bodily humanity and is destined to be resurrected along with the rest of His Body: it is bound to be "reabsorbed" in His new glorified Body on Easter morning and thus be no longer present on Earth. In 1462, St. James of the Marches—a Franciscan friar—disagreed with this concept, and this led to one of the many arguments between Dominicans and Franciscans that gave Catholic theology a unique flavor. The Shroud and the other Passion cloths, if genuine, demonstrate the presence of human blood that perhaps—in theological jargon—is no longer hypostatically united with the Word. Instead, it would seem as if this Blood was left to us as a "relic" or evidence of the ransom Jesus paid for our salvation.

Dear reader, this is the end of my small survey. God willing, more information will become available in the future, and perhaps someone else will take over my work from where I left it and continue the onward journey. Praise be to God!

Bibliography

Venter, J. Craig, Mark Adams, Eugene Myers, et al. 2001. "The Sequence of the Human Genome." *Science* 291 (5507): 1304–1351.

The historical presentation of the huge Human Genome Project that unveiled the complete sequence of the human DNA.

Noble, Denis. 2006. *The Music of Life: Biology Beyond the Genome*. Oxford University Press.

Passionate essay that critically revisits the role of genes and DNA in the complexity of the living organisms.

Oppenheimer, Stephen. 2003. *The Real Eve: Modern Man's Journey Out of Africa*. New York: Basic Books.

Oppenheimer, Stephen. 2004. *Out of Eden: The Peopling of the World*. London: Little, Brown Book Group.

Passionate story of the conquering of the world by the human species, based on the genealogic tree that is hidden in the Y male chromosome.

Coble, Michael, Odile Loreille, Mark Wadhams, et al. 2009. "Mystery Solved: The Identification of the Two Missing Romanov Children Using DNA Analysis." *PLoS One* 4 (3), p. e4838.

Summary of all the investigations on DNA that brought about the certain identification of the remains of the whole Romanov family, after the findings from 1991 to 2007.

Woestendiek, John. 2010. *Dog, Inc.: The Uncanny Inside Story of Cloning Man's Best Friend*. New York: Avery Publishing.

Sagi Ido, and Nissim Benvenisty. "Haploidy in Humans: An Evolutionary and Developmental Perspective."

Developmental Cell 41 (6): 581–589. https://doi.org/10.1016/j.devcel.2017.04.019.

Journal article on experimental haploidy in the human species. One section explains the natural barriers that make the existence of a haploid human impossible.

Castañón Gómez, Ricardo. 2011. *Más allá de la razón*, 3rd ed. Mexico: Centro Internacional de Estudios Humanos.

The best book (in Spanish) about the investigations of the Buenos Aires events.

Tesoriero, Ron, and Lee Han. 2013. *Unseen New Evidence: The Origin of Life Under the Microscope*. Australia: Ron Tesoriero.

Personal reflections by the Australian lawyer involved in the investigations of the Buenos Aires events: he makes interesting references to all the other eucharistic miracles that have been studied in the modern ages.

Castañón Gómez, Ricardo. 2014. *Crónica de un milagro eucarístico: Esplendor en Tixtla Chilpancingo, Mexico*. Grupo Internacional para la Paz.

The best book about the events from Tixtla.

Kiernikowski, Zbigniew. 2017. *Bóg przemówił w Legnicy*. Kraków: Wydawnictwo M.

Official summary of the Legnica events, written and published by the Diocese of Legnica in 2017.

Vernesi, Cristiano, Giulietta Di Benedetto, David Caramelli, et al. 2001. "Genetic Characterization of the Body Attributed to the Evangelist." *Proceedings of the National Academy of Sciences of the United States of America* 98 (23): 13460–13463.

Study of the mitochondrial DNA from a tooth from the body remains associated with Luke the Evangelist, held in St. Giustina Cathedral in Padua.

KakaTonyLa. 2012. *National Geographic HD: Head of John the Baptist.* Documentary. YouTube. Accessed July 12, 2021. https://www.youtube.com/watch?v=e-QjoorU03g&has_verified=1. From min. 39:40, Hannes Schroeder and Eske Willerslev (University of Copenhagen) analyze the mitochondrial DNA sequence of the bones from a suspect relic of John the Baptist. In the film, a A188G mutation is revealed, resulting in a J1c2 haplogroup.

History Channel. 2017. *The Jesus Strand: A Search for DNA.* Documentary. Accessed July 12, 2021. https://www.dailymotion.com/video/x5m17zd.

2017 History Channel documentary in which a flamboyant Californian Baptist pastor and an Oxford geneticist take us on a journey to discover DNA fragments on sacred relics. Alas, the television style is rather shallow and fast-paced. Here the Danish scientists reveal that the mitochondrial DNA previously attributed to John the Baptist was a modern contamination.

Lucotte, Gérard. 2016. "The Mitochondrial DNA Mitotype of Sainte Marie-Madeleine." *International Journal of Sciences* 5 (12): 10–19.

Summary of the analysis of mitochondrial DNA from the remains attributed to Mary Magdalene and the sensational discovery of their belonging to the Jewish haplogroup.

Casarino, L. et al. 1995. "Ricerca dei polimorfismi del DNA sulla sindone e sul Sudario di Oviedo." *Sindon Nuova Serie* 8: 39–47.

First study on the Shroud's DNA polymorphisms.

De Stefano, F. 1996. "Automated Profiling of Multiplexed DNA Markers: An Italian Database of Four Co-amplified STRs Loci." *Advances in Forensic Hemogenetics* 6: 174–176.

Barcaccia, Gianni, Giulio Galla, Alessandro Achilli, et al. 2015. "Uncovering the Sources of DNA Found on the Turin Shroud." *Scientific Reports* 5: 14484.

Original study about all vegetable, animal, and human mitochondrial DNA traces found on the Turin Shroud.

Alonso, A. et al. 2007. "El DNA del Sudario de Oviedo: Oviedo relicario de la cristianidad." In *Oviedo, relicario de la cristianidad: Actas del II Congreso Internacional sobre el Sudario de Oviedo.* 1st ed., 167–173.

The official communication by Dr. Alonso in which he admits of knowing the DNA mitochondrial sequence of the blood on the Oviedo Sudarium.

Van Cauwelaert, Didier. 2005. *Cloner le Christ?* 1st ed. Canal Albin Michel.

An investigation on the improbable possibility of the cloning of Jesus Christ. It includes an interview with Prof. Lucotte, who anticipates the results on the Tunic from Argenteuil.

Marion, André, and Gérard Lucotte. 2006. *Le linceul de Turin et la tunique d'Argenteuil: Le point sur l'enquête.* 1st ed. Paris: Éditions des Presses de la Renaissance.

The second part of the book is dedicated to the original studies on the Tunic. For the first time, the CODIS code of a relic of the Passion is published.

Lucotte, Gérard, and Philippe Bornet. 2007. *Sanguis Christi: Le sang du Christ. Une enquête sur la tunique d'Argenteuil.* Guy Trédaniel Éditeur.

The French geneticist explains everything he knows and has discovered about the Argenteuil relic.

Lucotte, Gérard. 2001. "Study of the Mutation M694V of Familial Mediterranean Fever in Jews." *Genetic Testing* 5 (1): 53–56.

Gharib, Georges. 1993. *Le icone di Cristo: Storia e culto*. Edizioni Città Nuova.

A mine of patristic quotes regarding Jesus and His Mother's physical appearance.

Untitled website. Accessed July 12, 2021. http://www.najumary. or.kr/English/signs/preciousblood20.htm.

Website on the genetic studies related to Julia Kim's prodigious events.

One Last Observation

A few more words before saying goodbye.

At the end of this survey, I am still left with an odd feeling that warrants one last reflection.

So many tests. So much data obtained from just five eucharistic events. So many incredible "coincidences" suggesting that these biological tissues originating from consecrated bread point toward that suffering crucified man.

Still, I must admit that eucharistic miracles are somewhat strange compared to others. They have certainly sustained Catholics of all times in their faith in the Eucharist. Indeed, the presence of the Son of God in a small bread wafer is such an excessive truth to believe. However, the light radiating from these miracles is never a dazzling one. These miracles are restrained. They are self-limited and do not mean to crush the necessary but fragile treasure of our personal faith under the weight of overpowering displays. The Eucharist ultimately wants to be believed. It does not want to become an imposition on our senses. Perhaps this is why the tissue samples on the microscope slides were always strongly suggestive of heart muscle tissue, but their appearance was never textbook-like, never looking as if taken straight out of a histopathology encyclopedia. This was because surface proteins were often degraded to the point of no longer being recognized even by the most specific immunohistochemical markers. Likewise, common DNA polymorphisms could almost never be identified.

Let's try to imagine this: let's suppose that both the Buenos Aires and Tixtla DNAs could be sequenced and an unequivocal match was found between the two: half a dozen concordant STR polymorphisms would be enough to obtain a match with an error margin of only one in a million or one in a billion. This would turn into *breaking news* on all press agencies and global networks—CNN, BBC, Al Jazeera. The blood or the heart of the same person found to be undoubtedly present in two or three eucharistic miracles: the same man left a trace of His presence centuries apart and on different continents across the oceans. This would be nothing less than the unarguable scientific demonstration of the reality of the Catholic Eucharist. Such an overwhelming event would trouble the consciences of many people and compel all men and women to turn toward a Catholic Church once thought to be out of date, dying, and alienated from history. The following day, Protestant churches would shut down. A week later, the Dalai Lama would ask to be publicly baptized. A month later, the Mass would once again be celebrated at Hagia Sophia in Istanbul, which would then also be called Byzantium once again. Enough daydreaming—this is obviously not God's will, at least not in these terms, or otherwise all this would have already happened.

What else should we be thinking about, then? How could we not admire the gentleness of a God in keeping His modesty, even when fully displaying His power and overriding all natural laws to make Himself visible for us in the Eucharist?

About the Author

Dr. Franco Serafini lives in Bologna, Italy, where he grew up and received his education. He enjoys his work as a cardiologist at a local country hospital, to which he rides his bicycle on most days, weather permitting.

In his spare time, Dr. Serafini collects and appraises available clinical evidence about five eucharistic events officially recognized as miraculous by the Catholic Church. In the process, he has made connections with the Polish, Mexican, and Argentinian scientists who were involved in the most recent investigations. He travels around the world to meet these experts along with local eyewitnesses.

Since 2018, Dr. Serafini has reinvented himself as a public speaker on eucharistic miracles. He gives talks around Italy, has given multiple radio and television interviews, and has been involved in film and documentary shoots.

He and his wife are happily married and have two children.

Sophia Institute

Sophia Institute is a nonprofit institution that seeks to nurture the spiritual, moral, and cultural life of souls and to spread the gospel of Christ in conformity with the authentic teachings of the Roman Catholic Church.

Sophia Institute Press fulfills this mission by offering translations, reprints, and new publications that afford readers a rich source of the enduring wisdom of mankind.

Sophia Institute also operates the popular online resource CatholicExchange.com. *Catholic Exchange* provides world news from a Catholic perspective as well as daily devotionals and articles that will help readers to grow in holiness and live a life consistent with the teachings of the Church.

In 2013, Sophia Institute launched Sophia Institute for Teachers to renew and rebuild Catholic culture through service to Catholic education. With the goal of nurturing the spiritual, moral, and cultural life of souls, and an abiding respect for the role and work of teachers, we strive to provide materials and programs that are at once enlightening to the mind and ennobling to the heart; faithful and complete, as well as useful and practical.

Sophia Institute gratefully recognizes the Solidarity Association for preserving and encouraging the growth of our apostolate over the course of many years. Without their generous and timely support, this book would not be in your hands.

www.SophiaInstitute.com
www.CatholicExchange.com
www.SophiaInstituteforTeachers.org

Sophia Institute Press® is a registered trademark of Sophia Institute.
Sophia Institute is a tax-exempt institution as defined by the
Internal Revenue Code, Section 501(c)(3). Tax ID 22-2548708.